P.T. PHILLIPS is Associate Professor of History at St Francis Xavier University, Antigonish, Nova Scotia.

This comparative study deals with the important social phenomenon of sectarianism in four medium-sized cotton towns of northwest England – Bolton, Preston, Stockport, and Blackburn – between 1832 and 1870.

Professor Phillips examines the social role of sectarian animosity in a period of rapid economic expansion and population growth. Placing this conflict within the dense mosaic of religious, social, and economic factors he delineates sectarianism's crucial role in politics and class strife. He also assesses the activities of Churchmen (Anglicans), Nonconformists, Roman Catholics, and members of the new sects.

The author relates his findings to the operations of sectarianism in other parts of the country and takes into account some of the most recent work in urban, religious, social, and political history. This volume has important implications for the understanding not only of cotton towns, but of Victorian society, religion, and politics as a whole.

PAUL T. PHILLIPS

The Sectarian Spirit: Sectarianism, Society, and Politics in Victorian Cotton Towns

UNIVERSITY OF TORONTO PRESS
Toronto Buffalo London

© University of Toronto Press 1982
Toronto Buffalo London
Printed in Canada
Reprinted in 2018
ISBN 0-8020-2406-8
ISBN 978-1-4875-8071-1 (paper)

Canadian Cataloguing in Publication Data
Phillips, Paul T., 1942–
  The sectarian spirit

  Bibliography: p.
  Includes index.

  ISBN 0-8020-2406-8
  ISBN 978-1-4875-8071-1 (paper)

  1. Social classes – England – History – 19th century. 2. England – Social conditions – 19th century. 3. Sects – England – History – 19th century. 4. England – Religion – 19th century.
  I. Title.

  HN385.P55   305.5'0942   C82-094677-X

To my parents

Contents

PREFACE ix

MAP 2

1 Introduction 3

2 Bolton: the Geneva of Lancashire 10

3 Proud Preston 37

4 Stockport and the 'Dark Satanic Mills' 72

5 Blackburn: an Archetypal Cotton Town 107

6 Wider Perspectives 140

APPENDIX 145

NOTES 147

NOTE ON SOURCES 183

SELECT BIBLIOGRAPHY 185

INDEX 203

Preface

This book is an outgrowth of my 1971 Toronto doctoral dissertation, also entitled 'The Sectarian Spirit.' My thesis gave a prominent place to the cloth region of Wiltshire as well as to the north of England. Time, the appearance of new secondary literature, and subsequent research on the spot, however, have deepened my appreciation of the historical complexities of life in the textile region of northwestern England. The result has therefore been a geographical contraction of my concerns, accompanied, I hope, by an expanded and more profound analysis of developments within the cotton towns.

In the preparation of this study I have incurred a great many debts on both sides of the Atlantic. The staffs of many libraries and record offices have been enormously helpful in pointing to valuable sources of information. Clergymen, chapel secretaries, and others have been most kind in granting access to records of various sorts often held outside the conventional repositories that attract historians.

Stretching back to 1967 when my research in this area began, I must thank many academics who gave me good advice along the way, including E.J. Hobsbawm and R.B. Pugh of London University, G. Martin and the late H.J. Dyos of Leicester, A. Temple Patterson of Southampton, E. Royle of the University of York, Brian Harrison and B. Wilson of Oxford, W.H. Chaloner of Manchester, H.J. Perkin and J.D. Marshall of Lancaster, J.P.B. Kenyon of Toronto, and the late R.W. Greaves of Kansas. I must also give special thanks to W.R. Ward of Durham and T.O. Lloyd of Toronto for reading an earlier version of this manuscript. At all stages of my work, whether as a thesis or as a book in progress, I owe my greatest debt of gratitude to my former supervisor, R.J. Helmstadter of the University of Toronto. Needless to say, any errors or weaknesses in the final product are of my own making.

As a final note, I must extend my thanks to Jean Houston and Rosemary Shipton, my editors, and the academic readers of the University of Toronto Press and the Social Science Federation of Canada. Their advice and encouragement were most helpful. I am also grateful to the Canada Council for allowing me to draw upon its financial resources in support of my research through the years.

The book has been published with the help of a grant from the Social Science Federation of Canada, using funds provided by the Social Sciences and Humanities Research Council of Canada, and from the Publications Fund of the University of Toronto Press.

PAUL T. PHILLIPS
Antigonish, Nova Scotia

THE SECTARIAN SPIRIT

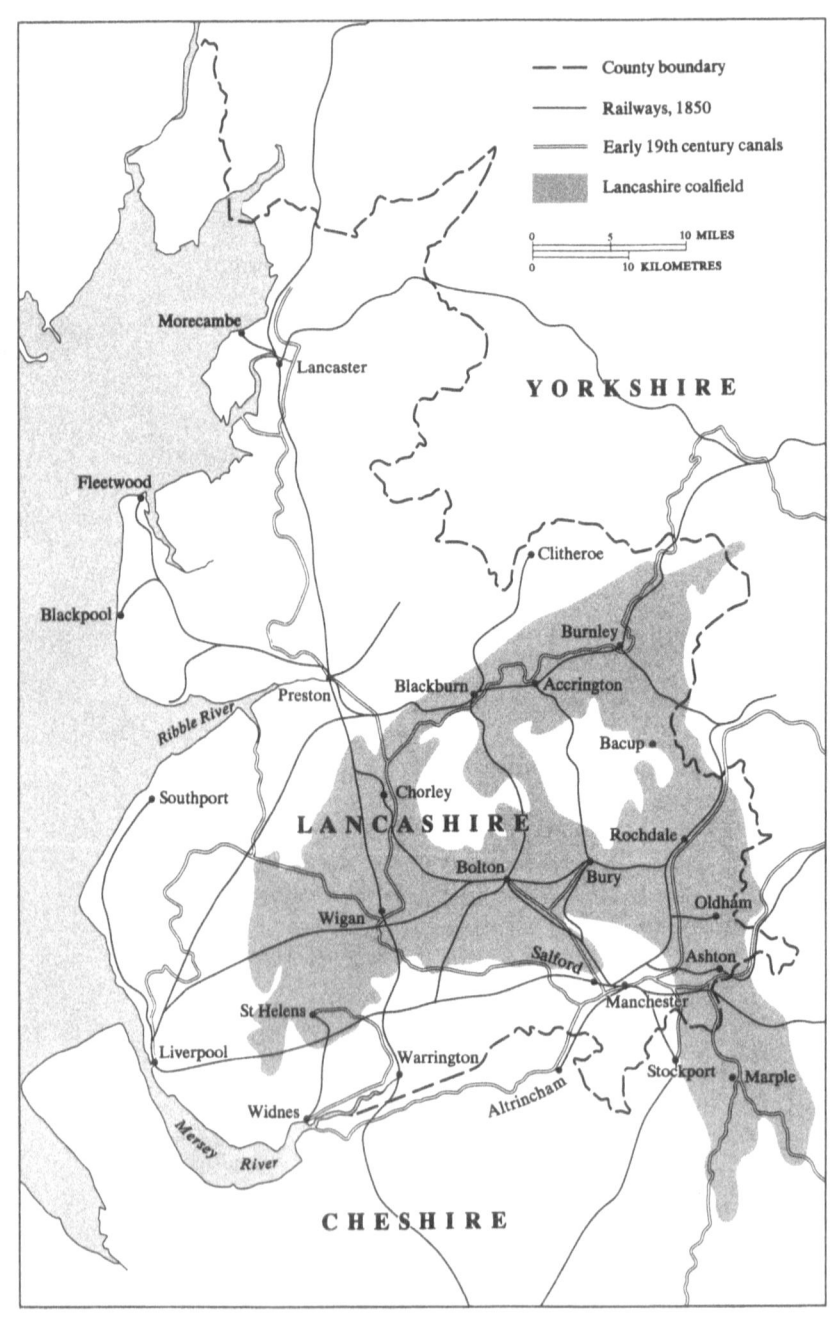

MAP Lancashire and North Cheshire in the mid nineteenth century

1
Introduction

> 'There was more religious strife in Manchester or Bradford in the forties than in the Roman Empire under the rule of Augustus.'
>
> B.L. and J. Hammond, *The Age of the Chartists*, 1930

The Hammonds have not been alone amongst historians in recognizing the religious upheaval in northwestern England in the mid nineteenth century. Yet little detailed analysis of this important phenomenon has been undertaken for specific urban areas within Victorian England.

The essence of this particular study is an examination of the social role of sectarianism in several Victorian industrial towns, with politics as its primary focus. More specifically it is a study of sectarianism, politics, and society in Bolton, Preston, Stockport, and Blackburn roughly between 1832 and 1870. Both of these dates were politically significant. The first was the year of the Great Reform Act, which symbolized a new era of great expectations and potential social power for Nonconformists in the great industrial towns. The second enacted Forster's Education Act which, in some areas of the country, saw the first glimmerings of sectarian compromise over a volatile social and political question. It was also the year in which James Fraser, a great opponent of sectarian strife, became bishop of Manchester and thereafter powerfully influenced social relations in northwestern England for the next fifteen years.[1]

The definition of 'sectarianism' employed here is the classical one, which was in widest currency in the nineteenth century. It is defined as 'religiously' related segregation and attendant animosity within a society, rather than the newer technical definition used amongst sociologists to mean the formation and maintenance of 'sect-type' religious groups.[2] Elements of the second definition may be found within the first (though not as part of a passive withdrawal), but the intention of this study is not to introduce sociological concepts or methodology per se. Such approaches might be useful in discovering, for example, the psychological impact of sectarian strife on individuals in these communities. There are fundamental differences in the outlook and concerns of social and religious historians as compared with those of sociologists who investigate historical developments. For that reason it might be well to indentify this work as falling especially within the boundaries of the discipline of history.

This book is concerned with the most important social ramifications of the operations of sectarianism within four cotton towns. As such, it is not concerned with strife arising out of questions of church order or doctrine which, in any case, might more properly be categorized 'religious' conflict. Sectarian conflict, of course, can take many forms – overt and covert. The overt operations are visibly obvious in Northern Ireland at the present time. In Victorian England, and in the cotton towns in particular, however, these alarming proportions of overt, physical sectarian conflict were never reached. The religious riot, while not unknown, was hardly a common phenomenon. Indeed, organized sectarian conflict may well have inadvertently helped to support the social status quo.

The lines of animosity were sharply drawn and ran deep into the fabric of Victorian town life. This was most obvious and important in the area of politics. The nature of politics, especially municipal politics, also mirrored the very nature of sectarianism in the quest of those involved for guidance of or control over the society about them. The two were intimately entwined in the cotton towns in the mid-Victorian decades. Indeed, 'politico-sectarianism' may have reached its high point in this period, though P.F. Clarke has observed that sectarianism remained an important influence in Lancashire politics even at the end of the century.[3] Bishop Fraser feared this close association to the point of seeing it as a major threat to the religious and social life of his diocese. He could clearly make the distinction between sectarianism and religiosity. Sectarianism was always a more self-conscious operation after Fraser's appointment and therefore began to lose some of its effectiveness in the years following 1870.

The intimate connection with politics may also have helped to produce the dominant type of sectarianism found in the cotton towns – the struggle between Nonconformist and Church forces for hegemony. As A.D. Gilbert has recently noted, emphasis upon particular denominational divisions often obscures the basic social importance of the 'Church' and 'chapel' cleavage in industrial England.[4] Apart from the Wesleyan Methodists (until 1850) and the occasional oscillations of Roman Catholics, most non-Anglican Christians gave their support to the Liberal-Nonconformist camp in their battle with Tory-Churchmen in the cotton towns. In both economic resources and members the forces were more evenly balanced than often supposed. Exceptions, of course, were always possible. One must especially include here the frequency of Churchmen as

Introduction 5

Liberal candidates in parliamentary elections and some moderate Churchmen as rank-and-file supporters. Perhaps W.A. Abram gave the best detailed synopsis of the religious-political situation in Lancashire (1868):

On the side of Toryism:
1 Churchmen by conviction, sentiment and tradition.
2 Minority of Methodists, and small minority of other Nonconformists.
3 So many of the Indifferents as may be moved thitherward by secular convictions or interests.

On the side of Liberalism:
1 A small party of Liberal Churchmen.
2 Dissenters of all sects, with few exceptions.
3 Vast majority of Methodists.
4 Roman Catholics, almost without exception.
5 Free Thinkers.
6 Indifferents, not otherwise influenced.[5]

The close relationship between sectarianism and politics in the cotton towns reminds one of G. Kitson Clark's well-known statement about the impossibility of separating religion from politics in Victorian England after the second quarter of the century.[6] The picture is further complicated by introducing other factors such as the struggle for an expansion of the parliamentary franchise, economic and administrative questions, and the all-important area of class strife, all of which had a bearing on nineteenth-century politics. Such questions raise the even more profound question of what factors are prime movers of social developments in a given community. Sectarianism was both a moulding force and a reflector of social developments; as with religion, it was an active as well as a passive agent in the social setting.

Though sectarianism was in some sense a greater phenomenon embracing more people under its shadow than the institutional churches in Victorian times, it was of course itself related to the social position of organized relgion. Religion formed the basis or at least ostensibly the origin of sectarian positions. For that reason the recent work of many historians examining the social roles and social position of the churches in Victorian society is relevant.

Ecclesiastical historians have often divided themselves into optimistic and pessimistic schools of thought on the subject of the churches' social strength by the mid nineteenth century. G. Kitson Clark, Desmond Bowen, Owen Chadwick,[7] among others, have stressed the positive achievements of the churches in relation to the needs of mid and late Victorian society. K.S. Inglis and others within the pessimistic school have seen the shortcomings of institutional religion

6 The Sectarian Spirit

especially in relation to the increasing alienation of the masses. Most recently A.D. Gilbert and W.R. Ward have enriched the latter position.[8] There is no question of the poor showing in attendances for industrial Lancashire on Census Sunday, 1851.[9] However, the suitability of a head-count on that occasion as an accurate measurement of religiosity, much less the social strength of the churches, is debatable. The social strength of sectarianism is also one step further removed and is much more difficult to measure.

The social roles of the churches or of religion in general have been a hotly debated topic. Karl Marx and Frederick Engels were most concerned about the negative effects of religion upon the people. This tradition has continued amongst Marxist social historians to the present day. Accepting to some degree the same assumption that the Christian religion acted as a social pacifier, contemporaries of Marx such as W. Cooke Taylor, Andrew Ure, Henry Ashworth of Bolton, and 'A Citizen of the World'[10] were interested in encouraging the positive aspects of this influence upon the masses. Ure even thought the factory in alliance with religion might be a valuable instrument in this indoctrination. Religious and social historians more recently have questioned the simplicity of both views. A good example is T.W. Laqueur's work on Sunday schools, *Religion and Respectability* (1976).

There have been many interpretations of the role of the churches in class relationships in mid-Victorian England. Harold Perkin, in a study of the small textile town of Glossop in Derbyshire,[11] saw the antagonisms between rival religious groups cutting vertically through class lines as more important than those of class. He also noted that the employing class 'inculcated in their workers their own principles, ideals and animosities.'[12] My view is that, in terms of the evidence uncovered thus far, this does not seem to have been a conscious effort on the part of most employers in the various denominations. Perhaps the employers shared much of the sectarian animosity held by the populace as a whole. J.C. Lowe has likened this popular sectarian conflict in nineteenth-century Lancashire to that of the mass enthusiasm for local football teams in this century within the same region.[13] The result, in any case, was much as Perkin has described for religion in Glossop. In the process sectarianism acted to subdue class tension in three of the cotton towns; in the fourth, Preston, it may have tended to reinforce it.

Another work, already mentioned, is W.R. Ward's *Religion and Society in England, 1790–1850* (1972). According to Professor Ward, by the 1830s the Nonconformist churches began to be pushed to the 'fringes of national life,' joining the Established Church which had been there for some decades. Exactly when the churches are fully pushed to the fringes he does not specify, but the trend is clearly there by 1850. About this time denominational divisions and sectarian hatreds began to mount, ending for all purposes the undenominational, popular spirit of the original Protestant Evangelical revival. As class tension then moved into the foreground of early Victorian society, religious developments, as all else, began to be influenced by it. Denominationalism in the 1830s and 40s only incompletely transformed class conflict into denominational conflict. The divisions within Methodism and to some extent Dissent eventually themselves reflected class tension and became even an outlet, almost a vehicle for class conflict. Ward uses the separation and segregation of middle-class groups (from their more plebian brethren) into new congregations and the subsequent decay of many of the older popular chapels as one source of evidence. His view of mid-Victorian sectarian conflict is therefore contained within his overall belief in the declining role of religion in general in this period – of which heightened sectarianism was a symptom. Denominational conflict was also in essence a reflector of class tension by mid nineteenth century. Ward's evidence is basically rooted in developments within rank-and-file Methodism, particularly in the Manchester area. His overall study is focused on a wider topic in a larger urban setting and in an historical period other than the one in this book. This may also explain the rather different conclusions for the most part drawn by Professor Ward on the nature of mid-Victorian sectarianism. My book is more concerned with the opposite end of the picture than Ward's – the effect of sectarianism on class politics.

The four cotton towns chosen for this study lay in an industrial region famous for its high degree of social tension. John Foster's *Class Struggle and the Industrial Revolution* (1974) has enriched the discussion by putting forth an ambitious, marxist interpretation of class conflict in the town of Oldham.[14] Bolton, Preston, Stockport, and Blackburn had much in common with Oldham. All were medium-sized towns (average population 58,000 in 1851) with a reliance on the cotton industry, making early working-class cohesion more likely.

There are, however, complicating factors in this picture. Social structures even amongst cotton towns experiencing the same rate of demographic and industrial growth in the same period were never the same. As the first shock wave of factory building passed, more concentration and specialization within the cotton industry led to a pattern of structural differentiation peculiar to each town. Sepcialization was often the product of historical factors in a particular locale. Where cloth merchants were large in number in the eighteenth century, weaving often predominated in the nineteenth. By 1850 it was clear that Bolton was a spinning centre, Blackburn a weaving town, Stockport men favoured weaving over spinning, and Preston manufacturers struck a balance between the two.[15] Such factors might be important if they bore on the pace of social dislocation, of, for example, large numbers of handloom weavers.

The insecurities of factory life bred by competition as well as the 'boom-bust' cycle which characterized the cotton industry may also have increased social tension. The cotton magnates dominated the industrial scene in these towns. Gentlemen of independent means, bankers, professional men, large merchants, the owners of mines, iron foundries, engineering firms, and breweries were also large property owners but were not as prominent. The extraordinarily powerful position of such families as the Horrockses of Preston or the owners of industrial suburbs such as the Ashworths of Turton (Bolton) truly made them factory lords dispensing employment and often housing and social services to their people. Paternal generosity could be found in their actions as well as ruthlessness.[16] What was constant, however, was the concentration of property in the hands of the few. Though most factory owners in this period were still resident in these towns, the social distance from their employees was growing. Social mobility from operative to owner was increasingly difficult. This widening social gap probably added to whatever sense of alienation was felt by the labour force as a whole.

The role of other social 'classes,' especially the lower middle class or upper strata of working men, was especially important. These groups, whether independent tradesman, the most prosperous of factory workers, or even small shopkeepers, also sometimes designated as 'petty bourgeoisie,' 'middling classes,' or 'the labour aristocracy' (in the case of the skilled and well-paid), occupied a crucial position on the social scale.[17] Frequently they were working-class political leaders in the first third of the century. Thereafter they were often members of the polite, mid-Victorian trade unions exuding respectability, responsibility, intelligence, and self-improvement. They are the focus of the 'embourgeoisement' controversy amongst historians of the working class. Many writers have viewed them as passive tools of the propertied classes through the mid-nineteenth century. More recently writers such as Geoffrey Crossick and Trygve Tholfsen have argued their active and positive espousal of Victorian values, minimizing the idea of bourgeois middle-class cultural and social encroachment.[18] The truth of these arguments must be tested in the context of particular towns. Such factors could certainly contribute in a variety of ways to the pattern of class tension found in a particular industrial area.

Bearing the complexity of the question in mind, I believe that class tension was a number of degrees higher in Preston than in the other three towns. The sources of evidence are most frequently found in recorded events in newspapers and journals rather than in an elaborate quantification of new sources of data. In any case there is as yet no generally recognized measuring instrument used by historians for either social conflict or class consciousness within a given community. One important reason for this higher degree of class tension in Preston is

9 Introduction

found in the operations of sectarianism within that community. This conclusion, at least for the social historians who specialize in quantification, must also be considered somewhat impressionistic. It is, however, a judgment based upon weighing and integrating the role of the various factors previously mentioned affecting class relationships and social tension.

It is also my belief that, among the social classes, the propertied classes, composed of industrialists, professional men, and the like, divided into Anglican and Nonconformist elites, largely guided the political sectarianism appearing in the mid-Victorian decades. They did so for historical and cultural reasons, not primarily as a method of dominating their economic inferiors. Such guidance was also given in co-ordination with other social groups below them to be found in the two sectarian-political camps in the four towns. The exception to this, as we shall see, was Preston, where the Liberal-Nonconformist side did not possess a Dissenting elite. The resulting situation in that town was something that resembled a class struggle between the two political factions that may well have allowed for even sharper forms of tension between classes to emerge in other areas of urban life.

Since the pattern of sectarian conflict antedated the Industrial Revolution of the late eighteenth century, it is logical to conclude that sectarian conflict was an active, complicating factor in the general picture of class tension resulting from the new industrial order. Sectarianism was therefore not in essence a function of class conflict. However, as industrial capitalism was a national system as well as a local phenomenon, the impact of the class structure upon sectarianism must also be considered. The propertied elites who directed the Liberal-Nonconformist alliance or the Tory-Church forces were also part of another elite – that created by wealth in the new industrial order.[19] Similar comments could also be made concerning other groups lower on the social scale. However, it is the local social setting which must ultimately be consulted in clarifying and refining our concepts. It is the final arbitrator in these questions.

2
Bolton: the Geneva of Lancashire

Bolton, like many industrial cities, was little more than a small town in the eighteenth century. By the early nineteenth century, however, profound demographic and social changes had already taken place as a result of the Industrial Revolution. William Cooke Taylor once noted that 'the most striking phenomenon of the Factory System is the amount of population which it has suddenly accumulated at certain points' and the new habits 'of thought and action' among its manufacturing population.[1] There is no question of the staggering social effects of the rapid build-up of the cotton industry. However, aspects of the older society did survive, including, among other things, sectarianism.

Bolton had a legacy of sectarian bitterness stretching back to the seventeenth century. In the early Stuart period the fervent commitment to Puritanism of many of its citizens earned it the title 'Geneva of Lancashire.' As a parliamentary stronghold it came under heavy attack by the Royalists in the Civil War. On 18 May 1644 occurred the famous Bolton Massacre. The Cavalier army of the Earl of Derby and Prince Rupert captured the town, and within an hour some 1500 men, women, and children were put to the sword, including 400 Royalist supporters by mistake. Anglican and Royalist persecution continued into the Restoration period. The events were faithfully re-recorded in most chapel histories and commemoratives written throughout the nineteenth century.

Religion itself remained a vital force in the lives of Boltonians into the Victorian age, in spite of industrialization and rapid urban growth. An anonymous writer in *St. James's Magazine* noted on first seeing Bolton in 1869: 'The first glimpse a stranger gets of it impresses him with the idea that it is a well-to-do and prosperous town. The next impression is that it must be eminently religious – churches and chapels and conventicles for the worship of every religion under the sun, Turks, heretics, jumpers and Jews.'[2] A survey of the various religious groups within Bolton society shows the Church of England to have had greater

11 Bolton: the Geneva of Lancashire

social strength in the Victorian period than one would imagine in the Geneva of Lancashire. Anglicanism experienced a revival in the early nineteenth century and, under the diligent vicarship of the Reverend Mr Slade from 1817 to 1857, fourteen new churches were consecrated, giving it a strong foothold in the period of Bolton's greatest development. Anglican laymen, including new cotton magnates, contributed to this expansion in several cotton towns. Especially notable was their assistance to the building of All Saints Chapel and St Paul's, Astley Bridge, in Little Bolton and Emmanuel District Chapel, Great Bolton.[3] Among the wealthy supporters of Bolton Anglicanism were such cotton families as the Heskeths, Bollings, Hardcastles, Ormerods, and Crosses, together with W.F. Hulton, owner of the Hulton Collieries, the Hargreaves and Dobsons in engineering, and James Greenhalgh, a prosperous lawyer.

The Anglican congregations, of course, embraced people well below this group of manufacturers, merchants, bankers, professional men, and gentlemen. But the clergy and the zealous laity clearly looked to the elite[4] for leadership. Sermons concerning the shortcomings of the industrial order were directed toward the workers. In his sermon preached before the weavers society in 1774, Vicar Whitehead stated that weavers had a moral duty to live up to all of their social obligations.[5] This meant hard work in the factory. Sermons against laziness, theft, and deceit among workers were common in the late eighteenth and early nineteenth centuries, one of the few areas beyond doctrinal disputes with which early printed sermons concerned themselves. This close liaison between Bolton's wealthy manufacturers and clergy was a target for attack by at least one Anglican clergyman, the Reverend Walter Chamberlain, in his pamphlet, *Parochial Centralization*, published in 1850.[6] Chamberlain's main concern was to point to the overriding power which vicars had over their lesser clergy in such large northern parishes as Blackburn and Bolton. But much of his work expresses very directly a distrust of the alliance between senior clergy and wealthy masters of industry. Chamberlain, being incumbent of the new parish of St John, had direct knowledge of the Bolton situation. He even went so far as to assert that these manufacturers might inspire the senior clergy to run the church on the lines of a factory with 'the Rector being the master, the district Incumbents, spinners; the Curates, piecers.'

The Anglican elite did not command the entire industrial wealth of the town, however. In a letter to the National Society requesting financial help for parish schools, the Reverend John Lyons outlined the situation from the viewpoint of St George's Church:

To show you how little I can expect from the district I will enumerate the mills within it.
1   Mill owned by a Methodist.

12 The Sectarian Spirit

2 Bankrupt.
3 Owned by a member of the Church of England, but far from wealthy.
4 Mill owned by an Independent.
5 Mill owned by an Anti-Corn Law-Leaguer.
6 Mill owned by a Church of England man, family struggle to keep above water.
7 Warehouse owned by a Methodist.
8 Warehouse owned by an Independent.[7]

This assessment of the church's position among the propertied class of the district was confirmed by a later incumbent of St George's who stated, 'Our congregation is by no means wealthy.'[8] Yet mills and foundries abounded in the area. Anglicanism, then, while having an elite in Bolton, could certainly not claim a monopoly of the important persons in all areas of the town. During the 1840s, 50s, and early 60s there was some reduction in the pace of church building. In 1862 the *Bolton Chronicle*[9] claimed that church expansion had not kept pace with the population, arguing that only half the church-going Anglicans could be accommodated by that date. Only two new churches appear to have been added in the period from 1851 to 1871, though Peter Ormerod did manage to rebuild the parish church at a cost of £40,000.

Many of Bolton's most prominent citizens were in fact members of Nonconformist congregations. Among these groups the Unitarian chapel seems to have claimed the greatest number of influential people. A town councillor, J.J. Bradshaw, once related the following incident told to him by his friend, Richard Carling, in the 1850s: 'A young man who for a good many years had heard Unitarians spoken of with the usual horror as heretics determined, after much screwing up of his mental courage, to go to the chapel and see what it was like. Selecting a quiet Sunday morning, he made his way, after the service had begun, into the gallery, and found a place from which he had a good view. Looking down, he saw, sitting below, the leaders in every good movement in the town or in business, whose character and standing gave weight and authority to all they took in hand.'[10]

The Bank Street Chapel, which traced its origins back to the mid-eighteenth century, owed much of its prosperity to the allegiance of such prominent families as the Pilkingtons, Brandeths, Deans, Heywoods, Darbishires, Crooks, Harwoods, Taylors, and Bromleys.[11] Almost all of these families controlled large cotton concerns in town. Indeed, in the religious census of 1851, of 614 sittings in chapel, 600 were appropriated.[12] These 600 seats were not by any means entirely the property of the wealthy. The membership lists (an amplification of the list of seat-holders) recorded by the chapel ministers at various times between the mid 1820s and mid 1880s include a large number of shopkeepers and tradesmen as

13 Bolton: the Geneva of Lancashire

well as factory workers. These occupational categories, hard to apply (especially with small shopkeepers),[13] straddle the line between working and middle class. Similarly, some skilled groups within the ranks of factory workers were labelled the 'aristocrats of labour.' The estimates for manufacturers and factory operatives, however, were minimal, representing only those who without doubt were in those categories.[14] The figures in Table I reveal the growth in selected occupational groups within part of the period as well as the social composition of the entire congregation in 1850.

Chapel business and the character of the chapel membership contributed to local pride in many Nonconformist congregations. This was especially true of the Bolton Unitarians. Though marriage records and institutions such as 'the Circle'[15] reveal that the wealthy chapel elite did not mix readily with the working classes[16] at Bank Street, their relations with those lower on the social scale were cordial. Trustee lists for 1833 and 1863 include some tradesmen and shopkeepers. Power was therefore shared to a degree by various classes. The new Unitarian business giants nevertheless found their power in the local community reinforced by the chapel. They directed the financing, choice of minister, and many of the social activities of their congregations. The traditional local autonomy of the Nonconformist denominations therefore complemented the local power of its leading sons. It was no accident that Bank Street Chapel could boast that the first two mayors of the town were members.

The attitude of the leading members of the chapel was predictable on the subject of the factory system. Manufacturing on a large scale had given Dissenters a disproportionate influence (according to their numbers) in the local community. This was the basis of their new social power. Franklin Baker, the most famous minister of the chapel, wrote to the bishop of Manchester in 1850 going so far as to claim that factories had moral as well as economic advantages for the people: 'The order and regularity enforced upon the operatives are so nearly akin to moral habits, that they cannot but be viewed as having a tendency highly beneficial to the character. Instead of being a school of vice, a well-ordered factory gives the initiative to feelings and habits greatly conducive to self-culture.'[17]

Baker may have been referring to the mills of his friend Henry Ashworth, the Quaker industrialist. Ashworth enforced strict moral codes on workers at his New Eagley factory as well as providing for their physical well-being. Ashworth factories were models of cleanliness and efficiency. 'Evangelical' Quakerism[18] and Utilitarianism prompted him to believe that under such circumstances workers would respond with hard work. He did not see his workers as belonging to another class but rather as fellow members of the new industrial order[19] – one destined to bring happiness and prosperity to all. The relationship between

14 The Sectarian Spirit

TABLE I

Bank Street Chapel: membership and selected occupations, 1835-56

	July 1835	5 Dec. 1844	Midsummer 1856	Xmas 1856
Total number:	128	193	211	213
Floor pews	60	76	79	67
Gallery	68	108	132	146
Gentlemen and manufacturers	9	9	13	13
Shopkeepers	9	20	37	25
Tradesmen	15	17	39	36
Factory hands	23	30	32	44

Occupations of members, midsummer 1850

Minister	1
Gentlemen	8
Gentlewomen	11
Manufacturers	5
Surgeons	3
Vet. Surgeon	1
Schoolmasters	3
Schoolmistresses	2
Relieving officers	3
Innkeepers	5
Clerks	9
Shopkeepers	37
Tradesmen, independent Artisans	39
Factory workers	32
Farmers	4
Warehouseman	1
Slater	1
Agent	1
Labourer	1
Railway porter	1
Letter carriers	4
Servants	6*
Illegible	7
No occupations listed	26
TOTAL	211

The congregation lists for November 1823, 1828, July 1835, 1 January 1841, 1 October 1843, 5 December 1844, Christmas 1848, Midsummer 1850, and 1854 can be found among the MS letters of Bank Street Chapel held at the library of the Unitarian College, Manchester (C1/54). The 'names of seat holders, Christmas 1856' are in the vault of Bank Street Chapel, Bolton. These lists containing occupations are an unusual discovery for a cotton town - at least before 1870.
* Women listed were usually single and employed or widows.

15 Bolton: the Geneva of Lancashire

employer and worker was based on a freely arranged contract entered in good faith by all. Religion was the instigator of this good faith being 'a popular power.'[20] Ashworth believed that disharmony in the industrial order was the work of atheism, communism, socialism, and trade unionism. Though his thinking on the subject of industrial relations was more advanced than most, in his general views he spoke for much of the Nonconformist elite of the town. The real enemy was the old landowning interest, which was Anglican and authoritarian. The Industrial Revolution had liberated Dissenters socially and opened new horizons for progress for all men – materially and spiritually. Beyond politics, Ashworth's support for the Nonconformist cause in such organizations as the British and Foreign Schools Society was well known.[21] Though Ashworth's own Quaker congregation in Bolton was small, it was socially prestigious and included at various times among its members and adherents other prominent cotton manufacturers such as Joshua Woodland, George Groofield, Thomas Thomasson, the Horrockses, and even the parents of John Bright.[22]

The Congregationalists or Independents, the single most numerous body of Dissenters in Bolton, also had wealthy members such as the cotton spinner Peter Martin in their midst.[23] The census figures for 1851 indicate a large number of appropriated seats in the chapels. In contrast with Bank Street Chapel, however, the survival of the denomination as a whole rested on the working classes. General subscription funds were usually responsible for financial well-being, and the administrative direction in the chapels was in the hands of many lower middle-class persons. The trust deed for the new chapel on St George's Road, dated August 1863, shows that of the thirty-one trustees, seven were shopkeepers and ten were tradesmen.[24]

The best known Congregationalists in the period were decidedly not affluent men. Many were identified with the causes of the workingmen. For example, Alderman John Brown (1792–1878), a shoemaker, was a leading Radical and municipal reformer of the period. William Hope Davison, the pastor of the St George's Road Chapel, was the secretary of the Bolton Poor Protection Society in the 1860s and first editor of the pro-working class *Bolton Evening News*. Ralph Almond, a timber merchant, at the age of twenty founded the Wheelwrights' and Blacksmiths' Society in 1830. The list of such men is impressively long. The emphasis in Congregationalist chapels on education reflected this working-class interest. Activities ranged from the first working-class Sunday schools established by James Hay in 1774 to the great Bible classes and missions for working men in the late 1860s.

For the last remaining Nonconformist denomination of considerable size in Bolton, the Methodists, I have uncovered, as in my other towns, somewhat less evidence as to their social composition. As their numbers were large and growing (compare the census figures for 1829 with those of 1851 in Tables III and

16 The Sectarian Spirit

IV), we can assume that many must have been of humble origins, though a few, such as the Musgraves in cotton and the Knowles family in coal, were known for their wealth. John Foster has noted similar facts for Oldham where the Methodists, with the least number of big employers, scored the most impressive gains in numbers of adherents.[25] Looking at Wesleyan Methodists in particular, Professor Walker[26] has argued that the membership of ten cotton town circuits (Bolton, Preston, Stockport, Blackburn, Chorley, Ashton, Oldham, Rochdale, Burnley, and Padiham) rose between 1861 and 1864 by 15.1 per cent and in the case of Preston and Chorley circuits by 38.6 per cent. Drawing evidence supplied by the Minutes of the Wesleyan Methodist Connexion, he estimated that of 34,892 members in the Lancashire circuits affected by the Cotton Famine in 1863, 14,263 were cotton operatives. These circuits included Preston, Stockport, Blackburn, and a number of other cotton towns as well as Bolton.

In contrast, growth figures for Primitive Methodist membership in the four towns of Bolton, Preston, Stockport, and Blackburn, as outlined in Table II, tend to be far less dramatic. However, apart from the fact that Primitive Methodist membership did not keep pace with population growth, there seems to be no substantial evidence, despite early Victorian schismatic tendencies within Bolton Methodism,[27] for Professor Ward's pessimistic views of the decline of institutionalized methodism as a whole. Geoffrey Best[28] has also commented on the strength of Methodism, and in particular Wesleyan Methodism, in northern industrial towns in the mid-Victorian period. In Bolton this success may also have been a product of the religious revival of the late 1850s that reached the town by 1860. *The Revivalist* recorded early that year that an average of 1200 to 1400 were present each night at the Temperance Hall to hear a series of sermons by Charles G. Finney, the American revivalist.[29] The religious impact of the revival is confirmed in local sources.[30] The Wesleyans themselves initiated a 'great revival' on 13 October 1861 with a series of sermons by a local preacher – James Wardle Greenhalgh. This reinforced a new spree of Methodist chapel building in the town and, as Walker points out generally for these towns, it happened in the midst of economic depression during the Cotton Famine.

While Methodism was strong numerically, however, its social influence was negligible. Its nation-wide equivocal relationship politically with the rest of Nonconformity was one reason for this situation. The outlook of the Dissenting elite toward the working-class Methodists, however, was probably as benevolent as that which they displayed on occasion toward working-class people of their own chapels. As has been seen, Nonconformist manufacturers frequently engaged in and supported actions they thought were conducive to the betterment of the lot of urban workers. They co-operated with workingmen, though principally the upper strata of workers, within their own chapels and,

17 Bolton: the Geneva of Lancashire

TABLE II

Primitive Methodist circuit reports: membership

	18 May 1833	1872
Bolton	436	463
Preston	477	580
Stockport	499	510
Blackburn	192	480

These figures are, of course, for members only – representing only a fraction of the actual Methodist strength. From Consolidated Minutes of Primitive Methodist Connexion, Methodist Archives, London

occasionally, in organizations not overtly connected with chapels, as, for example, the Bolton Mechanics' Institution established in July 1825. While the trustees, honorary members, and principal subscribers were overwhelmingly drawn from the ranks of the Nonconformist elite, the general membership was completely formed of tradesmen.[31]

Roman Catholicism, according to the religious censuses of the period, had approximately three thousand adherents in Bolton. This may have represented only a fraction of their actual numbers as there was often insufficient space in church at the time of the service. Many of these Catholics were Irish and were in the position, described by the Catholic Poor School Committee, of 'numbering among them not even a single shopkeeper, with work uncertain and wages low.'[32] An Irishman, according to Timothy Grimshaw, was also a 'most frightful and obnoxious creature'[33] in early Victorian Bolton. The attention and energies of the Catholic church were largely absorbed in ministering to these Irish. Catholicism was basically a religion of an ethnic minority within the labouring mass.

The old denominations, of course, were not alone in their interest in the working classes of the town. As W. Cooke Taylor noted in visiting the Ashworth family's industrial suburb of Turton in 1842: 'Nowhere did I see a book of immoral or even questionable tendency, unless the writings of the Mormonites or Latterday Saints may be considered as such, for this strange form of fanaticism, which we have imported from America appears to be taking deep root in Lancashire. Enthusiasm in everything, indeed, appears to be a marked characteristic of this branch of the Saxon race, and it is equally manifested in new forms of religion and in new forms of machinery.'[34] At the general conference of the Mormon Church in 1840, Bolton was reported to have sixty members, one elder, two priests, and one teacher.[35] In general in the country this new sect was known to have a strong working-class following.[36] This was probably the case in Bolton as well.

18 The Sectarian Spirit

The Mormons, however, were not the only 'new form of religion' making inroads among the working classes of Bolton. The Swedenborgian or New Church congregation in Little Bolton, according to its baptismal register,[37] had a strong following among mill hands. The congregation's growth between 1829 and 1851 can be seen by inspecting the religious censuses for those years. Most of these organizations, however, seemed to share the same withdrawal syndrome which sociologists tell us is characteristic of 'sect-type' groups. They made no criticism of the state of industrial society. Even the Teetotallers, so dynamic in places like Preston, seemed to lack independent initiative, being more of a sub-group under the direction of the old denominations.[38] Most of the new sects (and Roman Catholicism), therefore, while ministering primarily to the masses, did not stir up the people against the existing social order.

There was, however, one sect that did offer a systematic criticism of the new industrial social order in Bolton, as in the other three northern towns under consideration – the Secularists. Secularism, having most of the characteristics of any 'religious' sect,[39] offered an alternative philosophy to the working classes from that of the old denominations and the other new sects. It did not accept the status quo in the new industrial social order and offered practical criticism through specific political and social goals for the labouring masses. At the foundation of its creed was a new class division in society: Secularism opposed Christian denominations, among other reasons, for ignoring and indeed exacerbating the breach between the propertied and the propertyless.

The sect owed much to the previous activities of the Owenite Socialists in Bolton.[40] As a result of a series of Secularist lectures given at the local hall of science in 1851, a Secularist society was formed within the next year. By 1857 the society had absorbed most of the socialist groups in town and had established its own offices in Cheapside Street, complete with portraits of Paine and Owen. Thanks to the society's leading member, J. Moss, a bookseller, Secularist literature was fairly well distributed in the town as a whole. In the late 1850s the membership soared.[41] The primary appeal was among the upper strata of workingmen.

All was not talk with the Secularists in Bolton. Even before the formal establishment of their society in 1852, Secularists, together with related socialist groups, had begun a friendly co-operative society on the Rochdale model. Capital for this enterprise was raised slowly as money was contributed almost completely from working-class people – each person donating £2.[42] A provision store was finally opened in the Great Bolton area in 1859 with sixty-six members. Two months later a branch was established in Little Bolton. This practical exercise in self-improvement on the part of the working-class Secularists was not welcomed by many higher up in the town society with a stake in the

19 Bolton: the Geneva of Lancashire

old economic processes[43] – especially the larger shopkeepers and merchants. The stresses of the Cotton Famine in the 1860s caused some working-class people to forsake the Secularist cause for more practical and immediate help in their distress, and membership declined. The co-operative stores, however, managed to survive the famine in good order. In 1866 new central premises were established, complete with pub. The Cotton Famine, of course, did not hit Bolton as badly as the other cotton towns because so much of the local industry was devoted to the making of 'fine counts' using Egyptian rather than American cotton. In the late 1860s the Secularists expanded into new activities and an education department was established by the co-operative society. There is no evidence to suggest, however, that the Secularists supported the so-called workingmen's candidates[44] in the 1870 election for the new school board. No doubt the denominational and political affiliations of the candidates made Secularists disinterested in such support.

The general social strength of the institutional churches within Bolton (as in the other cotton towns) is a difficult phenomenon to measure. Though Richard Cobden and a few other national figures may have wondered about the role of churches as major vehicles for social engineering by mid century, it is by no means certain that the churches' general influence in the northwest was dwindling before the 1870s. Religious influences, of course, like those of sectarianism, went well beyond the institutional churches. As A.A. MacLaren has also pointed out,[45] standardized, reliable measurements of religiosity in Victorian Britain have not yet been developed. Church attendance and accommodation have been used as one gauge by some religious historians in recent years. Because such data are available they are supplied here but with reservations concerning their use.

Inexact though this social survey of religion may be in some respects, it does give us in particular some idea of the types of social classes and interest groups adhering to the various denominations in Bolton. It is obvious in the case of the Church and Nonconformity that both groups possessed propertied elites within their numbers as well as people lower on the social scale. The ramifications of this latter fact are difficult to ascertain completely because of the virtual impossibility of discovering the inner thoughts and motives of individuals in this period. Dr Patrick Joyce believes, at least in the case of Blackburn, that millowners may well have attempted to use churches and schools for their own political and social purposes.[46] Apart from the fact that millowners were not the only element among the propertied interests in these cotton towns, I think that two important points should be raised in objection to this view. First, it presumes the emergence at this time of an essentially secular view of town affairs, including politics, with the propertied members of churches being mainly influenced by concerns other

20 The Sectarian Spirit

TABLE III

Places of worship not of the Church of England, 1829, in townships eventually to form the Municipal Borough of Bolton

Number in each sect	Designation of each sect	Chapels
*Township of Great Bolton** (population in 1831: 28,299)		
520	Independents	1
850	Independents	1
100	Baptists	1
10	Baptist Gadbyites†	1
200	Unitarians	1
750	Presbyterians	1
300	Wesleyan Methodists	1
450	Kilhamite Sect	1
300	Ranters, Primitive Methodists	1
3000	Roman Catholics	1
Township of Little Bolton (population in 1831: 12,896)		
400	Independents	1
1400	Old Established Methodists	1
60	Quakers	1
100	Catholics	1
120	New Jerusalemites	1
Township of Tonge with Haulgh (population in 1831: 2201)		
No Catholics resident in the township		'No place of Worship of any persuasion'
50	Unitarians	
40	Independents	
50	Wesleyan Methodists	
20	Swedenborgians	
Tonge		
'There is about 550 persons in the Township of Tonge and of that Number there is only about 40 but what are of the Church of England.'		No chapel or place of worship
40	Methodists	

These are the original returns found in the LRO, Records of the Clerk of the Peace QDV/9. The poor grammar or peculiar comments on these and other returns can be attributed to the constable conducting the census. The returns for Lancashire were also printed up in Parliamentary Papers, 1830, IX. They are inaccurate in many ways in both forms, though the original return sheets are better. The printed tables usually under-represented Nonconformists and Roman Catholics.
* The municipal borough was formed out of the townships of Great Bolton, Haulgh, and the major portion of the chapelry of Little Bolton.
†Possibly Lancashire Baptist hyphers

21 Bolton: the Geneva of Lancashire

TABLE IV

Religious census of 1851, Municipal Borough of Bolton (population: 61, 171)

	Church	Others
Percentage of sittings to population	15.7	19.9
Percentage of sittings to total number of sittings	44.1	55.9
Estimated percentage of population at divine service	26.2*	

Denomination	Number of places of worship	Number of sittings Free	Number of sittings Appropriated	Total attendances Census Sunday
Church	9	3024	5134	9373
Presbyterian Church in England	1		500	200
Independent	5	370	2040	2593
Particular Baptist	2	163	377	552
Friends	1	300		100
Unitarians	1	14	600	710
Westeyan Methodist	5	1608	1792	3538
Methodist New Connexion	2	600		339
Primitive Methodist	3	450	306	926
Wesleyan Association	1	150	350	456
New Church	1	20	350	400
Brethren	1	70		55
Isolated Congregations	2	150	550	292
Roman Catholics	2		600	2953

PP, 1852-3, LXXXIX
* This estimate was arrived at by adopting the much debated formula of Horace Mann, registrar of the religious census. The figure represents all morning attendances, plus one-half of the afternoon and one-third of the evening attendances taken as a percentage of the total population.

than those of religion in church affairs. Secondly, it assumes that Church and chapel affairs were *solely* governed by the propertied members of congregations unchallenged by other social groups within the various denominations. Neither of these conditions were wholly true before 1870 in the cotton towns. As has been noted, some of these secular considerations may well have influenced the

The Sectarian Spirit

TABLE V

Bolton Chronicle census, 12 April 1862

Denomination	Percentage of population	Building programme
Roman Catholic	7	3 churches built in 12 years
Wesleyan and Protestant Dissent	19	8 or 9 churches built in 25 years
Church-going Churchmen	22.5	No church built in last 25 years. Can only accommodate one half church-going Churchmen
35,000 non-worshippers		

It is interesting to note that the 1862 figures claim some 48.5 per cent of the population was church-going – a total considerably higher than the Mann estimate of 26.2 per cent for Census Sunday 1851. The figures given in Appendices I and II also indicate that the increase in total sittings in town between 1851 and 1871 was 66.4 per cent compared with a population increase of only 35.4 per cent. The bulk of the accommodation increase was the work of the Nonconformists. By 1880 church accommodation increased by almost 10,000 sittings – approximately the same increase as in the general population for that period.

actions of some wealthy members within their churches, but it is doubtful that they were generally the pattern. Joyce appears to have made an *a priori* assumption that sectarianism, among other things, was less important than the social power of factory owners in places like Blackburn by the 1860s. It is conceivable that the factory owners' influence increased among the masses while that of sectarianism diminished in the later nineteenth century. In the period under discussion in this book, however, I shall argue for the primacy of sectarianism as a motivating force in politics and certain other facets of town life.

The propertied elites of Churchmen and Nonconformists were of varied backgrounds, as we have already seen. Men who earned their wealth from the Industrial Revolution – particularly the actual cotton manufacturers – were certainly an important component. The Church elite were usually groomed and co-opted into the leadership of town Anglicanism by the old pre-Reform social and political oligarchy, thereby continuing the spirit of the oligarchy after the era of Reform. The Nonconformist men of wealth created, as W.G. Rimmer described for Leeds, 'their own small social hierarchy and institutions, around which they would eventually rally opposition to the oligarchy in the town.'[47] They too carried on after the Reform Era of the 1830s. As the *Liberator* noted: 'Dissent is

23 Bolton: the Geneva of Lancashire

respected; it is seen in alliance with intelligence, probity and wealth.'[48] Wealth, of course, for either the Anglican or Nonconformist elites, did not arise exclusively from the Industrial Revolution. Indeed, these elites, especially for Churchmen, could trace their origins back to an earlier society of the eighteenth century. The propertied classes, however, increased enormously in wealth because of the Industrial Revolution. The prominent role of Dissenters in these economic developments is better known than that of Anglicans. However, both groups prospered in the cotton towns.

The basic economic facts for Bolton's cotton industry, as for the other three towns, are impressive enough. At mid-nineteenth century approximately one-third of all males and 20 per cent of all females, twenty years old and over, worked in the mills.[49] There were forty-two factories at that time with an average work force of 315. These firms were owned by fifty-seven individuals, all but two of whom were resident.[50] Table VI, taken from an earlier period, indicates that spinning was the main concern of these Bolton manufacturers. 'Fine counts' (or high counts) became their main product, especially after the invention of the mule. Before this rapid expansion of fine-spinning, however, Bolton had been known as the main producer of coarser or unfinished cotton articles in the northwest. A few merchant families from this period remained, such as the Ashworths, who made the transition to large-scale spinning. On the whole, however, spinning was more a business for 'new men.'

The relationship between millowners and workers was a strained one through much of the Victorian period. Though wages in the cotton industry were relatively high, the environment tended to be ruthless. As an anonymous writer in *St James's Magazine* stated in 1869: 'there is in fact no golden link of sympathy between master and man – apathy on the one hand and solemn distrust on the other.' The attitudes of 'new men' of wealth in the cotton industry were probably less paternal than those of the older merchant families, notably the Ashworth family's industrial suburbs of New Eagley, Bank Top, and Turton. Some industrialists believed that a man could cross class lines and progress from operative to small owner of a cotton concern. After 1830, with the appearance of an increasing number of larger factories, such social mobility was in actual fact very difficult. All in all, the precarious nature of the trade, with its cycles of prosperity and depression,[51] the widening social chasm between owners and workers, and the general conditions of men, women, and children in the factories produced tension between the classes. At the same time, as John Foster indicated for Oldham, class solidarity, or at least mutual identification of interests amongst the labouring masses, was also an earlier and easier achievement in a cotton town.

It is not surprising, then, that urban Lancashire was famous as a region of high social tension in the first half of the nineteenth century. Strikes and other

TABLE VI

People employed in the different branches of the cotton industry in the Parish of Bolton, 1833

Cleaning and spreading cotton	156
Carding	1521
Mule-spinning	2833
Throstle-spinning	125
Reeling	375
Weaving	351
Roller covering	21
Engineers, mechanics, firemen, etc.	87
Total number of operatives	5469

Report of Factory Inquiry Commission, Supplementary Report, Part I (U), PP, 1834, XIX

types of breakdown in industrial relations were a logical product of this situation. Violence was also a part. Machine-breaking riots were among the worst in England in the three decades before 1832. The sources of this protest were a combination of food prices, wages, the introduction of power looms, Luddism, trade unionism, and perhaps overzealous magistrates. The violence recurred at certain points after 1832. Chartist activity in 1839 and 1842, for example, resulted in much destruction of property in Bolton. In the latter year a defence association was formed by some of the large property owners against future working-class violence. Such violence, however, never achieved the level of the Luddite unrest of 1812.[52] Some of this working-class violence pre-dated the factory system and much of it thereafter involved men outside the factory as well as those in it. The 'shopkeeper/craftsmen class'[53] could be found in various forms of working-class protest and violence as well as in the more political trade unions and movements, such as Radicalism and Chartism. More often than not they spoke for workingmen to the propertied classes. At a time when the existence of a completely separate and unified working-class culture is debatable, their voices should be all the more important to historians. These voices were directed as much in the service of sectarianism as class conflict. The pattern of sectarian conflict was shared through them with the propertied denominational elites. This form of social conflict may well have helped to subdue the lines of class conflict in the critical mid-Victorian decades.

There were different types of sectarian conflict in the cotton towns – spontaneous as well as organized. The theological differences amongst individual denominations or sects, such as that between orthodox Dissent and Unitarianism, as well as the strident Toryism and aloofness of many Wesleyans (before 1850) which separated them from Nonconformity, were all tensions within these societies. Perhaps the most explosive force was the wide-spread hostility toward

25 Bolton: the Geneva of Lancashire

Roman Catholicism. Nevertheless the main organized sectarian conflict, at least in relation to politics, lay between the forces of Liberal-Nonconformity and Tory Churchism.[54] Sectarian propaganda tended to be directed between these two groupings rather than against particular denominations. The relationship between sectarianism and politics was more in the nature of mutually-reinforcing companions than as parent/child in the period 1832-70. Though sectarianism did on occasion assume the dominant role in motivation, political or otherwise, Kitson Clark's observation on the intertwining of politics and religion in the mid-Victorian era certainly is relevant for these societies.

The Reform Act of 1832 saw the immediate end of a series of sharp contests which involved Nonconformists and Roman Catholics on one side and Tory Churchmen on the other. These contests mainly concerned Repeal of the Test and Corporations Acts, Catholic Emancipation, and later the sectarian-related issue of representation for some of the great northern towns in Parliament – all basically within the period between the late 1820s and 1832. The period after 1832 can be characterized as one of well-organized sectarian-political strife relying less on specific issues of confrontation.

By 1832 the Evangelical revival had also shot its bolt and the period of greatest recruitment for the churches amongst the masses was over. As W.R. Ward has pointed out, petty denominationalism increased at the expense of the older, undenominational fervour of the revival. Methodism in particular experienced a great deal of internal schism. Class strife also on occasion broke into internal denominational affairs. The 1834 split in Hanover Street Congregational Chapel over the question of writing instruction in their Sunday school, for example, refected separatist militancy among working-class members.[55] However, social cohesion was more the rule in the affairs of congregations and their associated institutions, with religion rarely reflecting class tension. In fact the churches, and even more, sectarianism, tended to subdue it.

Churchmen in Bolton were not particularly anxious to incur the wrath of Nonconformists over purely religious issues after 1832. The church rate was put on a voluntary basis early in the nineteenth century to avoid the trouble experienced in other towns. Institutions associated closely with Dissent were allowed to grow unchallenged. A Church Institute, for example, was not established until 1841 – sixteen years after the formation of the Mechanics' Institute, associated with town Dissenters. In the late 1860s the Bolton Hesperus Literary and Christian Association witnessed many open displays of aggressive Nonconformist criticism of the Church.[56] Yet Churchmen made no public counterattack against the association or its leading members.

Only in the area of education did the Church interest actively oppose Dissenters. Even here, however, it can be argued that Churchmen acted primarily out of the desire to defend essential elements of their own religion, which included the right to raise their children as they saw fit. In the late 1830s Churchmen supported their own schemes for a national programme of education as a reaction against the current Nonconformist system. In 1837, for example, Henry Ashworth read a paper before the British Association entitled 'On the State of Education in the Borough of Bolton.'[57] The main point of his paper was that half the town's children received no education. His statistical evidence also revealed that Dissenters provided educational facilities for three times as many children as did Churchmen. The result was an attack by the pro-Church press against Ashworth's alleged attack on Church schools. In 1870 the thorny question of a national scheme of education came to a head. But even in the complicated manoeuvrings in the fall of 1870 one can see a willingness to compromise on the part of both the Churchmen and the Nonconformists. In fact, had it not been for a sudden shattering of the electoral truce five minutes before the polls closed on 26 November 1870[58] a compromise list of thirteen candidates would have satisfied the leaders of all the old denominations, avoiding the need for a contested election to set up a local school board.

The only other important area of direct denominational conflict – that between protestants as a whole and Roman Catholics – was also kept in check. Much of the anti-Catholic rhetoric of the period was against the Irish community in town. The fear of cheap Irish labour undoubtedly explained much of the hostility of the English working class towards them. This form of sectarian hatred was harmful to the potential unity of the working class (English and Irish together). Though English workingmen were not always to be found in church on Sunday, the Reverend E.A. Verity, incumbent of Habergham, Lancashire, was correct in claiming that 'the convictions of the industrious classes of this country were soundly Protestant.'[59] The civic authorities, police, and newspapers also kept up a constant but low-key pressure against the Irish. But the respect among Boltonians for Canon Carter,[60] for over four decades, helped to lessen hostility toward the Irish and Catholic community as a whole. In any case, there were no major riots involving the Irish in the town before the election riots of 1868, which engulfed many urban areas in northwest England.

Local politics offered the most immediate and relevant rewards for power to denominational interest groups as well as to various social classes. The concerns of local politics were close to many people in the community. In contrast, parliamentary politics were often remote, and the usually smaller electorate made contests less exciting.[61] It was because local politics was so important to the local community, and not just because this type of politics was fought out in small and manageable administrative bodies, that zealous denominationalists sought involvement.

Politics also in turn influenced sectarianism and religion. The principal religious groups with social significance were Church and Dissent and this was

27 Bolton: the Geneva of Lancashire

revealed in politics. If you were a Nonconformist you were normally Liberal, if you were a staunch Churchman you were usually Tory.[62] There were, of course, exceptions and amendments to this statement. Andrew Knowles (1830-90), for example, a prominent cotton spinner and Churchman, was a life-long Liberal. The Nonconformists were both numerous and admirably led by their own elite of manufacturers, professional people, and other prominent, wealthy townsmen. This elite was the backbone of the town Liberal party. The Anglican elite of the town was likewise the backbone of the old regime, controlling many of the pre-Reform local government bodies and the local Tory party. Both elites realized by the mid 1830s that control of local government was the best way to maximize their influence in society.

The Liberals were influenced by the sectarian zeal of the Nonconformist element in the party from the very start. Much of the movement for administrative reform in local government in the 1830s,[63] supported by the Liberals, was the product of this zeal. Some of the old pre-Reform bodies, in particular the Courts Leet of the two Boltons, were controlled by Anglicans. The Courts Leet were self-elected and determined the qualifications for new members. In a speech favouring incorporation in January 1838, C.J. Darbishire, a Reformer and a Unitarian millowner, stated that he could not remember a Dissenter ever being appointed to the Great Bolton Court Leet and only one to Little Bolton.[64] In Little Bolton Court Leet a transcript of the proceedings for the 1830s indicates that members of this body were drawn from all walks of life except the working classes.[65] For some 'corporationists,' then, resentment against these bodies was based primarily on their religious exclusivity rather than on social grievances.

The incorporation controversy of 1838 was the first test of strength for the two political groupings. The controversy, of course, also involved issues such as the cost and necessity of incorporation, the possible destruction of the distinctive character of each of the Boltons, and the possibility of an increase in rates among townspeople. These other issues, however, seemed of secondary importance to the primary issue of the need for a new form of local government – which reflected the Nonconformists' desire for a greater voice in the town. The question of incorporation produced numerous meetings, pamphlets, placards, and petitions on both sides. The following statistics on the petitioners reveal some interesting facts. Of the 4150 persons who signed the petition in favour of incorporation, 3100 were ratepayers with property rated at £31,000. The 3422 persons who signed the petition against incorporation were all ratepayers with total property rated at £55,661.[66] From these figures it is obvious that though there were many wealthy persons (usually members of the Nonconformist elite) within the corporationists, this group was numerically larger but held less property as a whole than the anti-corporationists. The difference in wealth may have been the result of the Nonconformists having a smaller wealthy elite and more lower middle-class adherents than did the Anglicans in the anti-corporationist camp.

This strong lower middle-class element in the Nonconformist ranks was probably impelled to support the reform of local government, at least in part, as a way of acquiring political power. The old government bodies were obviously heavily laden with wealthy citizens. The first group of town councillors elected under the new charter in November 1838 shows an upswing in representation from the tradesman and shopkeeper classes. Since the Tories refused to participate in the election (taking this to mean de facto recognition of the charter), the new group of councillors was totally Liberal. The social composition of the council thus reflected that of the Dissenting chapels: there were seven designated as gentlemen, six owners of cotton spinning concerns, six owners of other industries, one coal merchant, two tea dealers, one spirit merchant, one tobacconist, one flour dealer, one yarn agent, one pawnbroker, one linen draper, one druggist, one grocer, one tailor, one shuttle maker, one chairmaker, one shoemaker, and one bleacher.[67]

The incorporation controversy did not end with the granting of a charter in 1838. Local Tory leaders continued to refuse to recognize the legality of the new document. The Anglican-Tory elite in town clearly felt that the charter was a serious blow to its prestige, and prestige was the issue here far more than the actual exercise of administrative power. The Courts Leet, the central showpieces of the Anglican elite, had ceased to be important in governmental bodies long before the 1830s. The more active and less prestigious boards of improvement trustees were neither vigorously defended by the Tories nor seriously criticized by the Liberals.[68] The Tories continued their opposition to the charter until the Boroughs' Incorporation Act of 1842 ended the legal disputes and confirmed the status of the charter. Between 1839 and 1842 many of the financial and administrative problems of the new corporation were a product of this opposition.[69]

On the Liberal-Nonconformist side the new corporation provided an opportunity for this group to assert its influence over town life. Under the guidance of the first two mayors, C.J. Darbishire and R. Heywood (both Unitarian mill-owners), the Liberal regime in the new corporation attempted to create a new style of government for Bolton. The hopes of these politicians ran high. Committees were set up, by-laws and regulations were passed, corporation officers were appointed. This regime was definitely partisan in its actions. The new borough justices appointed in 1839 were almost all Liberals and large property owners. At least five can be identified clearly as leading members of the Nonconformist community. Their Teetotalism was also well known.[70]

The intermingling and mutually reinforcing relationship of politics and sectarianism could be seen in many of the Liberal leaders. Thomas Thomasson

29 Bolton: the Geneva of Lancashire

(1806–1876) is a good case in point. Owner of a number of mills in Bolton, Thomasson entered politics staunchly on the side of the Liberal corporationists in the late 1830s. He was of Quaker background and was a close friend of the Nonconformist Liberal town leaders. Yet personally he was not a member of any specific church. After his marriage in 1834 he even attended the parish church on occasion with his wife, as he did Quaker services. Nevertheless, his allegiance was always to the political cause of his Nonconformist friends. In 1855, as a result of a pro-Crimean War sermon, he resolved never to attend the parish church.[71] His decision not to be seen in the spiritual company of Churchmen again was as much political as moral.

The tension between Liberal-Nonconformist and Tory-Anglican factions in this period did not completely obscure class tensions in town. The attitude of a significant section of the Liberal regime toward the working classes was one of benevolent friendliness. This was also the personal outlook of many Nonconformists as, for example, C.J. Darbishire, who was very sympathetic to working-class political movements, including Chartism. In August 1839, however, violent Chartist riots took place, causing much property damage and a temporary breakdown in civil order.[72] The renewal of working-class violence in 1842 only served to remind people again of the breach between propertied and propertyless. Unemployment and the unhealthy living conditions of workers were put forth as explanations for the unrest. A Society for the Protection of the Poor[73] was even established to supplement official agencies in relieving the poor. Class tension, nevertheless, dominated the scene. In 1842 a defence association was formed by the 'respectable' citizens, whatever their politics or religion, to protect property from working-class violence. After this brief crisis in 1842, however, there was no chance of the Liberal-Nonconformist and Tory-Anglican elites being drawn into permanent alliance for the protection of property. In the municipal elections of November 1842 the Tories launched a vigorous campaign against the Liberal regime. Two years later they gained a controlling majority in town council. The two political factions were as polarized as ever.

Denominational conflict remained as the root cause of political positions in local government throughout the period up to 1870. As the *Bolton Chronicle* noted concerning the 1862 municipal election: 'Some are chosen because they are teetotallers, and others because they are not. Some because they are Roman Catholics – others because they are Protestants. Some because they are Radicals – some because they are Conservatives. Strangely enough, the last thing municipal electors seem to think about is whether their nominees are well fitted for the discharge of the duties of the office to which they elect them.'[74] Administrative skill or naked opportunism was not enough to secure a man a position of importance on the heavily politicized town council. In local politics itself there were almost no expressions of secular political philosophy on record. Relationships of rivalry or friendship with local gentry do not appear to have been important by the early nineteenth century. As Table VII shows, there were few social and occupational differences between Liberals and Conservatives on council,[75] except a greater number of manufacturers in the Conservative ranks at this particular time. One may assume, therefore, that denominational differences were amongst the determinants of party preference.

Overt sectarian quarrels between the two political groups in council were rare. Robert Heywood's diaries covering the period up to 1868 make no mention of such occurrences.[76] There was just enough friction, however, to reinforce the relationship between local politics and sectarian conflict. In May 1840, for example, the Liberal-dominated council convened a special meeting to investigate the recent action of Liberal MP Peter Ainsworth in his support of the River Weaver bill. The bill allowed trustees of the river commission to use surplus revenue from navigation dues for the building of new Anglican churches in Cheshire. At a second meeting convened for the same purpose, a Conservative councillor opposed the Liberal inquiry by asking if Ainsworth would have been investigated had the surplus revenue helped to build Unitarian chapels.[77] Such arguments, however trivial, served on occasion to reinforce allegiances on both sides.

The condition of the town and its population were of some concern to both Conservatives and Liberals. The 'gas and water socialism'[78] of the Tory regime between 1844 and 1853 was matched by even more vigorous civic projects under the Liberals between 1853 and 1869. Much was done to improve the sanitary and housing conditions of the masses. Certain Liberals such as Alderman John Brown and Thomas Thomasson could be singled out as zealously concerned with improvements in public utilities in the interest of the people. But the greatest project most identified with this period, the town hall, built between 1863 and 1873 at a cost of £166,418, was of little direct benefit to the people. An anonymous writer in *St James's Magazine* stated that poverty, illiteracy, crime, and disease were still rampant in Bolton in 1869.

If this was the case, the working classes failed to register any special protest against this style of politics. They were not without potential power in this period. There was a sizeable increase of municipal voters owing to the Rating of Tenements Act in 1850 (13 and 14 Vic., c 99). In 1868 the electorate also increased.[79] Political machinery in the town, however, was successfully controlled by the denominational elites and their allies throughout the period. The cant and promises of the political factions, of course, could sway the masses. The Liberal victory of 1853 brought in a regime with many Nonconformists dedicated to local government. Millionaire Thomas Thomasson, at the first meeting

31 Bolton: the Geneva of Lancashire

TABLE VII

Bolton Town Council, 1852-3

Occupation	Liberals	Conservatives
Gentlemen	3	2
Solicitor	1	
Surgeon		1
Manufacturers		2
Iron founder		1
Iron master		1
Cotton spinners	3	8
Cotton waste		1
Manager		1
Overlooker		1
Timber merchant		1
Tea dealers		1
Corn dealers	1	
Machine maker	1	
Engineer		1
Spirit dealer	1	
Publican	1	
Drapers	2	
Tanner		1
Druggists	1	1
Tobacconist		1
Butcher	1	
Currier		1
Bleacher	1	
Unknown	4	2
Total	21	27

This information was compiled from Whelan's *New Alphabetical and Classified Directory for 1853* and local newspapers. This is the normal way of constructing such tables unless the information is supplied by the newspaper.

of council under this regime, made a speech describing Bolton as 'a little empire of 63,000 subjects' which could look forward to a great era of civic enterprise.[80] The gospel of civic improvement inspired by Dissenters in other towns and the obvious interest of leading Dissenters in Bolton society could not fail to impress many a common man. It is always possible that the average man might have had town halls in mind as well as drains.

Sectarian fervour was implicit in this Liberal-Nonconformist gospel of improvement, an enthusiasm which could be shared by many Dissenters well below the elite. The refusal of the mayor's gold chain of office by P.R. Arrowsmith in November 1853, because it was a symbol of the Established Church, was a triumph for all Nonconformists.[81] Because such actions were trivial for the denominational elites, this did not mean they were not popular, especially with Dissenters lower on the social scale. The anti-authority positions of Thomasson and Darbishire also helped.[82] Overt sectarianism was experimented with more consciously on the Conservative side. The Tories used anti-Catholic rhetoric against the Liberal regime in the municipal election of 1868. The Irish Church question in national politics undoubtedly assisted them, but so did such local events as the decision of the Liberal magistrates to arrest the great Orange orator, William Murphy, in July of that year.[83] In the election, feelings ran high between English and Irish working classes. There was even a riot in one ward. The expanded working-class electorate was, therefore, embroiled immediately in new sectarian conflict, with questions involving class conflict being largely ignored.

All-out sectarian warfare, of course, was futile. The almost equal strength of the Nonconformist and Church elites and their respective followers made continuous overt clashes in politics absurd. Each openly sectarian action by one side always had the possible effect of unifying the other side. This was particularly so with the Tories. it was better for them to stir up Orange sympathies among the working class than to engage in anti-Dissent actions that might further unite the lower orders in the chapels with the Liberal-Nonconformist elite. The balance between the social forces of Dissent and Church was mirrored in the balance between Liberal and Conservative forces in council. Once again there would appear to have been little difference in the social standing of the two political factions other than a somewhat greater number of cotton spinners in the Tory ranks. As indicated in Table VIII, the council membership in 1869 was exactly one-half Nonconformist and one-half Anglican.

In the other area of reformed local administration – poor relief – the lines of political-denominational interest were to be found on the new union board. The first election of guardians for Great and Little Bolton in January 1837 did not see a great turn-out of voters. This was primarily due to the fact that both the Radical Association and the Conservative Operative Association refused to participate officially in the elections. Opposition to the New Poor Law in Bolton was great and was found in both political camps. Issues such as localism versus centralism, autonomy of overseers, often cut across party lines. The sectarian differences between the political parties, however, were quite clear. This factor may also have prevented local politics from sinking into a morass of alignments inspired by intensely local issues. Party lines were therefore roughly similar in most of the English provinces.

The first meeting of the union board on 9 February 1837 demonstrated these sectarian differences.[84] In the deliberations over the selection of registrar, J. Hamilton, a Liberal and Nonconformist, argued that the Registration Act had

33 Bolton: the Geneva of Lancashire

TABLE VIII

Bolton Town Council, 1869–70 (composition: 27 Conservatives, 21 Liberals)

Churchmen	24	Methodist Free Church	1
Independents	4	General Baptist	1
Wesleyans	8	Particular Baptist	1
Wesleyan Refuge	1	Unitarians	6
Methodist New Connexion	2		

Bolton Chronicle, 6 Nov. 1869

been passed for the benefit of Dissenters. Watkins, a Tory, and one of the six possible candidates (all lawyers) for the office of registrar, disagreed, arguing that the post should be open to Christians of all persuasions, including Anglicans. Watkins was thereupon elected over Gordon, a Dissenter, by a vote of 22 to 13. No doubt the large voting power of the Tory-represented out-parishes secured Watkins his victory.

In all four northern towns sectarianism was less well expressed in parliamentary politics at the local level than in local government politics. This is understandable as national politics was less immediately relevant to the special concerns of Bolton society.[85] The eyes of parliamentary members were turned toward Westminster; moreover, the use of all forms of bribery and intimidation[86] at election time tended to limit the pressure brought to bear on MPs by the public. This is not to say that the issue of free trade, for example, was not of extreme importance to Boltonians. However, even before the town received parliamentary representation, organizations for national political purposes were formed – organizations closely tied to denominational interests. On the Conservative side a Church and King Club was formed in the late 1820s. Initially opposed to repeal of the Test and Corporation Act, the club soon shifted its attention to a crusade against Catholic Emancipation. In the latter cause the Tory organization even attracted a few Dissenters, including W.Jones, the Independent minister,[87] and his father-in-law, John Ritchie, a Presbyterian and the owner of the Gilnow Blackworks. The Tories continued to emphasize their Anti-Catholic sympathies well into the 1870s. The Orangemen also allied themselves to the Conservatives quite early.[88] The anti-Catholic bias of the Conservative Operative Association in the 30s, 40s, and 50s was most obvious.

The core of the Liberal party was the local Nonconformist elite followed by rank-and-file chapel members. Franklin Baker, the Unitarian minister, was an important member of the Radical Union of the 1830s, as were C.J. Darbishire and other prominent Nonconformists. All prospective Radical Union candidates in the 1832 parliamentary election campaign, for example, made statements against the Church of England. Irish Catholic electors and non-electors gave their support to the Liberal cause. On 16 March 1831 Walter O'Carroll, a leader in the Bolton Irish community, urged Irishmen to support the Nonconformist Reform cause as staunchly as the Nonconformists had supported the cause of Catholic Emancipation.[89] The Orange propaganda on the Tory side throughout the nineteenth century probably confirmed their allegiance to the Liberals. Irish Catholics were more apt to act in a defensive manner politically (as they did socially) than put forth any positive approach. Their economic weakness and ethnic isolation were probably at the root of their helplessness.

The issues, platform speeches, propaganda, and public statements[90] by individuals associated with party conflicts in the period up to 1870 confirm the notion that denominational interests were more regularly at the centre of political activity than, for example, economic class interests. Both Tories and Whigs, of course, took their cues to a certain extent from the national political arena. Issues and organizations were often inspired from centres outside Bolton. But sectarianism made its way into politics consistently, regardless of where the influences originated. The parallel power of Church and Nonconformity was perhaps reflected in the almost even record of Liberal and Conservative successes in parliamentary elections from 1832 and 1868. National sectarian issues such as the Papal Aggression question propelled political activity in Bolton for decades.[91] Secular issues like the repeal of the Corn Laws could also be made partially into sectarian questions. For example, it was obvious in the case of the Corn Laws that the activities of the Anti-Corn Law League were being controlled by Henry Ashworth and other members of the Nonconformist elite in town. This brought forth criticism of both an economic and sectarian nature from the Tory ranks.

The principal organs of political propaganda in this period, the newspapers,[92] were carefully aligned with one or the other of the two camps in town. The Tory-Anglican interest was well represented in the pages of the *Bolton Chronicle* between 1824 and 1917.[93] The Liberal-Nonconformist interest fared less well with a series of short-lived newspapers throughout the period. Perhaps the most interesting of these was the *Bolton Evening News*. Founded in 1867 by John Tillotson, a Primitive Methodist, it was the first daily halfpenny evening newspaper in England. It tried to capture as many working-class readers as possible by presenting their views (always Liberal) on a variety of political subjects. Its first editor was William Hope Davison, a Congregationalist minister.

With sectarianism largely determining the political stance of the populace in this period, there was little surprise when ministers of religion involved themselves directly and openly in elections.[94] People voted in large measure as their denominational allegiance prompted them.[95] The results of the 1832 election, for example, reveal no great difference in economic interests between Liberal and

35 Bolton: the Geneva of Lancashire

Conservative voters. Table IX gives a sample of some of these voters, broken into occupational groups:

TABLE IX

Voter occupations, 1832 election (sample)

	Liberal (total 91)	Conservatives (total 121)
Manufacturers	7	7
Shopkeepers	20	16
Tradesmen	25	27
Weavers[96]	7	3

Voters listed here are those who voted for *both* of the party's candidates. Pollbook is reproduced in W. Brimelow, *Political and Parliamentary History of Bolton* (Bolton 1882), 156–92.

From an inspection of pollbooks from the election of 1832 to that of 1841, this general pattern of voting appears to persist. From the surveys taken as a whole, the Liberal condidates may have received a slightly greater portion of the tradesmen's and shopkeepers' votes than did the Tories. The large representation of lower middle-class people in the Nonconformist chapels may account for this. On the whole, however, the people voting solidly for Liberals and those voting solidly for Conservatives were not very different in economic background. The basis of preference in national politics for the voters of Bolton was not, as far as can be determined, one of economic class interest in the local community but one involving other sorts of considerations, including sectarianism.

Sectarianism was, then, a principal source of division among Boltonians in the mid nineteenth century. The people of this community could also potentially be divided on other lines – especially those of class. These other divisions and the tensions resulting from them, however, were submerged to a degree in the more elaborate organization and workings of denominational conflict. Though this conflict was elite-managed, many below the elites were directly or indirectly involved in it. The result was a fundamental division within society that did not challenge the distribution of economic and social power created through industrialization.

Though the propertied groups within the Tory and Liberal camps were hardly engaged in a bourgeois conspiracy to mislead and redirect working-class energies away from class conflict, they were in some sense concerned with the maintenance of their hold upon the masses right up to the 1870s. The sheep were not permitted to stray from one fold to the other. Thus Thomas Thomasson could write to George Jacob Holyoake in January 1868 concerning the workings of the Second Reform Act: 'The new constituencies are in need of political information and if they cannot be trained before the General Election the consequences will be disastrous. If the Tories in the manufacturing towns can spread money *safely* I fear for the result.'[97] The social consequence of the blind workings of sectarianism may well have led, as Perkin found for Glossop, to a degree of 'social pacification' in a region in which class tension or at least class consciousness was an established factor by 1832. P.F. Clarke has also noted of Lancashire that 'the militancy of working-class movements' appeared 'softened,' possibly by mid-Victorian prosperity. He also notes that 'the converse is not the case, however, since the Cotton Famine elicited a docile response.'[98] Perhaps a partial answer to Clarke's dilemma concerning Lancashire lies not in economics alone but in sectarianism as a contributor to mid-Victorian tranquility. That sectarianism influenced the degree of social tranquility in a measurable way is difficult to substantiate. There are no signs, for example, that sectarianism was always advancing in periods of social tranquility – at least in Bolton. However, its presence was a constant one throughout the period, powerfully influencing social relationships.

3
Proud Preston

Preston, an ancient borough by prescription,[1] had a far more glorious history than the other three northern towns before 1832. Since the Middle Ages the town had been the most important market centre for North Lancashire. In the sixteenth and seventeenth centuries its trading companies were famous and, until the early eighteenth century, it had been a major port of the region.[2] Gradually in the eighteenth century Preston became better known for its legal and administrative functions. Many of the nobility and gentry of the county maintained residences in the town. 'Proud Preston,'[3] however, from the late eighteenth century began to experience the same dramatic physical and social changes as the other three towns, owing to the rapid expansion of the cotton industry. The transformation was so complete that the casual observer, unaware of the borough's renowned past, would have thought that Preston was much like any medium-sized cotton town[4] by the early Victorian period.

The comparative isolation of Preston from the main centres of the cotton industry in Lancashire did not impede the growth of cotton manufacturing in the district. Canals and the railway helped to open the town to the rest of industrial Lancashire. Coal could be delivered, with some difficulty, from pits eight miles away, though its price was high when it reached Preston. The migration of agricultural workers from nearby estates supplied the town with a large labour force.[5] Preston's previous history of trade and commerce was an added factor in making it more receptive to the introduction of the cotton industry. Linen manufacturing was an important activity of Prestonians in both the seventeenth and early eighteenth centuries. By the eighteenth century the merchant companies had largely declined or disappeared in the area, but the experience of sorting and selling the wares of independent weavers was not forgotten.

38 The Sectarian Spirit

John Horrocks,[6] Preston's first great cotton manufacturer, was the largest employer of handloom weavers in the county. Approximately seven hundred weavers were said to be in his employ in the town itself, around 1800, with nearly ten times that number in the district as a whole. The function of an employer of handloom weavers was much like that of a merchant of the early eighteenth century. Horrocks and other early cotton magnates, however, were open to the adoption of machinery and a full-fledged factory system where possible. In 1777 Messrs Collinson and Watson erected the first mill in Moor-lane. Horrocks built his first mill, the 'Yard Factory,' in 1792. There was no greater opposition to technological improvements among working people in Preston than in the other towns. Many handloom weavers were still prosperous until the 1830s.[7]

The town produced a large amount of low-count, coarser cotton goods, characteristic of handloom weaving, in the early decades of the nineteenth century. As time passed, however, other fabrics were also produced. Though weaving retained an important position, Preston soon became noted for its fine spinning. Combined operations were favoured until 1850 when 'weaving only' factories began to be popular.[8] Preston maintained a better balance between the two branches of the cotton industry (spinning and weaving) than any of the other towns.[9] If structural specialization in one branch over the other could be a contributing factor to working-class solidarity and bitterness,[10] then one must look elsewhere for the cause in mid-Victorian Preston. There were no imbalances or outstanding peculiarities in the local industry.

At mid century approximately sixty men controlled a labour force of over 16,000 in thirty-eight cotton concerns in the town.[11] The social origins of these millowners are obscure, but two facts about them are obvious – their effective industrial leadership and their social unity. This accord between millowners and the propertied interests, in general, was vital to the development of both class division and sectarian conflict in Preston between 1832 and 1870.

The industrialization of the old town of Preston was accompanied by the usual population growth and social dislocation. The physical surroundings of ordinary Prestonians were, undoubtedly, better than those of the other northern towns – at least in the first two decades of the nineteenth century. Until 1835 the old town corporation and improvement commissioners were much more effective than similar bodies elsewhere in the provision of social services.[12] The well-known reports of the Reverend John Clay, referring to the poor living conditions of the Preston working classes, mostly cover the period after 1835.[13] The ineptitude of the reformed corporation in these areas contributed heavily to this situation.

Since Preston was a market and administrative centre, tradesmen and shopkeepers were resident in the town in large numbers, catering to both townspeople and the residents of nearby estates. As the population grew eightfold between 1801 and 1871, the number of tradesmen and shopkeepers kept pace. The number of grocers, for example, grew sixfold between 1831 and 1871. In a society dominated by gentry, professional men, and great millowners, these lower middle-class elements were aligned more with the working classes.

The propertied interests in the town were unified socially before 1832 – indicating the acceptance, by older propertied groups, of the cotton manufacturers (some of whom must have been 'new' men of wealth) into their fellowship. This was fortunate for the propertied classes as millowners were clearly the most important men in local society by the 1830s. Indeed, this acceptance could be traced back to the struggle between town and county interests which antedated the Industrial Revolution. The nobility and gentry of the county exercised influence over the town in the seventeenth and eighteenth centuries,[14] and used the services of the professional people, tradesmen, artisans, shopkeepers, and merchants. In return for their patronage, these great families could expect some loyalty from townspeople and the acceptance of their social and political leadership. Their great town houses stood as a constant reminder of their contribution to Preston society.

However, the landed interest was not completely paramount in town life. By the late eighteenth century there was already an influential group in Preston in opposition to the landed gentry that dominated the town council. In politics they were Tory, possibly because the Stanleys (the earls of Derby), an overwhelming influence in the county, were Whig at that time. The social background of these propertied Tories is not clear[15] but some of them most likely were professional men, bankers, merchants, and gentlemen of independent means.

In due time, millowners joined the town Tories, who were anxious to draw support from any quarter in their struggle with Whig influence in the county. Some friends of the Tory cause, who came from a variety of backgrounds, gained in prestige by joining the corporation.[16] John Horrocks,[17] and perhaps some of the other town Tories, were originally Nonconformists. However, they appear to have lacked the cohesion necessary to attract newcomers to their ranks and make Nonconformity into a power similar to that described by A. Temple Patterson in Leicester.[18] Their adherence to this predominantly Anglican political clique, in fact, ultimately made for their own social assimilation into the ranks of Anglican Toryism. Again politics reinforced sectarian and even religious allegiances as in Bolton, but in a slightly different way. This is another reason, besides pure historical accident, for the lack of a viable Nonconformist elite in Preston by 1832. The importance of the millowner to the town Tories was recognized very clearly by the 1830s. As early as 1796 John Horrocks was nominated by the Preston Tories to contest a parliamentary seat against the

Stanley family. The social composition of the pre-Reform corporation in its final years reflects the ascendant influence of millowners. In the last year of the unreformed corporation (1834–5) two of the seven aldermen and five of the seventeen capital burgesses were cotton manufacturers.[19]

The expansion of cotton manufacturing in Preston offered a threat to the traditional social structure, including the landed interest. With more and more people employed in the mills, the influence of manufacturers grew proportionately. In fact, their hegemony in town society was probably one strong factor in hastening the withdrawal of the gentry. The borough must have seemed socially less attractive to landed gentlemen with so many prominent manufacturers in their midst. The behaviour of the Stanleys is ambiguous until the mid 1830s, though for the 1802 parliamentary election they struck a compromise with the town Tories so anxious were they to retain political influence.[20] For the most part, however, the town houses of the landed families were being abandoned by 1800. Improved communications (by road and then by rail) made London society more accessible,[21] and their social activities in Preston began to decline. The disappearance of the Preston races in 1833 was a symptom of their waning interest. Finally, in 1835, the Stanley town residence, Patten House, was razed.[22] Still, in 1851 there were 604 male agricultural labourers resident in the town[23] who depended directly on the gentry for employment. County gentlemen continued to have extensive property holdings in Preston – more valuable as time passed with shops and houses built on them. Some may also have remained as residents or part-time residents. At mid century there were fifty-two gentlemen of independent means in Preston – a figure much higher than in other cotton towns.[24]

Factory owners, however, were clearly the most powerful figures in Preston society by the 1830s.[25] Proof of this may be seen in the Stanley family's belated attempt to regain political influence within the town by building Church Street mill.[26] Older elements in Preston's governing class accepted the manufacturers' help very early and they quickly became fellow leaders of the community. The struggle with the local Whig aristocracy and gentry gave the town government special cohesion. Though the reasons for this cohesion were largely political, the result had a bearing on the entire social development of the borough. By 1832 Preston had virtually one unified elite of large property owners, predominantly Anglican, governing the town. Without a rival Nonconformist elite to foster organized denominational conflict, class tension was more in evidence than in the other towns. Since the Anglican elite and the large property-owning class were virtually the same, sectarian conflict, when directed against this elite, reinforced the lines of class tension.

41 Proud Preston

TABLE X

Places of worship not of the Church of England, 1829, Township of Preston
(population 1831: 33,112)

Denomination	24 July 1829	14 Dec. 1829
Independents, Grimshaw St	700	600
Independents, Canon St	450	450
Scotch Independents	40	30
Baptists	28	28
Particular Baptists	261	261
Old Wesleyan Methodists	423	1,000
Wesleyan Protestants	65	65
Primitive Methodists	350	80
Countess of Huntingdon	800	800
Unitarians	164	164
Quakers	82	82
Roman Catholics	11,000	10,900

Clerk of the Peace's Office, QDV/9, LRO. For reasons unclear, two censuses were taken in 1829.

The religious censuses of 1829 (Table X) and 1851 (Table XI) show more clearly the relative social strength of the different denominations. The 1829 figures seem to represent the enumerator's estimate (by whatever method) of the numerical strength of denominations within the community. The 1851 census is clearly a measure of attendance. Such figures, as well as the formal position of the institutional churches, are, of course, miniscule in assessing the real social importance of religion, let alone sectarianism. Comparison between the two sets of figures, with some exceptions, reveals a similar pattern of growth to that of the other cotton towns, though the rate of increase was not as great. What is perhaps more important is the social survey of the churches themselves.

The Church was blessed with a powerful property-owning elite comprising both old-established families such as the Heskeths of North Meols, the Fleetwoods of Rossall, and the Parkers of Cuerden Hall, as well as new industrial wealth in such families as the Horrockses, the Collinsons, and the Swansons. Eventually new and old wealth became mixed in the elite again through the process of sectarianism and politics reinforcing one another. The material and social position of the Church was of course assisted by its wealthy sons. In the Civil Wars the town had initially been a Royalist and Anglican stronghold, much like nearby Wigan, a situation maintained in the nineteenth century. In 1839, according to the Archdeacon's Visitation Book,[27] there were six churches

42 The Sectarian Spirit

TABLE XI

Religious census of 1851, Municipal Borough of Preston (population: 69,542)

	Church	Others
Percentage of sittings to population	17.0	18.4
Percentage of sittings to total number of sittings	48.0	52.0
Estimated percentage of population at divine service	20.1	

Denomination	Number of places of worship	Number of sittings Free	Number of sittings Appropriated	Total attendances Census Sunday
Church	10	4900	6900	2196
Independents	5	410	1630	750
General Baptists				437
Particular Baptists	2	164	752	328
Scottish Baptists	1	60		
Baptists (not defined)				153
Friends	1	528		155
Unitarians	1		145	1545
Wesleyan Methodists	3	726	1487	1822
Primitive Methodists	1	300	500	345
Bible Christians				254
Wesleyan Association	1	150	340	470
Lady Huntingdon's Connexion	1	150	750	166
New Church	1	50	200	60
Brethren				120
Isolated Congregations	1	200		80
Roman Catholics	4	2212	2598	6339

Census of Public Worship, 1851

in the town; by 1851 the figure had reportedly risen to ten, though this may well have been too low an estimate.[28]

The financial state of the Church was not always adequate to its present needs and future plans, in spite of the benevolent attitude of the town's Anglican elite. Correspondence with the National Society by various town clergymen reflects special concern that Church educational facilities be maintained, that continued neglect of the children of the poor could result in the permanent loss of church influence among the lower orders of the town. Education was one of the few ways that the Church could reach the industrial masses.

Being thus identified with the propertied elite, it was to be expected that the Established Church clergy would speak for the existing social order. The Reverend Mr Parr, vicar of Preston, in his *Lecture on Capital and Labour* published in 1860, for example, argued that strikes were fruitless:[29] 'Then let the laws of justice, moral right, benevolence, and religion animate and govern the intercourse of rich and poor. Let Capital and Labour rejoice together in their appointed and blessed relationship and connection. God makes the rich for the poor, the poor for the rich, that each bless the other.' In contrast, the attitude of the working classes toward the Church is not clear. In February 1854, at a meeting of the Wages Movement held during the Preston strike, reference was made to clergymen urging women to work rather than remaining on strike with the male operatives. A millhand, Mr Waddington, attacked the clergy quite violently.[30] Aside from rather scant references, however, little is known about the general attitude of workers toward the Established Church,[31] or toward any other denomination for that matter. Their poor attendance at public worship is obvious from the statistics for 1851.

As to the numbers, but more particularly the social background of all churches in Preston, it is fortunate that we have in print the observations of Anthony Hewitson ('Atticus'), editor of the *Preston Chronicle*. In 1869 he published a series of articles entitled 'Our Churches and Chapels,'[32] which focused on every denomination and sect within the borough and presented the reader with first-hand comments as to the social background (and history) of each congregation. The statistical results of his survey are summarized in Table XII. While Hewitson's observations must be employed with caution and verified with other, more substantial records where possible, they remain the only source of information on the social background of the Established Church.

Hewitson noted of the parish Church that while the congregation 'is a fair sample of every class of human life,' 'money and fashion are well represented at it' (including the typical cotton manufacturer).[33] At St George's, where it was observed that very few poor people attended, 'the great majority of worshippers, either represent, or are connected with, what are termed "good families." '[34] Hewitson added that 'it is not healthy for a church to have a congregation too select and too fashionable.' Of Trinity Church the journalist went so far as to say that twenty years before, 'when nearly all the fashionable families went to Trinity Church, neither Platonic love nor current coin could secure a pew.'[35] Christ Church was also described as once very select socially (the Horrocks family was connected with this church), though in recent years it was less so.[36]

44 The Sectarian Spirit

TABLE XII

Anthony Hewitson's survey of churches and chapels in Preston, 1869

Denomination and place of worship	Accommodation	Attendance
Church of England		
Preston Parish Church	1500* (250 free)	
St George's Church	700* (70 free)	
St Peter's Church	1200* (660 free)	
Trinity Church	1400 (280 free)	'few and far between are the worshippers'
Christ Church	1000 (440 in galleries)	'pretty large attendance'
St James's Church	1300 (400 free sittings)	
All Saints' Church	1500 (400 free)	700–800
St Saviour's Church	800 (400 free)	'the congregation, considering the capacity of the church, is large'
St Thomas's Church	1000 (300 free seats)	
St Paul's Church	1200	800
St Mark's Church	1000 (500 free seats)	600
St Luke's Church	800 (¾ free sittings)	280 (160 children)
Chapel of Ease, Fishergate Hill	240	200
St Mary's Church	1450	500
Emmanuel Church	1000	not opened yet
Presbyterians		
Presbyterian Chapel		200 (112 members)
Independents		
Cannon St Chapel	1000–1200*	300 communicants*
Lancaster Road Congregational Chapel		230* (120 members)
Grimshaw St Chapel	500–600	300
Baptists		
Fishergate Baptist Chapel	400	200 (90 members)
Pole St Baptist Chapel	900	84
Vauxhall Rd Particular Baptist Chapel	500–600	200 (50–60 members)
Zoar Particular Baptist Chapel	200	70–80
Friends		
Quaker Meeting House		70
Unitarians		
Unitarian Chapel	200	60

45 Proud Preston

TABLE XII continued

Anthony Hewitson's survey of churches and chapels in Preston, 1869

Denomination and place of worship	Accommodation	Attendance
Wesleyan Methodists		
Lune St Wesleyan Methodist Chapel	1250*	(circuit 800–900 members; chapel 300–400*)
Wesley Chapel	800–900	600
Moor Park Chapel	900	'*more* sittings than sitters'
Croft St Wesleyan Chapel		250 (125 members)
St Mary's St Wesleyan Chapel	400	350
Marsh End Wesleyan Chapel	100	80–100
Primitive Methodist		
Saul St Methodist Chapel	700–800	500 (700–800 members in circuit)
Brook Street	150	66
United Methodists		
Orchard Chapel	700–800	350–400 (300 members)
Parker Street	200	100–200
Free Gospelers		
Free Gospel Chapel	95	50 (30 members)
New Church		
New Jerusalem Church	250	70
Roman Catholics		
St Wilfrid's	100*	
St Augustine's	1000	3290
St Ignatius's	1000	3500 (6000 in district)
St Walburge's	1000	3000
Church of the English Martyrs	850	1350
St Mary's Catholic Chapel	1000	'large congregations attend this chapel'
St Joseph's Catholic Chapel	560	'well attended'
Latter Day Saints		
Mormon Meeting		70 members
Brethren		
Pitt St Revival Tabernacle	70	51 (35 children)

Material taken from A. Hewitson, *Our Churches and Chapels* (Preston 1869), passim. See also note 32.

* From A. Hewitson, *History of Preston* (Preston 1883), 452–539. These must be taken as figures from the early 1880s which may or may not correspond with the situation during Hewitson's first survey published in December 1869.

The Anglican elite were responsible not only for the fine furnishings in the prestigious churches but in some cases for the financial backing of predominantly working-class churches. St Saviour's was the result of the purchase of a chapel from the Baptists in 1859 and its rebuilding in 1863 by a group of four Anglican laymen. Hewitson described the congregation as 'large and consists almost absolutely of working people.'[37] Mr J. Bairstow[38] gave £700 toward the building and £6000 for the endowment of a church in Ribbleton Lane, St Luke's, in which three-quarters of the sittings were free. Most of the congregation was working class.[39] Prominent Anglican laymen also contributed substantially toward the building and enlargement of St Mary's (1838), described as having a predominantly working-class congregation.[40]

Social mix, however, was also a distinctive feature of many Anglican congregations, in spite of the appearance of wealthy benefactors. St Paul's, All Saints', and even the Chapel of Ease for Chirst Church, Fishergate Hill (Hewitson called it 'Bairstow Memorial Chapel') were said to have a mixture of working and propertied people.[41] St Thomas's was also described as drawing attenders from all classes though 'there is a clear halo of respectability about the place.'[42] The only church without a good working-class representation, not mentioned before, was St James's which had a 'thin' congregation, mostly 'upper middle class.'[43]

Nonconformity in Preston never attracted a large number of wealthy citizens. This fact provides the key explanation for the course of sectarianism in this town. Unable to provide an elite of their own to rival the Anglicans, Dissent in Preston had to accept the fact that it could not hope to dominate, or even change, the basic structure of local society or politics. It also explains the impotence and lack of *esprit de corps* in Dissent, so evident to historians of the region.[44] Without a true elite, there were fewer extra-religious incentives to join these chapels. This may account for the smaller numbers of Dissenters in Preston compared with the other northern towns. A comparison of the Dissenting chapel figures for 1829 and 1851 reveals that while there was a substantial increase in the number of Nonconformists, some of this was attributable to Nonconformist immigration rather than local conversions. As the chapel report for the Preston Unitarian Church in 1872 stated: '... your committee cannot but regret that in this large manufacturing town, accessions to its only Unitarian congregation are due chiefly to the accident that professors of our simple faith are amongst those who, for various circumstances, become resident here. The distance of Preston from the centres of Unitarian activity in Lancashire is without doubt unfavourable to the diffusion of our views here.'[45]

The fact that there was no small established core of Nonconformist manufacturers, merchants, and professional men in the late eighteenth century meant that new men of wealth, coming to Preston, would not find an established Nonconformist avenue for the advancement of their social power. In the other towns, especially Bolton and Stockport, many Nonconformists were propertied before the industrial revolution in cotton. With capital they were in a position, therefore, to move into the cotton industry and form an important element in its ownership class. There may have been no Nonconformist elite in nineteenth-century Preston simply because there were no really wealthy Nonconformists to start it. Perhaps this is why John Horrocks, the founder of the Preston cotton industry, became a Churchman (he was brought up a Quaker) and probably influenced others by example to do the same.

The Unitarian congregation, so important to the development of political Dissent in many areas of the county, was, according to chapel records, in straitened circumstances throughout the first three-quarters of the century. This was the result of the meagre financial resources of the membership. The minute books note that 'the congregation, with the exception of a comparatively few individuals, consists of the labouring and poorer classes.'[46] The most notable, albeit not too prominent, of the 'few individuals' of substance were the Pilkington family (John, Richard, and William), attorneys, and Thomas Ainsworth, a cotton manufacturer. Trustee lists frequently included tradesmen among their number. The list of eight trustees in April 1844, for example, mentioned a reed maker, a plumber, and a tinman.[47] This deficiency in very wealthy members made the financial management of the chapel extremely difficult. In 1827 a subscription fund, organized by the membership to eliminate the debt of £374, amounted to only £125 12s 6d. In the same year the chapel was forced to bury its dead in the parish yard, the old grounds having been filled. The congregation as a whole must have been relatively poor, as the figures for Census Sunday indicate that this chapel was well attended. The contrast with the affluence of the Bolton Unitarians is striking and in itself an important factor in the different chain of social and political developments.

The Baptist congregation started under somewhat more optimistic financial conditions than the Unitarians, when four Baptist families came from London to invest money in the new calico-printing industry. Under its capable pastor, John Crook of Inskip, the Leamington Street Chapel grew in numbers. In 1829 there were forty members and over 260 regular attenders. In 1857 a new chapel, seating 500, was established on Fishergate Street at a cost of £5000, 'as chaste and elegant a temple of religion as is to be found within the precincts of our town.'[48] The chapel, however, underwent many problems throughout the period, such as the departure of Joseph Livesey, founder of the Teetotal movement, from the congregation.[49] Potentially dynamic figures in Dissent, like Livesey, found more important things to do than support purely chapel activities. They undoubtedly sensed that conventional Nonconformity was not strong enough to challenge the local Tory Church clique in its position of authority in town affairs.

The Independents were noticeably less numerous than in other towns, perhaps because their origins were somewhat diverse and confusing. The oldest known group began meeting in 1772, in the Preston Cockpit, in much the same way as the new sects of the nineteenth century would meet there. The Reverend David Carnson, in accepting the pastorate of the new Fishergate Chapel in October 1820, stated, 'I am in some degree aware of the prejudices that exist against the place.'[50] In 1829 the congregation moved to the much larger Canon Street Chapel. From the baptismal records of the congregation, from May 1821 to January 1837,[51] the following information is revealed: among the eighty-five fathers, there were ten shopkeepers, forty tradesmen, and five weavers. The bulk of the membership, then, seems to have been of the upper strata of working men or lower middle class. The trustee deed and minute books of the Canon Street congregation reveal a highly-disciplined, extremely rigid, and inward-looking congregation. Penalties and expulsions were strictly enforced for non-attendance, improper behaviour inside or outside chapel, and false creeds, from Antinomianism to Arminianism. In spite of this fact, the congregation grew. In 1820 there were 35 members; in 1847, 174; in December 1862, 248. The congregation's posture, however, continued to be one of withdrawal from commitment to the political and social concerns of the wider Preston community. No prominent Prestonian appears to have been associated with the congregation except T. Edelston, a cotton manufacturer.

The origins and development of the Grimshaw Street Independent congregation were quite different from those of the Canon Street group. The result of the secession of an evangelical minister and his followers from the Unitarian chapel in 1807, the congregation grew in numbers in the nineteenth century, especially under the pastorate of Richard Slate (1826–62). The bulk of the membership was similar to that of Canon Street, with perhaps an even greater working-class representation. Samuel Antliff, writing in the 1880s, declared: 'The church and congregation are composed almost exclusively of tradesmen and persons employed in the factories ...'[52] The chapel initiated several evangelical projects among its members. According to a report read into the chapel minutes on 25 December 1851 the congregation maintained the following institutions: a school with forty teachers and 375 scholars, a sickness society, a juvenile missionary society, a tract distribution agency, a total abstinence society, and a library. In the 1860s a mutual improvement society was established for the labouring classes.

As the various censuses reveal, the Quakers were not a numerous denomination in Preston in the nineteenth century. Gathering members gradually from outlying country centres, the Preston congregation was formed in the late eighteenth century. The Preston Register of Sufferers records resistance to the tithe and subsequent seizures of property (cheeses, pigs, and the like), especially in 1818, from ten Quaker households.[53] The Preston Preparative Meeting had eighty-two members in 1858, which was about average for the cotton towns.[54] Its membership, however, contained few names as illustrious as those found in the Bolton Meeting. Preston Quakerism did not appear to make any special efforts to enlarge itself in the Victorian era.

The last remaining Protestant denomination of any size were the various groups of Methodists. From the census it can be seen they were fairly numerous and expanded their following greatly between 1829 and 1851. It is possible that the relative unattractiveness of old Dissent may have made Methodism a viable alternative for some. Hewitson's figures indicate that this trend continued over the following twenty years. The first Methodist chapel was erected in 1778. In 1817 the large Lune Street Chapel was built, with a school attached. The chapels were, on the whole, not very numerous or extensive in these years, though this picture changed in the 1860s. Nevertheless, their indirect impact on town society was important. According to Pilkington[55] some of the most capable leaders of the Teetotal movement came from Wesleyan Methodist ranks. Henry Anderton, the temperance reformer, was one of their number. Methodist trustee lists are useful in enumerating the social background of the membership. Two lists[56] survive from the period indicating a numerically large shopkeeper and tradesman contingent. Teetotal activity may have robbed the Wesleyans of some important leaders. The Mormons, another new sect, managed to take considerably from the Primitive Methodists through conversions at the Vauxhall Street and Laurel Street chapels.

A baptismal register surviving for the Primitive Methodists gives some idea of the social composition of that denomination. Out of the 117 baptisms registered for Preston in the Preston circuit[57] between 1824 and June 1837, the fathers' occupations were two shopkeepers, thirty-five tradesmen, twenty-four weavers, and eighteen spinners. The impression of an impoverished membership in the Primitive Methodist chapel was conveyed by Sir George Head when he wrote about his visit to the town in 1835.[58] It is interesting to note that the census figures reveal a sharp decline in the membership of the Countess of Huntingdon's chapel. It is possible that the novelty of this sect had worn off by the mid nineteenth century, with the appearance of other new sects.

Aside from the low prestige associated with Dissent, another possible reason for the relatively small number of Nonconformists in Preston into the mid-Victorian era was the effect of class divisions operating within this society. Professor Ward contends that class consciousness forced its way into

50 The Sectarian Spirit

Nonconformity at this time, fomenting schism and the migration of the middle class away from its working-class brethren within the chapels.

Nonconformist chapel migrations in the large towns were the special interest of the Reverend Abraham Hume, vicar of All Souls, Vauxhall (Liverpool). Of the four cotton towns in this study, Preston is the only one named by Hume in his book, *The Church of England: the Home Missionary to the Poor* (London 1862).[59] He noted that two Dissenting chapels in the poorer districts were abandoned by the migrations of middle-class Dissenters and taken over by the more pastorally-minded Established Church.[60] The Baptists of Leeming Street Chapel clearly moved to better quarters at Fishergate in 1858. Hewitson noted that in 1869 there were few poor people in the congregation at Fishergate; rather, it consisted 'almost entirely of middle-class persons – people who have either saved money in business or who are making a determined effort to do so.'[61] In contrast, St Saviour's (founded at the Leeming Street premises) was working class[62] – the 'missionary and ragged church' noted by Hume. The second church named by Hume, St James's, was hardly a working-class church, though it may have been 'surrounded by the cottages of working men,'[63] and was vacated by Dissenters who were designated as the Fieldingites or the Primitive Episcopal Church. This sect was originally formed at the Vauxhall Road Chapel – a building which was used by the 'Round Preachers' or General Baptists before Fielding and the Mormons and particular Baptists (Gadbyites) after him. Hewitson said that the series of changes at Vauxhall Road 'beats Plato's theory of transmigration; and is a modern edition of Ovid's Metamorphoses.'[64]

Just as the reasons for chapel migration were often more complicated than Hume realized, so too were the reasons for schisms within chapels. Though Ward may be partially correct in seeing the influence of class tension, in Preston as elsewhere theological debate must also be considered. Hewitson stated 'a stiff quarrel is about the surest and quickest thing we are acquainted with for multiplying places of worship, for Dissenters, at any rate.'[65] Perhaps legitimate doctrinal and personality clashes were as responsible as class divisions for schism in Preston.

Based on Hewitson's observations of Nonconformist congregations it seems that few schisms could have been influenced by class division. Among the Congregationalists, Lancaster Road Chapel was formed out of part of the older Canon Street congregation in 1860. Its members, like those in the parent congregation nine years later, were basically working-class.[66] Pole Street Baptist Chapel, the remaining Baptist congregation not yet mentioned, was formed from a schism at Leeming Street Chapel in 1855 and its members were described as 'poor.'[67] It was this group that split from the more select parent group rather than the other way round. Of course, it is possible that this 'working-class migration' may well have been instigated for social reasons.

Among the Methodists, the group most frequently discussed by Professor Ward, there was a tremendous number of national and regional schisms beginning in the late eighteenth century. In the Lancashire area itself in 1834 there was a massive secession from the Wesleyans led by Dr Warren of Manchester (the Wesleyan Association). To further complicate the situation, in 1857 the Wesleyan Association merged with James Everett's Wesleyan secession group (formed in 1849) to produce the United Methodist Free Church. These national and regional controversies impinged on local congregations, raising the possibility of splits and secessions even among socially cohesive chapels.

The Primitive Methodists at Saul Street, Ashmoor Street, and perhaps Brook Street were, not surprisingly, working-class in majority.[68] The Wesleyan Methodists reflected a greater mixture of classes. The old Lune Street Chapel was 'the fashionable tabernacle' for Preston Methodists though it was observed that poor people were in the congregation.[69] Wesley Chapel, North Road (1838), and Croft Street Chapel (1840) were predominantly working class, as was St Mary's Street Chapel (1866) and Marsh End Chapel (1866).[70] In fact, the newer chapels were more likely to be working-class, with the possible exception of Moor Park Chapel (1862). If there was indeed a class-motivated migration from an older chapel it was more likely to be working-class (perhaps influenced by the high degree of class solidarity). The constant building and setting up of new circuits contributed, of course, to the proliferation of chapels as well as increasing numbers of religionists. As a result of a dispute at Orchard Street Chapel the Parker Street congregation was established in 1857 as a second circuit of United Free Methodists. The dispute, it appears, was of no consequence and short duration but the chapel was conveniently situated at the school premises built for the denomination by the Haslam cotton mill somewhat earlier. There is no evidence of any significant difference in social background between the two circuits.

On the whole the evidence supplied by Anthony Hewitson on Preston Nonconformity seems to suggest that some chapels had a number of members who were reasonably prosperous. While some would be reasonably well-dressed, he was probably safer in seeing 'a middle-class shopkeeping halo' around the more prosperous members (as he commented of the Canon Street Independent Congregation in general). Elegance and social leadership were not characteristics one would readily apply to Preston Nonconformists.

Preston, or 'Priest's Town,' had been known as a stronghold of Popery since the Reformation. Though apparently playing little or no role directly in the Pilgrimage of Grace, the local vicars were often suspected of harbouring Popish priests or of being Papists themselves. The proximity of recusant nobles' estates ensured that many former agrarian labourers, who migrated to the town, would be Roman Catholic. In addition to this migration, the Jesuits maintained a mission in Preston from at least the beginning of the eighteenth century.[71] All of these factors made for a flourishing Catholic population long before the nineteenth century. Estimates vary enormously for the Catholic population of the town. However, most sources put their number at about 15 per cent of the total population in the early decades of the nineteenth century.[72]

Though most of the English Catholics were tradesmen, shopkeepers, and industrial workers, there were a few prominent families. Some of these were connected with the legal profession, some were in small manufacturing, such as iron founding, a few were in the cotton waste business, and a very small number were landowning gentlemen, such as the Cliftons of Lytham Hall and the Towneleys of Towneley. The list of the presidents of the Catholic Charitable Society of Preston, from June 1731 onwards, contains the most prominent family names, the most notable being Gradwell, Saygar, Arrowsmith, Gillow, and Brown,[73] almost all being in the professions. Preston also received its share of Irish immigrants in the nineteenth century. The 1851 census stated that there were 5822 Irish-born persons residing in the town. This gave Preston an Irish population second only to that of Stockport among the four northern towns studied. Such a large influx of Irishmen into the town's labour force was not welcomed by the native working class. At times of industrial strife the Irish, as a surplus labour force, were often an important factor in determining which side – employers or working-class – would triumph. The Irish were also, of course, identified with Catholicism.

In spite of the impression conveyed by the National Society correspondence and other sources of information, the Roman Catholics were hard pressed to finance the building and upkeep of their churches and schools. Brother Thomas Berry, in an undated memorandum to the Reverend William West,[74] of St Ignatius Church, Preston, estimated that of one hundred boys over the age of ten in his school, about one-quarter would soon be found in neighbouring factories. In another letter he indicated that a high proportion of Catholic boys did not attend Catholic schools, going instead to Protestant schools where 'they receive impressions which perhaps may never be effaced,' working in factories, or living in 'idleness and ignorance, and consequently in vice.'[75] In spite of occasional assistance from wealthy Catholics, schools depended on collections taken at Mass and on parliamentary grants. In 1866 parliamentary grants amounted to £1477 for six schools, with a combined average attendance of 2524.[76] Hewitson also confirms the large numbers of working-class people attending the Catholic churches in 1869.

Such pressing internal problems, and the disinclination of the Catholic Church to embroil itself in questions of class conflict, lessened the combative instincts of many working-class Catholics toward the social order. The Irish

Catholics were roused to religious and racial conflict by English workers, rather than by seeking confrontation with their employers. In addition to this, the old English element in the town's Catholic community was very conservative in its attitudes. As J.T. Hogg, one of the Municipal Commissioners noted: 'Native Roman Catholics usually form a very small part of the population of English towns, it is but just, however, to observe that these persons ought not to be included in the same sentence with Dissenters, being eminently disposed by the influence of their ancient faith to respect whatever is established, and excessively addicted to Church and State; for their apparent enmity to the former is but the too conservative regard of over-zealous friends.'[77]

The social factors contributing to the development of new sects were many. In general, they were connected with problems generated by social dislocation, which was caused in turn by rapid industrialization and urban expansion. In Preston this pattern held true for the development of most of the new sects – religious or secular. There were, however, additional factors peculiar to the social structure of this particular town. The absence of an elite group among Dissenters in Preston diminished any prospects of challenging the Anglican elite. For a brief time in the 1830s some Dissenters were active in the cause of Radicalism, in both local and national politics, but as this involvement declined late in the decade there was a sharp upswing in the development of new sects. It is entirely possible that many of the talents that could have been used in the build-up of a machine for political Dissent were now devoted to these new movements. Certain members of the lower middle class, largely recruited from Dissent, were well represented in these new sects – in fact they provided the leadership. Other working-class people who might have been brought under the sway of political Dissent, via the lower middle-class element in the chapels, were allowed to drift into the new sects. The infatuation of members of the working class with these sects shows a form of alienation from the industrial social order.

Mormonism, or the American religion, was first introduced into England in the 1830s by North American missionaries. In July 1837 Herber Kimball, along with a missionary group consisting of two Americans, three Canadians, and one former Bedfordshire man, landed at Liverpool. The group immediately proceeded to Preston where they stayed with the Bedfordshire man's brother, the Reverend James Fielding.[78] Fielding, a preacher of Methodist leanings, had recently taken the Vauxhall Road Chapel to form his own sect, and it was here that Kimball preached his first sermons in England. Within a year the Mormons had gained converts, particularly among Wesleyan, Primitive Methodists, and Fieldingites in the town, and had begun to establish other congregations in the north. 'Cockpit Fever'[79] as it was called, was particularly successful among the working classes. As the report of the religious census of 1851 stated concerning

Mormonism in England as a whole: 'The preachers, it appears, are far from unsuccessful in their efforts to obtain disciples. The surprising confidence and zeal with which they promulgate their creed, the prominence they give to the exciting topics of the speedy coming of the Saviour and his personal millennial reign, and the attractiveness to many minds of the idea of an infallible church, relying for its evidence and its guidance upon revelations made perpetually to its rulers – these, with other influences, have combined to give the Mormon movement a position and importance with the working classes which, perhaps, should draw to it much more than it has yet received of the attention of our public teachers.'[80] The British Church Conference of 1840 announced the following figures for Preston: three hundred members, seven elders, eight priests, six teachers, and two deacons.[81] Preston at this time had the largest Mormon church group in the country.

The attitude of Preston society and institutions toward the Mormons varied. While there was little actual violence perpetrated against the new sect, there was some initial hostility. Their customs were suspect, and criticism mounted when it became known that polygamy was practised by Mormons in America. In late July 1837 the town corporation gave the sect special protection for a time. In the late 1830s anti-Mormon tracts began to appear in Preston[82] which, similar to anti-Catholic pamphlets of the same era, denounced the rituals and beliefs of the new sect. As time passed Mormonism became more fully accepted, but eventually shrank in influence in Preston and elsewhere. No attempt was made to combat lingering Mormon influences on the labouring classes.

The New Church was also present in the town from 1815 onwards. According to one source[83] the sect was particularly associated with weavers – both hand-loom and power-loom. The most prominent leaders in the early period were of the lower middle class – Hugh Beconsall, a grocer, and Richard Parkinson, a linen-draper. No information is available on the Brethren[84] or the Pitt Street Revival Tabernacle.

Preston was a pioneer area for Teetotalism in England, in which the involvement of lower middle-class and working-class Dissenters was of great importance. The overall retiring quality of Preston Nonconformity was offset by the aggressive spirit of Teetotalism. Basically a working-class movement, Teetotalism aimed at making deep inroads into as much of the general population as possible. Its creed was total involvement in the social and, at times, the political life of the town. Teetotalism in Preston involved a more serious effort at developing a distinct sect than in any of the other towns. Its somewhat blurred class membership made for a marriage of ideas that were both working-class and middle-class in origin. To old radical working-class ideas of self-improvement was added the middle-class desire for the general social improvement of the community.[85] The Teetotal sect, led mainly by members of the tradesman and shopkeeping classes,[86] had as much vitality as elite-led Nonconformists in Bolton or Stockport.

The most famous pioneers of 1832, the 'seven men of Preston,'[87] were drawn from the various strata of workingmen.[88] It was an illiterate Preston fishmonger by the name of Dicky Turner who actually coined the word 'teetotal.' By 1835 the Teetotallers had organizations, and even a salaried missionary, to spread the word of the gospel throughout the land. Teetotallers aimed at reforming the morals and, from that base, the physical condition of the working classes. Many disagreed with their basic premise but their influence on society was obvious to most people. Joseph Livesey[89] once described their impact on Preston where, 'the attempt to change the fashions has been made, and most successfully. There is now much less drinking in respectable society, and even those who like it are almost afraid of being known to drink. Some club and society meetings are now held in schoolrooms or at the Temperance Hotel, and some which are held at public-houses have made great reduction in the allowance of drink. We have now a teetotal band of musicians. Temperance christenings, temperance weddings, and temperance funerals are occurring almost every week. On these occasions, instead of ale and wine, or spirits, the guests are supplied with tea and coffee, and sometimes with ginger-beer and lemonade.'[90] Livesey's efforts to organize the working classes for the Teetotal cause eventually made his participation in purely Nonconformist causes less vigorous. Realizing the limitations of Dissent in the local community, he preferred to organize a sect that could challenge the existing values of society in a dramatic way. So did many of his earliest followers. Henry Anderton, for example, was a Radical who turned to Teetotalism as the only way to combat drinking and hooliganism, the tools of Toryism, at elections.[91] It is perhaps contentious to claim that Preston Teetotalism reached the status of a denomination but its behaviour went beyond its usual subordination to existing churches, especially Nonconformity.

Secularism was another new sect which, like Teetotalism,[92] challenged traditional patterns of behaviour. Unlike the Teetotallers, however, Secularists directly attacked the institutions responsible for old behavioural patterns in society. The Secularists in Preston began with an organization called 'The Friends of Political and Social Reform' which met every Sunday afternoon in 1851 in Gardner's School. One year later the group was formally organized into a Secularist Society by James Lennon, a bookseller. At the first Secular Conference in Manchester in October 1852 the Preston society was assessed: 'The number of Freethinkers associated here is about twenty, but 300 might be organized under the name of the Secular Society. We have a small room for meeting in, but a hall capable of holding 700 is available.'[93] The society had good and bad times in the 1850s. The defection of their secretary, William Singleton, late in the decade to the Urquhartites dealt the society an almost fatal blow.

The area of direct denominational conflict between Churchmen and Dissenters was kept to a minimum, as in the other towns. Since Dissenters were not numerous or powerful, the Church elite could afford to be tolerant. Of course, the weakness of Dissent meant that many of the ancient Church privileges would persist. The church rate, for example, was a tradition dating 'from time immemorial,' yielding a standard revenue of £50 from each of the three divisions of the town parish. Not until it was abolished nationally by Act of Parliament in 1868 did it disappear in Preston. Occasionally an extra rate was also laid for very special reasons. There was rarely much opposition.[94]

There was also a certain spirit of ecumenism evident among some of Preston's Nonconformists and Churchmen. Robert Halley noted in 1869 that many 'Calvinists' in Preston (as well as Manchester) objected to the liturgy being read in Dissenting chapels; when Dissenters wanted to worship in high-church style they preferred to attend the Established Church.[95] This phenomenon of 'crossing-over' was not unusual in older, more settled societies – as in nineteenth-century Wiltshire. This ecumenical spirit may have been an added inducement for some to abandon Dissent for the more vital ways of the new sects or for propertied people to join the Anglican elite.

In the broad field of education there was ample opportunity for conflict between Church and Dissent, yet little happened to disturb the social relations between the denominations. The local grammar school was accused on one occasion by the Liberal Nonconformist press of being 'elitist.'[96] Dissent was too weak to maintain concerted opposition to such quasi-denominational institutions or to institute viable ones of their own, as in Stockport or Blackburn. The activities of the Mechanics' Institute were often more the work of dynamic new sect groups[97] than of the old Dissenting elite. They could not compare with those of the Church Institution in any case.

The Education Act of 1870 brought a small crisis to Preston's interdenominational relations. The Church union party, led by Canon Parr and supported by many Roman Catholics, took up a petition in April 1870 denouncing the alleged secularism of the act, which they ascribed to the Nonconformists. Nonconformists, in turn, denounced the act, holding fast to the rather outmoded principles of Voluntaryism. In a letter to the *Preston Guardian* Joseph Livesey even questioned whether education would help to improve the habits of the masses significantly, especially in the area of drinking.[98] The attitudes of Churchmen, Dissenters, Roman Catholics, and Teetotallers made the institution of a school board difficult. In addition to this, it was realized that Roman

Catholic children, both English and Irish, would be involved in future school-board projects. Fear, not only of Catholics on the board but of possible Irish integration with the English children in these schools, helped some Prestonians to decide against the board. For all of these reasons the idea of a school board in Preston was defeated. The town council simply issued a statement deeming the existing school facilities satisfactory.[99]

It is difficult to measure the impact of the denominational schools on the hearts and minds of both children and their parents in the mid nineteenth century. As John Foster has pointed out, their potential social influence was enormous before the establishment of compulsory and secular education.[100] The denominational day and Sunday schools embraced large numbers of school-age children in the cotton towns. Their influence on the course of sectarianism can only be speculated upon but one is reminded of Frederick Engels's comment in 1845: 'As it is, the State Church manages its national schools and the various sects their sectarian schools for the sole purpose of keeping the children of the brethren of the faith within the congregation, and winning away a poor childish soul here and there from some other sect.'[101]

The position of the Catholic community, no matter how shaky financially, was of importance to Preston. Anti-Catholic rhetoric and activity were always tempered by the sobering thought that Catholics were much more numerous and better organized in this town than in the other northern communities. For example, a note from the Catholic clergy to the mayor and borough magistrates, complaining of Orange provocations at a Catholic Whitsuntide procession in 1860, was taken seriously. The warning, sounded by the clergy in this letter, referring to possible failure in controlling their people in the event of future Orange activity, was ominous.[102] A few aggressively Protestant clergymen, such as the Reverend Owen Parr, managed to turn out anti-Catholic pamphlets and, at special times, such as the Papal Aggression crisis, some Nonconformists joined in the No Popery crusade. Despite the fact that anti-Catholicism did not markedly increase in the town, Catholic sensitivity to it did. As a result, the sectarian tension between English and Irish workers, as mentioned before, was a factor of some importance in inhibiting full working-class solidarity.

As in Bolton, Stockport, and Blackburn, the force of sectarianism was felt in Preston politics, but was lessened by the dominance of the Anglican elite. Before the nineteenth century this elite included both Whig and Tory elements. The pre-Reform corporation, however, was largely Tory and influenced heavily by the new industrialists. The Whig interest in town was generally supported by the landed families in the neighbouring country areas (some of whom had industrial interests). With the decline in country family influence in Preston, Toryism became even more powerful. There were, however, a few millowners who had been Whig and later were supporters of the town Liberal party after 1832. The preponderant power of the Anglican elite in town society assured their ultimate control of local politics, whether Tory or Liberal. Their tolerance of Dissent was understandable, the opposition being so poorly led and organized and so weak economically. The old pre-Reform corporation, though self-elected, had at least one Dissenter – the Unitarian attorney, W.O. Pilkington – among its members in its last year of existence (1834–5).

The members of the old corporation and the local Tory party did not resist municipal reform. Though the Municipal Reform Act outwardly changed much of the local government apparatus of the town,[103] the social background of the members in the new corporation remained more or less the same as the old. In the first municipal election of November 1835, therefore, the only change from the old corporation was a small increase in the number of tradesmen and shopkeepers in the council. The fact that there was no vibrant Nonconformist elite capable of putting up an effective challenge to the Anglican elite probably explains the lack of firm political lines in the new corporation. The pro-Tory press was not alarmed that there were more avowed Reformers in the council than Conservatives. As *The Times* noted,[104] twenty-two of the forty-eight councillors had no declared party affiliation, in spite of the fact that published pollbooks and other sources probably revealed their political preferences to the public. There seems to have been little argument among reformers on council concerning the largely political appointment of the new justices in 1836 – nine out of the ten were known to be Tories. At election time there was little activity, many wards going uncontested. As the Liberal *Preston Guardian* stated on 3 November 1838: 'At our municipal elections, if it were not for gangs and agents, and a few public spirits, too honest or too chivalrous for the occasion, it would be difficult to get up a contest.'

The organs of Tory propaganda, however, never ceased to beat out the message that the town council was being taken over by the Radicals in the early years after municipal reform. There was some basis in fact for this assertion. Radical militancy was exhibited by some reformers – especially by the Teetotal wing led by Joseph Livesey and Thomas Swindlehurst, both councillors after the 1835 election and definitely partisan in politics. The Tory *Preston Pilot* once stated that Livesey was 'the very god of idolatry of the silly worshippers in the nicknamed temple of reform.'[105] Teetotalism aimed at the reform of the people, as did Radicalism, and Livesey thus became part of a cause that was sweeping many parts of the country in the 1830s. It was also a cause well suited to the tastes of upper strata of workers, the shopkeeper / craftsmen class. The Teetotallers were quite capable of supplying leadership for this political attack upon the propertied interests of the town, but their single-minded fixation could only make their forays into politics of short duration. Their swift withdrawal from the political scene when their main purpose was not achieved made them appear to have all the characteristics of the sociologist Max Weber's 'sect type' – a political sect in any case. There was also some similarity in their attitude toward parliamentary politics.

The early elections for the new Preston Poor Law Union were more spirited than those for town council. The electoral contests seemed to have attracted both a large number of candidates and a disproportionate representation from the retail and service industries, groups associated with the Radical wing of the Liberal party. In the first election of January 1837 thirteen of the twenty-three candidates were of these occupational groups, as were three of the six winners, two of them being the well-known lower middle-class Nonconformists Joseph Livesey and Michael Satterwaite, a Quaker and leather-cutter. The six members for the town of Preston were particularly noticeable among the thirty-four on the new union board. Livesey earned special publicity because of his opposition to the New Poor Law, causing some embarrassment to town Liberals and illustrating the independence of thought among these Radical Teetotallers. Ostensibly Livesey supported the Whig-Liberals in national politics – the party that had implemented the New Poor Law. On 6 April 1837 he declared that he was 'determined by every legal means in his power, to resist the introduction of the odious New Poor Law into this part of the country.'[106] Obviously he made a popular move with the lower orders in the town, for in the union's second election in April 1837 he was returned at the top of the poll.

Livesey's objection to the New Poor Law was based not only on his concern for the people but also on his fear of centralism. Being a Nonconformist in origin, Livesey could appreciate the importance of local institutions[107] such as those connected with the chapel, but unlike many Nonconformists he saw the New Poor Law as an actual threat to local autonomy and initiative. He strenuously objected to the fact that information on the local workhouse could be sent to the bureaucracy in London without the Preston union's permission, and to the regimen of required weekly meetings set down by London. At a meeting of the Poor Law Union he moved that a petition be sent to Lord John Russell stating that acceptance of the poor law in an area should be up to the ratepayers of each district. The motion passed by a vote of nineteen to one. His localism was typical of Nonconformist politicians from Newcastle-upon-Tyne to Bath, though his views on the poor law were not.

The decline in opposition to the New Poor Law among members of the board, evident by 1840, was an inevitable consequence of time.[108] The new law was there to stay. Politics on the town council also became much less spectacular by 1840.

In the late 1830s the local Tories began to mount a campaign of some magnitude against the Radical Liberals on council. The *Preston Pilot* stated in 1837: 'The viciousness that was once wont to be ascribed to the system of self-election in the old corporations, were purity itself compared with the depravity that shamelessly displays itself under the reform rule.'[109] The article referred to bribery and intimidation, often in the form of the beer barrel, that was a part of elections in the town. The fact that Teetotallers were the most zealous part of the Reform party seemed to make such methods even more reprehensible. By 2 November 1839 there was not a single Liberal in the council. Never again in the period up to 1870 did the Radicals or the Liberal party, in general, attempt to capture control of the town council. The so-called 'mania' of the reformers in corporation affairs had only lasted three years. In that time a few changes had transpired in local government. A watch committee was set up by the council and committees regulating other areas of town life came into being. None of these actions, however, were unusual for a town corporation at this time. In point of fact, the old corporation had already involved itself in these areas. The most distinctive and impressive step of the reformers had actually been the sale of the corporation wines at the instigation of Thomas Swindlehurst, the Radical roller-maker.

By 1840, however, it was evident that Teetotallers were more interested in spreading their faith than engaging in concerted political action. Obviously, the Anglican elite was not going to disappear as a result of a few attacks in municipal politics. The tradesmen and general lower middle-class groups, associated with the Teetotal Radicals, had already achieved some status satisfaction by being in the council. The status of a member of the reformed corporation was debatable. As the *Preston Chronicle* stated,[110] in commenting on the ineffectiveness of the corporation and the low level of electoral activity in the mid-1840s: 'Had the office of councillor been one for arousing higher ambition, either by the honour it was supposed to confer or the responsibilities it was understood to involve, we should long since have had a less sleepy corporation than now repose some half-dozen times annually in the town hall, and Preston would have rejoiced in institutions more worthy of its magnitude and importance.'

The decline of sectarianism in local politics also saw the decline of politics itself between 1840 and 1870. In Preston, politics and religion were not as rigidly aligned as in the other northern towns. Men of diverse religious and political commitment sat in town council. On 31 October 1868 the *Preston Chronicle* bemoaned that 'It matters not who may be in our Council Chamber – they may be Fifth Monarchy Men, Praise God Barebones fanatics, sly eyed Whigs, savage Tories or fierce Radicals – it is unimportant what their political creed may be – crazy, wise, antiquated or modern ...'

The Anglican elite, of course, was basically in command of the political situation in local government. Only on certain occasions, however, was it useful

61 Proud Preston

to display this fact, as at the installation of Townley Parker as mayor in November 1861. Parker, the parliamentary politician, had been brought forth as a Tory candidate in St John's Ward. When elected, he was then installed as mayor with his son, the Reverend Arthur Townley Parker, vicar of Burnley, officiating at the ceremony. The vicar's sermon, delivered before 2000 of the assembled faithful, was on the responsibilities of local government leaders.[111]

After 1840 the Nonconformists and Roman Catholics usually attempted to express their sectarian feelings directly to the agencies of local government, rather than through the elaborate political groups constructed to represent their interests. There were many incidents involving these denominations (and sects) and local government, but none of any significance. The only incident that held out the possibility of an ambitious new political grouping occurred in November 1856 when the council discussed the possibility of appropriating part of Moor Park for a race track. The 'Nonconformist conscience' in the town was repulsed by the idea and a committee was formed to sponsor candidates at the municipal election to oppose this plan. Joseph Livesey returned briefly to municipal politics to lead this anti-race track party,[112] he and his son, William, standing as candidates at the election. Though the council did not promise to abandon the project, the race track proposal was shelved. Local politics, therefore, lacked the discipline of strong party alignments found in many other urban areas.

In spite of the absence of deep sectarian conflicts, the town corporation was peculiarly ineffective between 1840 and 1870. The 'Solomons of civic existence' failed to live up to their duties in dealing with 'drains, water pipes, street paving, police, lighting, night soil and our pockets.'[113] The pre-Reform corporation and police commissioners had been among the most progressive in the country, introducing lighting, paving, provision of water pipes, police, and new burial grounds. The reformed corporation did not carry on the traditions of 'Proud Preston' in this respect. Though corporation expenditure increased, improvements were slow in coming to the town, often being enacted only on the threat of action by the central government. This civic inactivity in dealing with social problems probably assisted in raising working-class tempers.

In November 1853, during the Preston strike, the *Preston Guardian* suggested that, in the current industrial unrest, any increase in the number of municipal voters would lead to the defeat of candidates connected with millowners. In point of fact, there was vigorous activity in Fishwick Ward during the November election on the part of operatives, under the direction of John Hansen, a London labourer.[114] Concerted working-class action in local politics was highly unusual in these four northern towns. In Preston it was made difficult by the relatively small size of the municipal, as compared with the parliamentary electorate (at least until the 1850s).[115] An additional complication was the anti-Irish feeling, which absorbed the energy of many workers. Moreover, some of the new sects

62 The Sectarian Spirit

TABLE XIII

Preston Town Council, 1869-70

Name	Occupation	Political party	Religion
ST JOHN'S WARD			
Aldermen			
D. Arkwright	Cotton manufacturer	Neutral	
W. Birley	Cotton spinner and manufacturer	Conservative	Churchman
Councillors			
R. Robinson	Wine merchant	Conservative	Baptist
W. Hayhurst	Brewer	Conservative	Churchman
R. Benson	Wholesale grocer		Quaker
J. Parker	Large farmer		
S. Simpson	Gold thread manufacturer	Liberal	Churchman
J.J. Myres	Land surveyor		
TRINITY WARD			
Aldermen			
E. Birley	Cotton manufacturer	Conservative	Churchman
C.R. Jackson	Cotton spinner	Conservative	Churchman
Councillors			
B. Halden	MD	Conservative	Scotch Presbyterian
T. Grime	Beerhouse owner		
J. Grudgeon	Retired grocer	Conservative	Wesleyan Methodist
S. Cragg	School teacher		Quaker
W. Gilberton	Solicitor	Conservative	Churchman
T. Dewhurst	Farmer	Liberal	Baptist
FISHWICK WARD			
Aldermen			
J. Isherwood	Coal merchant	Conservative	Churchman
M. Myres	Solicitor		Churchman
Councillors			
J. Woods	Cotton spinner	Conservative	Churchman
J. Watmough	Coal dealer		
W. Smith	MD	Conservative	Churchman
J. Robinson	Wine and spirit merchant	Liberal	Wesleyan Methodist
T. Lancaster	Cotton manufacturer	Conservative	Churchman
R.G. Watson	Solicitor	Conservative	Churchman

63 Proud Preston

TABLE XIII continued

Preston Town Council, 1869-70

Name	Occupation	Political party	Religion
CHRIST CHURCH WARD			
Aldermen			
L. Spencer	MD		
T. Walmsley	Gentleman		Churchman
Councillors			
J. Gerrard	Tailor	Conservative	Churchman
W. Sowerbutts	Cotton waste dealer	Liberal	Wesleyan Methodist
J. Rawcliffe	Cotton spinner		
P. Catteral	Solicitor	Conservative	Churchman
P. Park		Conservative	Churchman
J. Whitebread	Coal proprietor	Conservative	Churchman
ST GEORGE'S WARD			
Aldermen			
S. Smith	Cotton spinner		
W. Humber	Cotton spinner		
Councillors			
W. Dobson	Journalist		Churchman
H. Ormandy	Rope spinner		
J.B. Hallmark	Ironmonger	Conservative	Churchman
W. Hayes	Grocer	Liberal	Catholic
T. Ridings	Cotton manufacturer	Liberal	Churchman
E. Alston	Pawnbroker	Conservative	Churchman
ST PETER'S WARD			
Aldermen			
R. Pedder	Tobacco manufacturer		
J. Goodwin	Cotton spinner		
Councillors			
T. Talbot	Pawnbroker	Conservative	Churchman
J. Haslam	Cotton manufacturer	Liberal	Unitarian Methodist
R. Sims	Wine merchant	Conservative	Churchman
T. Edelston	Cotton manufacturer	Liberal	Independent
W.J. Plant	Solicitor	Liberal	Independent
J. Ware	Solicitor and victualler		

Data were compiled primarily from newspapers and town directories. The series 'Our Town Council,' which appeared in the *Preston Chronicle* from January to May 1870, was especially useful.

64 The Sectarian Spirit

diverted their attention to other-worldly concerns, away from economic and social questions, thereby lessening feelings of class antagonism. This was not true, however, of Teetotalism. Even in the Cotton Famine, when almost 50 per cent of the population was on relief by November 1862, Teetotallers did their work. Edwin Waugh, in his treatise on the Cotton Famine, noted how active they were among the working classes. They published a poem, *The Cotton Famine and the Lancashire Operatives*, in Preston in 1862:

My native town! I must remember thine,
For dark vicissitude has frown'd on these;
Thine are the woes of want and poverty.
But how much misery may yet be traced
To drunkenness; the greatest ill of all,
Compar'd with this the rest are only small.
This wastes more lives, and works more ruin far,
Than famine, pestilence, or even war.

Class conflict was allowed to come into parliamentary elections much earlier and more visibly than in local government politics in the first three-quarters of the nineteenth century. There were some special factors assisting this development. Before the Reform Act of 1832 Preston was known as a potwaller borough,[116] in which all male householders normally enjoyed the privilege of voting. In practice, however, bribery, intimidation, and sheer influence did a great deal to limit the independence of voters. The overt understanding between landed elements and town industrialists, led by John Horrocks in the 1802 parliamentary election, may have been a catalyst for the more organized behaviour of workers in parliamentary politics. Horrocks was by far the largest cotton manufacturer and was most probably seen, by many operatives, as a leading representative of the propertied classes in town. The Radical or Independent party, therefore, began to evolve in the first decade of the nineteenth century as one expression of working-class resentment against the propertied. The vulnerability of some in service and retail trade industries to the town and county ruling classes[117] may also have made Preston Radicalism much more proletarian than in other towns such as Blackburn.

In 1807 Joseph Hanson ran for parliament denouncing both the Stanleys and Horrockses and promising a minimum wages bill for weavers. He was easily defeated, as was his brother in the 1812 election. William Cobbett and Dr Crompton of Liverpool were also Independent party candidates before 1830. Orator Hunt became the great hero of the Radicals by winning the 1830 by-election against Stanley. Table XIV shows a sample of voting preferences in

65 Proud Preston

TABLE XIV

Voters whose names begin with A, B, C, and D

	Stanley	Hunt
Tailors	9	23
Shoemakers	27	44
Weavers	66	328
Spinners	56	97

From *An Alphabetical List of Persons who Polled for a Member of Parliament to Represent the Borough of Preston, 8 December 1830* (Preston 1831). J.R. Vincent has used this technique for names beginning with A and B in *Pollbooks* (Cambridge 1967), 160–2. I simply enlarged on his base of evidence, with similar results.

certain selected occupations during that election. It is clear that Henry Hunt received overwhelming working-class support when compared with the Whig candidate, E.G. Stanley. Hunt's victory, according to Hardwick,[118] was partially accidental, Lord Stanley[119] being so confident of victory that he neglected to 'treat' his electors according to 'ancient usage.' The result was that the people felt they could vote the way they wanted at polling time. Town Tories were said to have helped Hunt, being opposed to Stanley's ideas of parliamentary reform. The alleged 'Black Fleet,' which was said to be composed at least in part of industrial workers, in the meantime continued to agitate and riot on every occasion for the Radical cause.[120]

Between 1832 and 1870 the defeat of Radical candidates, such as Henry Hunt and Captain Forbes in 1832, and Colonel T. Perronet Thompson in 1837, continued to be the rule. In 1833–4 there was actually a decline in the number of parliamentary voters in town, as franchise qualifications were tightened. This decline continued until 1867.[121] Bribery was used to erode the willpower of electors. As James Heywood wrote to George Melly, an aspiring Liberal candidate in 1859, 'Preston is an expensive place.'[122] The Conservatives were said to have spent over £12,000 in bribes during the 1862 election alone, 'the canvasser's orders being not to lose a vote if money would or could prevent it.'[123] The allegiance of certain groups of workers to the Liberal Radical cause remained fairly stable up to 1870.[124]

There was also the tradition of continuing collusion between Whigs and Tories to defeat Radical candidates. Whether true or not, by the late 1830s the Conservative and Whig-Liberal parties were the only groups operating on anything like a permanent basis. Without successful Radical spokesmen, working-class antagonism was expressed more in election riots than anywhere else.[125] Since wealthy Anglicans were to be found in both of these political camps, the issues dividing the parties were varied – sectarianism being only one.

Anglicans were not, of course, unusual in Liberal ranks but it was an unusual situation when they were not diluted in a stream of Dissenting wealth. The Whig-Liberal group was known to have the support of Dissenters (and of Catholics before 1850). Many partisan Dissenting petty bourgeoisie, such as Joseph Livesey, however, were associated with the Radical cause *per se*. The Liberals were really the party of a minority of manufacturers in town, such as George Wilding and Joseph Edge,[126] and a number of the old landed families. The Anglican support in the Liberal party was very important. As William Croke reminded the Liverpudlian George Melly (perennial Liberal candidate and Unitarian) in 1862 in discouraging his attendance at the opening of an Independent school: '... to attend a soiree in a *denominational building* is to throw yourself altogether on the sympathies of Nonconformists, and endanger the friendly feelings of those moderate Church of England men, without whose support you cannot succeed.'[127]

Secular questions were often raised between the parties. The issue of free trade, for example, was particularly important in the late 1830s and early 1840s. The Liberals, under such august figures as Sir George Strickland and Sir Peter Hesketh-Fleetwood, no doubt made a few converts to free trade among the manufacturers of Preston. There are indications, however, that many, if not most, factory owners remained loyal to the Tory banner at this time.[128] Localism and town interests versus county interests were some of the other questions raised at elections which had significance for industrial workers.

When sectarianism was introduced as a factor in parliamentary politics its use was more sporadic than consistent. The mechanism of organized, elite-managed political sectarianism was simply too weak in Preston. Dissenters and Catholics were known to be associated with the Liberal cause, therefore Tory propaganda at election time sometimes concentrated on this fact, especially after 1868. More frequently, however, the Tory propaganda machine concentrated on the long-lived *Preston Pilot*, operated by the Clarke family whose financial resources remain a mystery. Joseph Livesey, Lawrence Dobson, and even a joint-stock company were incapable of maintaining a permanent, pro-Liberal paper in the town, though the figures, issued on stamps before 1851, indicate that the *Preston Pilot* actually had a smaller circulation than the Liberal press. Some of the Liberal editorial policies probably offended the powerful Tory leadership group. The *Preston Guardian*, for example, refused to join the *Preston Pilot* in condemning the workers during the strike of 1853-4.[129]

In numerical strength Roman Catholicism rivalled Nonconformity in Preston, but was prone to withdrawal from interaction in politics, adapting instead a defensive posture. In the 1850s both the Ecclesiastical Titles bill and foreign policy involving Italy caused grave suspicion among the priests and Catholic laymen of Preston toward the national Liberals. For twenty years after mid-decade the defeat of certain Liberal candidates – especially Charles Grenfell and George Melly – was said to be due to the hostility of Preston priests.[130]

Even that dynamic new Preston sect, the Teetotallers, despite its formidable political power,[131] seemed reluctant to become fully involved in parliamentary politics. Joseph Livesey was not anxious to tie Teetotalism permanently to the Radical cause. In the 1830s a link did exist. In the September 1838 issue of the *Moral Reformer* he attempted to weld the cause of Teetotalism with that of free trade and then with Radical Liberalism. The primary cause of Teetotalism, however, was never forgotten: 'I cordially join in the urgent demand at present put forward in favour of the repeal of the corn laws; but, at the same time, to be consistent, I would as strenuously urge the repeal of the *drinking laws*. By the latter *an immense quantity of food is destroyed*; by the former an immense quantity of food is prevented from being imported into the country.... The effect of both is the same, to produce *less food* in the country.'

The most vigorous attempt to bring overt sectarianism to the forefront of politics occurred at the 1868 election (as in other parts of the northwest), shortly after the expansion of the working-class electorate. In this campaign the Tories came out strongly as the champions of the Church. As the Tory vicar, the Reverend Owen Parr, explained, the issue of the election was rebellion on the part of Dissenters and Roman Catholics against the Church through the Liberal policy of Disestablishment. He stated: 'That revolution commenced forty years ago when the Test and Corporation Acts were repealed.'[132] The Tories tried to work with the Orangemen as much as possible in the election. It was vaguely hoped that such efforts might swing traditional working-class support from the Liberals. The Liberals, in turn, tried to present themselves as the party of religious liberty, though many of their leaders were, in fact, members of the local Anglican elite. They made a special effort to regain Catholic support by choosing as one of their candidates Lord Edward Howard, 'the scion of an old and faithful Catholic family.'[133] They also tried to secure the Irish vote by sponsoring a local Irish Reform Association.

Neither Tory nor Liberal electoral techniques were very successful. Large-scale Orange-Catholic riots did not occur in Preston as happened in other towns, such as Blackburn, with considerably smaller Catholic populations. But the proletarian masses, having barely recovered from the devastating effects of the Cotton Famine, were hardly in a position to make significant political strides on their own behalf. The working classes were just beginning to move into a new era of separate political consciousness, and in 1869 Thomas Stephenson, a workman, founded the *Preston Observer*[134] as an organ of advanced labour political thought. Although it would take time for the working classes to develop new lines of consciousness, the foundations were being laid by 1870.

The Preston situation clearly indicates that sectarianism did not have to be directed by propertied elites, though such leadership was common elsewhere. In this cotton town virtually the entire propertied class was the target of a social and political attack by a special sect composed of various strata of workingmen – the Teetotallers. The upper working class and those lower on the social scale were hardly the victims of bourgeois social encroachment through the agency of sectarianism. This has implications for all of the cotton towns. That the operations of sectarianism not only failed to subdue but actually reinforced the lines of class conflict can be readily seen in this particular area. That sectarianism was the principal factor in influencing the course of urban class relationships in general is as yet an unproveable fact. Much more research must be done on the impact of other social and economic factors as well as on the concept of class conflict itself.

It is also difficult to establish the fact that there was a higher level of class conflict in Preston than in the other cotton towns. This has been suggested and demonstrated to some degree in politics. In class relations in general, however, without recognized types of measurement[135] the evidence becomes even more impressionistic.

In the area of workers' organizations Preston was in the forefront of the earliest trade union movements. One of the first mule-spinners' unions was organized in the town, and had the reputation of having the biggest reserve of funds in the county.[136] Weavers were even more impressive in their huge demonstrations in 1808 and 1818 under their articulate leader, Richard Marsden, and in their support for the 'Independent' candidate[137] in the election of 1807. The wide franchise in pre-Reform Preston, of course, diverted many of the early working-class aspirations in the direction of politics. Food riots[138] and other primitive forms of protest against specific problems were decidedly secondary to organization. Class violence, of course, was linked to emerging class consciousness and Preston had its share of it. The Chartist riots in the summers of 1839 and 1842 involved virtually all of the industrial urban areas of the northwest, mob activity spreading from town to town. In Preston 'turn-outs' occurred months preceding the plug riots of 1842[139] and there was also separate agitation over the Ten Hours bill. Riots occurred in the early summer of 1826 against the introduction of power looms – as in the town of Blackburn. The waves of machine-breaking in 1831, however, did not seem to have happened in the other towns. Symbolic of these problems, it is perhaps no coincidence that the Preston House of

Corrections added Martello Towers to its fortifications in 1831. Even more to the point were the elaborate battlements constructed about the 'Big Factory' of Messrs Swainson and Birley in 1826 during the disturbances of that year.

More formidable than violence and sporadic protest was, of course, strike activity. Here Preston had a clear lead in terms of man hours of work lost compared with the other cotton towns. This is not to say that the other towns did not have some similar disputes. Bolton experienced a miners' strike in 1846, some industrial disputes in 1848, and an impressive strike of 7429 weavers and spinners over wage reductions in March 1861. In Blackburn there was a strike at Hopwood Mill in 1847, at Walsh Mill in 1848, and a colliers' strike and lock-out at Church and Oswaldwistle in 1860. In Stockport, where class tensions also ran high, there was a wage dispute (involving resistence to a wage reduction) leading to a massive lock-out of spinners and weavers from October 1828 to September 1829, and in June 1860 a strike of 6000 operatives.[140] 'Preston,' as the *Quarterly Review* stated in a sombre mood in 1842, 'has unhappily acquired a notoriety for its strikes.'[141] In 1810, 1821, and 1836-7 spinners staged most impressive strikes to raise their wages. The latter strike was one of the worst in Lancashire history lasting three months, bringing all of the mills to a halt and costing the town an estimated £107,006. Employers often tried to represent the 1836 strike as a defeat for the 660-man spinners' union, but this so-called defeat did little to dampen their spirits. As Cooke Taylor reported concerning the aftermath of the strike: 'On visiting the town at a subsequent period, I was perfectly astounded at the obstinate perseverance displayed by the operatives engaged in the strike: they stood out with a stubborn and dogged resolution which never yielded a jot until famine and its attendant disease had wasted away every particle of their physical energy, and then they sank exhausted rather than conquered.'[142]

The resolute opposition of cotton workers to their employers did not wane. This is clear when almost twenty years later the Preston strike took place. Between October 1853 and May 1854 all cotton operatives (both weavers and spinners) opposed all major millowners in a classic confrontation of labour versus capital. In late August 1853 the cotton workers went on strike at five mills in an attempt to raise wages at these factories to the general level of wages found in the town and in response to a successful campaign to raise mill wages in Stockport. Other employers soon joined these millowners in opposing this demand and a general lock-out was arranged in October, throwing eighteen thousand mill-hands out of work. The operatives then organized a Wages movement and received support from trade unionists all over Britain (including £105,000 in aid). The employers, for their part, attempted to solicit support from capitalist interests outside Preston as well as 'black leg' labour from as far away as Ireland.

The extremes to which both sides were prepared to go, and the extent of the general suffering and dislocation in the town over such a long period of time, point to the serious nature of this contest.[143] Both sides carried on the struggle in terms of principle. Henry Ashworth of Bolton believed that the strike was a struggle between capitalism and communism. Ashworth's chief communist culprit, of course, was trade unionism.[144] There is evidence that at least some workers were, in fact, suggesting a reorganization of the industrial system on collectivist lines, perhaps through co-operative mills. On 3 April 1854 an operative named Mortimer Grimshaw addressed a Wages movement meeting at Fulwood proposing the following: 'We must commence working for ourselves, and when manufacturers see our tall chimneys creeping up they'll begin to look about them. We must erect another town in Lancashire, and we can do it in a very few months. If the people have only the will, the means are within their grasp. We can raise a town with as many mills as there are in Preston and we'll call it "New Regenerated Preston." We can do this, and we'll emigrate every man and woman out of Preston; and what value will their mills be then? They are only valuable so long as you are here to work in them. Concentrate your funds; build factories of your own and then there'll be an end of cotton-lord tyranny, oppression and despotism ...'[145]

Though Grimshaw's plan for 'co-operative self-employment' in Preston was not realized, the dream itself illustrates the degree of alienation felt by many workers from the existing social order. That both sides conceived the struggle in terms of principle indicates the extent of the social chasm between them. Little dialogue was possible between these separate camps. As Charles Hardwick wrote from his vantage-point in the mid nineteenth century, 'Preston has become somewhat celebrated as the principal "battle field" where the capital and labour engaged in the cotton manufacture fight what each deems its respective rights or privileges.'[146]

It should be noted in viewing this evidence that little has been said here about the actions of employers – which is always part of the picture. The defeat of workers in dispute can reflect as much on the strength of employers as on the weakness of workers' organization.[147] Preston employers may have been more socially unified and a good deal more 'hard-headed' in dealing with their workers. There is no question of the fact that the slightly better wages paid, for example, to Bolton operatives as a result of the 'Bolton list' (prices agreed to by employers and workers in the spinning industry between 1814 and 1836)[148] probably got labour relations off to a better start in that town in the early nineteenth century. Wage figures, by themselves, of course cannot tell us much. Cotton workers did comparatively well everywhere.[149] Wage reductions were more often the cause of industrial disturbances and were common in all towns.

71 Proud Preston

In Bolton, for example, employers affected a reduction of 10 per cent in wages in 1842, 1848, 1853, and of 5 per cent in 1861, 1867, and 1869. Henry Ashworth in fact argued that Preston manufacturers, while paying on average lower wages than in the typical Bolton situation, did not adjust them downwards in times of bad trade as did Bolton employers.[150] The debate about Preston workers' standard of living continues. What is remarkable about the Preston operatives, however, was not only their higher degree of organization and solidarity in the face of wage reductions but their willingness to act in a disciplined fashion even for pay increases, as in the strikes of 1853–4, the spinners' strike of 1836–7, or the weavers in 1808 and 1818. It is interesting that Peter Stearns rates 'genuinely offensive wage strikes,' the often related demands for a reduction of hours, and on occasion, union and solidarity issues, high on 'a graded system for evaluating the sophistication of strike demands.'[151]

The breach between propertied and propertyless in Preston remained wide, in industrial relations as well as in politics. Manufacturers steered a sensible course, avoiding friction with the working classes.[152] Workers, even when preoccupied with disasters like the Cotton Famine, remained vigilant for their own interests. Sectarianism had not subdued these developments as in the other cotton towns before 1870. Preston appears to fit much more into the classic mould of 'capitalism versus the proletariat.'

4

Stockport and the 'Dark Satanic Mills'

Stockport, located on the Mersey,[1] was plagued with a history of industrial conflict dating from the late eighteenth century. Indeed, in the first two-thirds of the nineteenth century the town was second only to Preston in overt displays of class tension. Organized sectarian conflict, similar to the pattern observed in Bolton, was also very much in evidence, making politics and social relationships in general resemble the situation in Bolton much more than in Preston.

By 1832 Stockport was already a scene of impressive industrialism, accounting perhaps for the early appearance of class solidarity and tension amongst its workers. Large-scale manufacturing had developed quite independently of Manchester, in spite of the great town's proximity. Silk manufacturing was the first business pursuit of many of Stockport's wealthiest citizens. The construction of silk mills and the collection of a large labour force made the introduction of other forms of industry relatively simple. In 1783 Henry Marsland, a cotton manufacturer from Bosden, bought the large Park and Longwood silk mills and began converting them to cotton production. Soon others interested in cotton manufacturing were attracted to the town. The most notable of these was Samuel Oldknow, who began operations near Mellor in 1786.[2] Technical innovations followed, particularly in weaving but also in spinning, and the development of the iron power-loom by H. Horrocks in 1803 made factory production more attractive. Other cotton manufacturers, such as the spinners William Radcliffe and Samuel Oldknow, gave Stockport an early lead in power-loom weaving, and Henry Marsland and Joseph Goodair were among the first in England to use steam power-looms in their weaving sheds. The development of the cotton industry was very much a factory operation. Stockport's 'satanic mills' were already famous by 1832.[3]

There were, of course, handloom weavers in the neighbourhood who resented some of the factory innovations. Their criticism and early opposition

Stockport and the 'Dark Satanic Mills'

TABLE XV

People employed in the industry in Stockport and Heaton Norris (Lancs.) Parish, 1833

Cleaning and spreading cotton	112
Carding	1129
Mule-spinning	1345
Throstle-spinning	364
Reeling	153
Weaving	4236
Roller covering	28
Engineers, mechanics, firemen, etc.	104
Total number of operatives	7491

Factory Inquiry Commission Report, Part I, Supplement K, PP, 1834, XIX

contributed something to the class tension of the district. However, it is clear that their numbers were quite small by the 1830s. Duncan Bythell claims their number dropped from 5000 in 1818 to only 400 by 1834.[4] Other factory operations also hastened the departure of ineffective cottage industries. Calico printing was important to the economy, Thomas Marsland operating one of the largest such concerns in the kingdom.

Table XV reveals the degree of specialization in the different branches of the cotton industry in the first third of the nineteenth century. By the last quarter of the century Stockport was prominent as a spinning centre, indicating that the balance in the industry shifted to favour spinning sometime in the middle third of the century. Although silk and woollen concerns persisted into the mid nineteenth century and hat manufacturing, which was important by the Edwardian era, began about this time, the town's economy was overwhelmingly bound up in the cotton industry. The percentage of the town's population employed in cotton manufacturing was high – 37 per cent of all males and 22 per cent of all females twenty years old and over.[5] This work force was employed in forty-seven cotton firms owned by sixty-five men, fifty-four of whom were resident in this district.[6]

Class tension was as prevalent in Stockport as in any of the other northern towns, especially in the first third of the nineteenth century. The rapid adoption of machinery and the large-scale factory system in both weaving and spinning were reasons for this strife, as handloom weavers and those who opposed the factory system agitated violently. Early in 1812 Stockport's Secret Committee began the Luddite agitation in the Manchester area that, by spring, culiminated in riots.[7] On 14 April the homes and factories of the principal manufacturers using power-looms were attacked.

Low wages contributed significantly to the Luddite disturbances,[8] as can be seen from the frequent petitions to parliament on this subject from Stockport weavers.[9] Societies sprang up among workers offering mutual protection in times of personal or general difficulty. The parliamentary commission on the poor in Stockport in 1842 noted their spirit of independence with regard to help from charitable agencies sponsored by the propertied. Some of these societies also had a trade union character.[10] The Friendly Society of Stockport Spinners, formed in 1792, for example, had not only the purpose of helping its members in times of distress but of collectively opposing the reduction of wages.[11] Combination laws[12] failed to deter their formation.

The existence of spinners' and weavers' associations encouraged some authorities to suspect that the secret societies were subversive organizations. The correspondence between local magistrates and the Home Office shows a great concern about such influences among the working classes. In June 1829, for example, William Smith, a Stockport magistrate, wrote to the Home Office describing the alleged activities of secret operatives' committees during the severe industrial crisis of that year.[13] These committee men, according to Smith, not only were persuading operatives to strike but also to take a spinners' oath 'of a most awful and diabolical nature.' The oath might require them to assassinate 'oppressive and tyrannical masters' or destroy 'shops deemed incorrigible.' Paranoia seemed to grip magistrates[14] not only in thought but also in their actions in arresting leading Radicals.

Evidence from the Luddite agitation, the troubles at the time of Peterloo, and the Reform organizations all indicate that Stockport workers were actively involved in politics. The disturbances in the town, however, were related to the practical problems of low wages, unemployment among handloom weavers, trade depressions, and the evils of the factory system rather than to politics *per se*. Stockport stood out as an early centre for working-class agitation – the first known strike of power-loom weavers took place there in 1818[15] and many of Stockport's severest labour-capital confrontations occurred before 1832. The dislocation caused by the rapid adoption of power-looms and the factory system contributed heavily to class tension.

Located close to other centres of unrest in South Lancashire such as Manchester, Stalybridge, and Hyde, Stockport was affected by regional and national working-class movements. Chartist activities through the 1830s and into the early 1840s continued to pit workers against employers. In 1842 the plug-drawing riots witnessed violence and property destruction by an estimated 30,000 operatives from Stockport and elsewhere. The acute distress of spinners was a direct cause of much of this violence, though Kitson Clark sees a relationship between the Chartists and the Anti-Corn Law League mayor (as in Bolton)

75 Stockport and the 'Dark Satanic Mills'

as having assisted the mob violence.[16] In 1842 seventy-two mills were said to be closed (and the remainder on part-time work), and one-quarter of the houses and shops unoccupied.[17] After 1842, however, industrial class strife lessened significantly in the town, the Anti-Catholic riot of 1852 being the only major outburst of working-class violence in the period to 1870. With the introduction of free trade, moreover, the Chartists had fewer potential allies among the powerful and influential within the community.

Much of the working-class unrest in Stockport up to the mid 1840s was related to social problems. The expansion of the cotton industry led to rapid growth of the town[18] at least up to 1850, and the population suffered severely from insufficient physical facilities.

Violence was common and troops frequently had to be called out as a final solution to disputes, as in the summer of 1828 and in 1842. After 1820, however, houses were built at a tremendous rate to meet the demand. In 1835 a parliamentary study was made of the Irish population in Stockport, followed by a thorough investigation of poverty in 1842. By the mid 1850s employer-worker confrontations seemed to be less threatening to the social order. As the mayor of Stockport noted in a letter to the Home Office in May 1854, education and the threat of immediate punishment (from Stockport Barracks) had lessened the propensity toward violence among workers.[19] This working-class education was, of course, very much linked with religion in Stockport.

Institutionalized religion also made progress among the people in the middle decades of the century. In 1815 N.K. Pugsley wrote that 'the population of this place is immense – the estimated population is twenty-five thousand, twenty thousand of which never attend a place of worship!'[20] The situation improved slightly by 1829 in the various townships which, within a few years, would comprise the municipal corporation of Stockport. By 1851 the estimated attendances had greatly increased (Tables XVI and XVII). Church accommodation also improved throughout the first half of the century, though it declined (see Appendix) between 1851 and 1870 owing to the small growth rate in population. While the Church and the other Christian denominations grew in the years before 1851, the expansion of church facilities was a costly business. The Municipal Commissioners were uncertain about the financial resources of the Church in Stockport in the 1830s and the Church Building Commissioners and the National Church Building Society made grants to the parishes of north Cheshire. Special church rates were also levied in Stockport between 1812 and 1834, under a local act of parliament passed in 1810, in order to rebuild the parish church (£30,000).

Wealthy Anglican families could be found within the environs of Stockport. The seating plan of the parish church of St Mary's in 1810[21] reveals the names of

76 The Sectarian Spirit

TABLE XVI

Places of worship not of the Church of England, 1829, in townships eventually to form the Municipal Borough of Stockport

Denomination	Number of chapels	Number of adherents
Township of Stockport, Ches. (population 1831: 25,469)		
Wesleyan Methodists	1	900
New Methodists	1	700
Primitive Methodists	1	450
Ranters	2	500
Independents	2	1300
Unitarian Christians	1	120
New Jerusalem Room	1	150
Total	9	4120
Township of Brinnington, Ches. (population 1831: 3987)		
None		
Township of Cheadle Bulkeley, Ches. (population 1831: 4228)		
Cheadle Methodists	120	
Cheadle Methodists	200	
Cheadle Methodists	180	
Township of Cheadle Moseley, Ches. (population 1831: 1946)		
Roman Catholic Chapel	230	
Township of Heaton Norris, Lancs. (population 1831: 11,238)		
Independent Dissenters	1	800
Wesleyan Methodists	1	1500
Baptists	1	100
Total	3	2400

For the townships of Stockport, Brinnington, Cheadle Bulkeley, and Cheadle Moseley the returns can be found at the Cheshire RO–Quarter Session Records [QDR]. For the township of Heaton Norris the returns are at the LRO [QDV/9].

many gentry. As time passed, of course, cotton magnates such as Thomas Marsland and S.W. Wilkinson as well as other men of property such as Sidney Gedge and John Vaughan, attorneys, the Baker family, wine merchants, and the Sykeses, iron founders, became important members of the Anglican elite. These

77 Stockport and the 'Dark Satanic Mills'

TABLE XVII

Religious census of 1851, Municipal Borough of Stockport (population: 53,835)

	Church	Others
Percentage of sittings to population	16.3	25.7
Percentage of sittings to total number of sittings	38.8	61.2
Estimated percentage of population at divine service	29.8	

Denomination	Number of places of worship	Number of sittings Free	Number of sittings Appropriated	Total attendances Census Sunday
Church	8	3528	5278	8300
Independents	5	863	2223	3314
Particular Baptist	2	360	510	754
General Baptists New Connexion	1	150		70
Unitarians	1	50	400	400
Wesleyan Methodists	9	1910	3021	4911
Methodist New Connexion	2	340	989	1312
Primitive Methodists	2	360	322	810
Wesleyan Association	1	100	264	370
Independent Methodists	1	130	120	255
Isolated Congregations	1		200*	172
Roman Catholics	1		1050*	2000
Latter Day Saints	1			380

The original returns for the 1851 census have been lost at the PRO (marked missing 1955). Summaries are from the *Census of Religious Worship, 1851*, PP, 1852-3, LXXXIX, omitting 1 Wesleyan Methodist chapel attended by 43 at a service and a Mormon meeting place attended by 160 at a service (CCXIX).
* Total sittings

men of new wealth, especially the cotton manufacturers, gave some direct help. Samuel Oldknow, who seems to have switched from Unitarianism to the Church early in his career, donated £3000 to the rebuilding of the Anglican church at Marple. Other individual acts of charity can undoubtedly be found. However, as R.B. Walker[22] has pointed out, though there were many wealthy Anglican manufacturers in Stockport, the local branch of the diocesan building society

78 The Sectarian Spirit

had only six members – all of whom were clergy or the family of clergy. The attention of members of the Church elite seemed to be focused on matters other than church building.

The relationship between the Church elite and rank-and-file Anglicans, or indeed with the masses in general within the town, is unclear for much of the nineteenth century. Though the percentage of appropriated seats was smaller than in the other cotton towns in 1851 (perhaps indicating some desire to decrease class barriers within the Church),[23] the predominant early nineteenth-century image of the Anglican clergyman was that of a reactionary figure, assisted no doubt by examples such as the Reverend Charles Prescot, rector of Stockport and magistrate.[24] There was, however, some evidence of the relevance of the Church in the lives of workingmen. Perhaps the most puzzling example was the Chartist march to the parish church in the turbulent summer of 1839. Though similar marches occurred in the other three cotton towns, at least one historian[25] believes it began in Stockport. According to the *Times*, on Sunday, 28 July 1839,[26] about 1500 Chartists marched to St Mary's parish church, occupying the majority of pews, both free and appropriated. Their presence seemed to represent a traditional feeling that the Church was still a relevant agency in seeking redress of grievances.

Among the new, wealthy industrialists of Stockport was a Nonconformist elite, including the Wesleyans W.J. Smith (Mersey Mills) and Thomas Fernley (Weir Mills). As the Independent minister, N.K. Pugsley, stated, or perhaps overstated, in 1815, 'the Dissenters here are in an exceedingly perfect state – they are the most wealthy people in the town.'[27] Not all of these families, however, were in the political camp opposing the Tory Churchmen. Some, in fact, such as Jeremiah Bury, an early cotton magnate, and later James Heald, owner of the great bleach works at Brinnington, were avid supporters. This situation was not unique to Stockport in the first half of the century. Heald, in the tradition of John Wesley, was devoted to the preservation of the Established Church. He was the real leader of the town Tories for many years and the Conservative MP for Stockport from 1847 to 1852.

The large number of appropriated seats at Wesleyan chapels in Stockport, together with chapel accounts,[28] indicates a greater number of men of means within their ranks than normally found in the cotton towns. Other sources of evidence suggest, however, that many of the Wesleyans were also in the more plebeian occupations. An early baptismal register (1794–1837) indicates many operative weavers and spinners connected with Wesleyanism.[29] The marriage register of Tiviot Dale Wesleyan Chapel (the principal one in town opened in 1826 and attended by James Heald) also reveals a great cross-section in occupational background.

79 Stockport and the 'Dark Satanic Mills'

The Primitive Methodists, as usual, had a large number of workingmen in their ranks, as a baptismal register extant for the Ebenezer Chapel[30] clearly shows. John Ashton, a large cotton magnate of the early nineteenth century, was perhaps one of Stockport's better-known Primitive Methodists. For the old Mount Tabor Chapel, Methodist New Connexion (eventually within the Stockport United Methodist circuit), an early baptismal register survives with a remarkably high percentage of factory workers and labourers listed as occupations of fathers at christening.[31] Mount Tabor's fortunes were clearly related to the economic fortunes of the average working man. This very old building had to stand unrepaired and without replacement during the Cotton Famine because of the financial state of its members and attenders.[32] Even Mount Tabor, however, had some social mix, with a handful of manufacturers present in its ranks.

The Reverend Charles Prescot, rector of Stockport, noted in 1811 that 'the sectaries are numerous' in his parish.[33] Dissent, in general, had prospered as a result of the development of large cotton manufacturing concerns in Stockport. Dissenters could claim Samuel Oldknow, the great pioneering cotton manufacturer, as one of their number, at least in his youth. The Hanover Congregational Chapel boasted some of the leading cotton magnates of the town in the mid nineteenth century. These included the Howard, McClure, Kershaw, Andrew, and Eskrigge families. Other prominent Congregationalists in town were J. Walthew and W. Leigh, both cotton spinners, and S.R. Carrington, the hat manufacturer. Yet the campaign to pay off this chapel's debt in 1844 was said to have had a great deal of help from working-class Independents. Writing in 1859, Pugsley stated that some factory girls contributed as much as £5 to the fund.[34]

The Hillgate Congregational Chapel, or The Tabernacle, had a considerable number of cotton hands along with tradesmen and shopkeepers in its numbers. Of the 195 baptisms between May 1815 and July 1831 the occupations of the fathers were as follows: three manufacturers, three professional men, eleven shopkeepers, fifty-five tradesmen, forty-four weavers, forty-three spinners, and thirty-six other millhands.[35]

The Particular Baptist congregation was also known for its appeal to the masses. In the late 1830s Charles Baker became pastor of the chapel and officiated at many public baptisms in the Mersey River. The membership of the chapel grew from thirty-four in 1839 to 215 in 1844. Yet the chapel owed its very existence to the patronage of wealthy Baptists. The building itself, for example, was purchased for local Baptists by Joseph Leese, a Manchester Baptist and county magistrate. The trust deed for the first chapel also reflected considerable assistance from wealthy co-religionists in other parts of the county.[36] The most famous Baptist New Connexion preacher in town was Joseph Harrison, who had a long association with Radicalism going back to the days of Hunt.

80 The Sectarian Spirit

The concern of Congregationalists and Baptists for workingmen was not dimmed by the wealthy in their midst. Pugsley's correspondence, for example, reveals a great interest on the part of the wealthy for more pastoral activity amongst the lower orders. In November 1856 the new Stockport Ministerial Association[37] assessed 'the reasons why the working classes do not attend our religious services' and concluded:

One. The example of the upper and middle classes as to their own non-attendance.
Two. The distinction between the pews and the free seats.
Three. Dislike of ministers of the Gospel.
Four. Dislike of religious truth.
Five. Habits of self-indulgence.
Six. The evil heart the root of all.[38]

The Stockport Quakers were small in number and not particularly outgoing. Little was said about them.[39] The Unitarians, in contrast, though less numerous than the Independents, exerted great influence in the local community. The Unitarian congregation resulted from an eighteenth-century dispute in the old Tabernacle Chapel over the High Calvinism of the pastor. By the early nineteenth century the congregation was a viable, separate Unitarian group. The chapel by that time had also come under the control of a number of prominent families, including the Coppocks (a family of wealthy lawyers), and the Marslands and Orrells (two of the largest cotton manufacturers in town). Some of the other important chapel members can be found in the list of shareholders for 1842 and the trustees named in the chapel deed of 1861 (Tables XVIII and XIX). It is interesting to note that no tradesman, shopkeeper, or factory worker was ever a trustee.

That chapel business should eventually fall under the influence of the wealthiest and most distinguished members was perhaps natural; they were often the most suitable trustees. What was unusual in the Stockport Unitarian congregation was that the formal management of the chapel by the wealthy clique was so explicit and open. In 1829, for example, a resolution was passed that an additional minister ought to be selected by the chapel membership and that the final voting for the new minister ought to take into account the amount of money contributed to the chapel by each member.[40] Henry Coppock,[41] in particular, seemed to have a powerful say in chapel affairs. In 1832, for example, he was largely responsible for the dismissal of the minister, Samuel Allard. Coppock's political attitudes closely parallel his attitudes in chapel affairs. A confirmed localist and advocate of the rights of municipal government, he showed a localist spirit in chapel operations. In 1863, for example, he violently opposed the

Stockport and the 'Dark Satanic Mills'

TABLE XVIII

List of shareholders in the New Unitarian Chapel, St Petersgate, 1842

Name	Known occupation	Number of shares	Amount
Alfred Orrell	Cotton manufacturer	100	£500
Henry Coppock	Attorney	100	£500
Henry Marsland	Cotton manufacturer	60	£300
John Slack	Gentleman	50	£250
Peter Edward Marsland	Cotton manufacturer	30	£150
Edward Hollins	Cotton manufacturer	20	£100
John Alcock	Cotton manufacturer	20	£100
John Hall	Iron merchant	20	£100
Richard Heys		10	£ 50
John Barrow		10	£ 50
Mark Tomlinson		8	£ 40
R. Banks	Surveyor and clerk to corporation	5	£ 25
William Ashe	Shopkeeper	2	£ 10
William Shawcross	Druggist	2	£ 10
John Shawcross	Bootmaker	2	£ 10
Hiram Hall		1	£ 5
Mrs Mary Brown		1	£ 5
Ellis Shawcross	Victualler	4	£ 20
William Woollam	Attorney	10	£ 50
Hugh Townall		2	£ 10

Records of Stockport Unitarian Chapel, in care of chapel secretary

institution of a minister's stipend from Liverpool,[42] arguing that a stipend originating outside the town was opposed to the 'religious liberty' of the Stockport chapel. Just as political centralism from Westminster might infringe on the power of the Nonconformist elite in Stockport local government, so ecclesiastical centralism might also infringe on the local rights and the power of the elite in the Stockport Unitarian congregation.

The involvement of members of the Stockport Unitarian congregation in politics was well known. With a list of figures in local and national politics that included Henry and James Coppock,[43] the Marslands, Edwin Oldham, and many others, the role of the congregation in Liberal political activity was acknowledged far beyond the confines of Stockport. The congregation was regarded by its enemies as being the backbone of the Liberal interest in the town. However, the prominent position of the famous and wealthy in the chapel should not obscure the social background of the bulk of Unitarians in the district. It is clear from Table XX that tradesmen and factory workers made up

82 The Sectarian Spirit

TABLE XIX

Trustees of Stockport Unitarian Chapel named in chapel deed, 1861

Name	Occupation
Henry Coppock	Attorney
Henry Marsland	Cotton manufacturer
W. H. Heys	Silk manufacturer
David Bowlas	Cotton manufacturer
Alexander Loonie	Accountant
Samuel Benson	Cotton merchant
John Alcock	Cotton manufacturer
Edwin Oldham	Town clerk
George Brookes	Alderman
John Cooper	Iron merchant
J.G. Johnson	Stamp distributor
James Shawcross	Solicitor
J.H. Brooks	Solicitor
John Turner	Yeoman
Richard Potter	Paint manufacturer
William Forrester	Manufacturer
Alfred Orrell	Cotton manufacturer

Records of Stockport Unitarian Chapel, in care of chapel secretary

TABLE XX

Occupational categories of men married at Stockport Unitarian Chapel, 6 Aug. 1848–26 Feb. 1873

Gentlemen		2
Professional men		6
Shopkeepers		4
Tradesmen		46
Cotton industry workers		55
Spinners	7	
Weavers	17	
Other hands	31	
Silk weaver		1
Unknown		8
Total		122

Records of Stockport Unitarian Chapel, in care of chapel secretary

Stockport and the 'Dark Satanic Mills'

the majority of the congregation, yet no charitable or special societies were organized for their benefit in the chapel.[44] The opinion of this majority regarding the management of chapel affairs by the wealthy clique is not clear; certainly the propertyless element offered no opposition to the dominance of the wealthy. For a short time in the 1820s a separate and politically radical Unitarian congregation appeared in Swaine Street but had little lasting effect upon the town or upon Unitarians.[45] It is also obvious that socially and politically the Unitarians were not as noticeably helpful in the activities of the Nonconformist elite in Stockport as were their co-religionists in Bolton or Blackburn. The strenuous public opposition of such prominent Unitarian millowners as R.H. Greg and Thomas Ashton to the Ten Hours bill suggests that most working-class people would have felt uncomfortable in their company.

Figures for the Roman Catholic population vary greatly. There must have been Catholics in the area in 1829 – yet none were recorded in the townships of Stockport or Heaton Norris.[46] The figures given in the 1851 religious census seem to be low for Roman Catholic attendance. According to the Catholic Poor School Committee, for example, St Michael's parish contained 10,000 Catholics[47] – quite possibly an exaggerated figure.

Roman Catholicism in Stockport was inextricably linked to the local Irish community. Though not all Irishmen were affiliated with churches, the majority who went to church were Roman Catholic. By 1851 there were 5701 Irish-born persons in Stockport, most of them unskilled labourers.[48] Many were first brought into the town to work on the Waterloo Road and bridge in 1824. According to the testimony of Father William Keily in 1835, most of his parishioners were Irish, all having settled in the area since 1790. He described their social background as follows: 'All of them, with the exception of a few families, belong to the working population. For the most part, they are industrious and hard-working. The great proportion of the women and children are employed in the factories; the men are chiefly bricksetters, labourers, and excavators of earth. For the most part they receive good wages; many families get 20s. a week. They chiefly live in yards, courts and cellars, and a good deal in lodging houses. They retain, in a great measure, their former habits; in their manner of living they do not assimilate themselves much to the English.'[49] John Stanley Barrett, superintendent of police, painted a picture of a much poorer Irish community[50] where many Irish earned only 12s to 15s a week as labourers. Many Irish families sent their children out begging to supplement their incomes. Some specific occupations were dominated by Irishmen; four-fifths of the town's bricklayers, for example, were Irish. Barrett also added that a number of young men and children were employed in the mills. It can be assumed from various sources[51] that the number of Irishmen employed in the cotton industry increased as time passed. With the vast expansion of the Irish population through immigration in the 1840s, the building trade was undoubtedly an insufficient source of employment for many of them. The entrance of large numbers of Irish into the cotton mills was a factor making for great social tension with the English workers.

Even more than Roman Catholicism, the new sects were spectators in the power struggle between Nonconformist and Church elites in Stockport. Their adherents, in most cases, were neither members of old entrenched social circles nor those newer groups who benefited from the Industrial Revolution of the late eighteenth century. Both the Mormons and the Swedenborgians were active in Stockport at various times. Their numbers, however, were not great and their influence on local society even less than in the other three towns.

The Secularists were successful in Stockport for a variety of reasons. The proximity to Manchester (a metropolis of Secularism), early socialist activity in the town, and the exertions of a local Unitarian bookseller, John Hindle, all assisted in the growth of the sect. As early as 1847 Hindle could report twenty-one subscriptions to *The Reasoner*. About the same time a Rationalist Society developed in nearby Hyde in connection with J.R. Stephens' chapel. Following a lecture by Holyoake in 1852 a new Secularist Society was formed with John Hindle as president. In the same year he reported in *The Reasoner* a new society of twenty-four members: 'I take the opportunity to inform you that the nucleus of a party for the extension of Socialism and Free Thought has existed here since the delivery of your lectures here last October. This society is one without a name or unalterable objects, and on that account might readily be induced to form a branch of a national organization for the advancement of Secularism. Stockport does not seem as if it would take the initiative in a combined movement of free thought, but would not be tardy to accept and enforce any system of principles having for objects the reduction of the power of the churches and the rearing of the great social fabrick of Owen.'[52] The legacy of the town's early socialists was obvious. As late as 1858 the society sent a congratulatory note to Owen on his eighty-third birthday. The class divisions within the society of Stockport made Secularism ally very closely with socialism.

The Stockport Secularist Society continued as an advocate of aggressive new ideas among the working classes of the town well into the 1860s. Its gospel was especially successful in the prosperous 50s. In the summer of 1854 a new Hall of Science was opened in the town, described by *The Reasoner* as 'the most elegant, commodious and complete in the possession of our friends in the north'[53] (the old one had been built by the socialists). Secularism, however, in number of declared adherents, was the creed of only a small minority of the working-class population. As such, it had little hope of altering the power struggle between the

85 Stockport and the 'Dark Satanic Mills'

Anglican and Nonconformist elites. Depending on a program of systematic indoctrination, the Secularist gospel appealed to the most affluent of the working classes, who were not stirred as directly by the struggle between factory owners and operatives. The Secularists may also have contributed to the nonpolitical Stockport Great Moor Co-operative Society.[54]

The various ritualistic friendly societies were numerically a much greater influence amongst the working classes. According to the committee reports on the working of the Poor Law in 1842, the proportion of the common people involved in these societies was very high: '... The number and extent of provident institutions, such as sick clubs, benefit societies, funeral clubs, and the various secret orders of the Odd Fellows, Druids, Foresters, etc., which comprise many of the better-paid manufacturing operatives, form a strong barrier for the protection of the poor-rates in regard to cases of accident, sickness or death.'[55] The aims of these societies were social and economic, not political. Their objectives did not interfere with the power struggle between Nonconformist and Anglican elites. The only possible factor disturbing the hierarchical arrangement of local society would have been the spirit of partial economic independence instilled into the members of these societies. Occupational statistics exist for the 2164 Stockport Oddfellows for the year 1840 (Table XXI).

The sect-like qualities of some of these societies were obvious to many people, explaining perhaps why some Church clergy in the Manchester area opposed these groups early in the nineteenth century. Church clergy were soon joined by many in other old denominations in their criticism. In 1833 a pamphlet by Samuel Cooper, *A Treatise on Odd-Fellowship or an Address to Secret Orders in General*, was published in Stockport attacking the Oddfellows, Druids, and other ritualistic friendly societies. First, Cooper criticized the moral atmosphere of such societies, stating that they were intended to promote 'ale-house conviviality' and 'the ignorance and barbarism of Pagan Britain.' Second, and most important, he believed that these sect-like groups were a threat to the old Christian churches: 'I have also been told that some of the members of these secret societies, have said, that no other religion was necessary, and that if they did but keep the rules of the society, it would be sufficient for salvation.' The challenge to organized religion may have been in the minds of some Oddfellows and members of similar societies but was not marshalled by the groups themselves at this time.

The sectarian conflict over specifically sectarian issues was, as in the other towns, less important than its indirect manifestation through politics. There were spontaneous outbursts as well as those more carefully managed by the denominational elites. In the area of the church rate, Churchmen were wisely prepared to back down, and the rate fell into complete disuse by the late 1830s.[56]

TABLE XXI

Occupations for the Stockport District of Odd Fellows, 1840

Professional people		7
Civil Servants		11
Shopkeepers		36
Tradesmen		655
Cotton mill workers		1167
Weavers	261	
Spinners	301	
Overlookers	107	
Other hands	498	
Mill managers		5
Cotton manufacturer		1
Cotton waste dealers		2
Other services		5
Labourers		212
Farmers		19
No trade listed		12
Others not classified		32
Total		2164

Report on the Poor, PP, 1842, XXXV

In the essential area of education the Church and Nonconformist elites often waged bitter war. The establishment of a Mechanics' Institute in 1834 was quickly matched by a Church institute, known as the Stockport District Society for the Promotion of Christian Knowledge.[57] Churchmen and Dissenters attempted to avoid a contested school board election in late 1870 by proposing a compromise list of eleven laymen, which proportionally represented the various denominations in the town. The compromise failed and an all-out, fiercely contested election occurred. The result was the election of four Churchmen, three Independents, two Wesleyans, and one Roman Catholic to the board.[58]

In the area of primary education, however, there was an exceptional case of ecumenical co-operation – the Stockport Sunday school. Begun by Methodists in 1784, the school was intended to minister to the poor children of all Protestant denominations (including Anglicans).[59] In 1805 a new building was erected at a cost of £10,000 – the money raised from contributions mostly given by mill-owners. The school was managed by an inter-denominational board for the benefit of children of all backgrounds. In 1837 there were 5417 pupils registered and by 1870 85,390 scholars had been educated by the school. In many ways the Sunday school was perhaps the most important religious institution in Stockport. The real founder of the school, Joseph Mayer, devoted himself to an

87 Stockport and the 'Dark Satanic Mills'

unsectarian approach to mass education, though in the process he nearly made the school a sect itself. Mayer persisted in his dream, often being rebuked by various denominations, including Methodists, and at one low point was actually accused of fostering the ideas of infidelism, sedition, and Major Cartwright.[60] At all times Mayer vigorously resisted any attempt 'to narrow or sectarianize' the operations of the school.[61] His success in sheer numbers was obvious. He also had the respect of most town leaders by the mid 1850s. His thinking undoubtedly matched some of the more progressive thought on education in the nation, though, unlike Cobden, for example, he expressed little interest in a national system of unsectarian education.

Sectarianism could neutralize even the tireless efforts of the Stockport Sunday school. As late as 2 September 1872 the Reverend J.W. Clarke of St Thomas' Church had to write to the school withdrawing his proposal to lecture there 'in consequence of the very strong disapproval expressed by members of my own Church ... My position is not independent enough, to enable me to disregard the judgment of others on this subject. Nor is the length of time I have been in Stockport sufficient to warrant me, in taking a lead, that would be running counter to the action of all the local clergy.'[62] The Stockport Sunday school was never truly accepted by the Anglican and Catholic clergy nor by many in the Nonconformist fold – ministers or laymen.[63] Its influence as a counter force to sectarian animosity is not easy to determine. At least amongst Protestants, however, it may have eased the denominational frictions to some extent. Generally, the school stood against the divisive influences of class animosity as well as those of sectarianism. Perhaps this was why a Radical Sunday school was formed in 1818 and a Chartist one in 1842. It may also explain Andrew Ure's praise for Stockport's Sunday schools in the earliest part of the century: 'The unrivalled growth of the factory establishments of Stockport, which work up now, it is said, as much cotton as those of Manchester, may be fairly ascribed, in no small measure, to the intelligence and probity of the recent race of operatives trained up in the nurture of its Sunday Schools. It possesses a population considerably exceeding 50,000, quietly engaged in industry through the week, and devoted to the religious exercises on the Lord's day. I have never seen any manufacturing town of such magnitude so exemplary in this respect.'[64]

In spite of the early cotton magnates' patronage, however, the Stockport Sunday school was hardly an example of the uses of religion as a tool of social control. Indeed, as Thomas Laqueur has recently argued, it was a working-class institution existing on its own with its enrolments unaffected by political and social strife.[65] It may, as Ure stated, have been responsible for 'the general decorum that pervades this town and neighbourhood, and the regard for the liberties, lives and properties of others.'[66] It did not accomplish this, however, as a mere adjunct of middle-class influence. Joseph Harrison, a Dissenting minister, founder of the Political Union Society, and a working-class leader between 1818 and 1842, did recognize the benefits of the Sunday school to the millowners and denounced it on those grounds.[67] He was vitally interested in the positive effects on the working classes that might result from socially responsible churches, and ran his own Political Union much like a Methodist society.

As in the other towns, cultural facilities less directly associated with individual denominations also became targets for sectarian bitterness. Grammar schools, being ancient institutions, were associated with the Established Church, and in the north, where organs of Nonconformist opinion were best developed, criticisms abounded. The Liberal *Preston Chronicle* stressed the elitist nature of the local grammar school. In the Liberal-Nonconformist propaganda in that town, social exclusiveness was the target for criticism, especially since Nonconformists were not known for their affluence. In Blackburn and Stockport, on the other hand, criticisms were made of *religious* exclusiveness practised by Anglicans against Dissenters in the local grammar schools.

In Stockport, Dissenters were demanding separate religious instruction in schools by 1850. Fortunately for them there was a Nonconformist elite capable of doing something about the situation. The Unitarian Henry Coppock built the Stockport High School at a personal cost of over £1250,[68] specifically for the benefit of children of wealthy Nonconformists. The school opened in 1857 and was designed to accommodate eighty scholars. It did not have to be maintained for long, however, out of the pockets of the Nonconformist elite. In 1859 the Goldsmiths' Company announced its intention of relinquishing its support of the old Grammar School and offered the management to the corporation, together with an annual bounty of £300. The Liberal Dissenters in the town council leaped at the opportunity and on 26 March twelve new trustees were appointed by the corporation, half of whom were Dissenters, including Henry Coppock himself. The controversy over the management of the Grammar School eventually resulted in a decision in the House of Lords against Dissenters acting as trustees in this legally Anglican institution. This decision stimulated an increased antagonism on the part of Nonconformists in the council toward the school, shown immediately in the appointment of six Churchmen of low social rank to replace the six Nonconformists. The resulting decline of the school in the 1860s was due in part to the hostile attitude of the Liberal majority in the council. In this conflict social rivalry as well as religious scruple had played a part. If old established institutions would not recognize their new social standing in the community, Dissenters would either change them or create new ones of their own.

89 Stockport and the 'Dark Satanic Mills'

Denominational conflict between Protestants and Catholics made less impact ultimately on the social situation in Stockport than did conflict between Nonconformists and Anglicans. Catholicism had no thrusting social elite capable of challenging the basic patterns of the new industrial society. As has been stated, the vast majority of Catholics in Stockport, as in Bolton and Blackburn, were Irish. Irish Catholics, economically impoverished, could at times be the subject of intense sectarian hatred. A clash between elites, therefore, was clearly not a direct cause of anti-Catholicism in the town. The major social mechanism behind this phenomenon of anti-Catholicism was fear and insecurity on the part of the English working classes. The Irish normally formed an important part of the unskilled and semi-skilled work force in all four northern towns. By mid nineteenth century, however, Irishmen could also be found in the mills of the town, doing work approximating that of their better-paid English counterparts. The fear among English workers that the factory owners might use cheap Irish labour in their place was a real one in these northern towns. In a town with a record of particularly poor industrial relations this was an explosive situation.

Latent racial prejudice against Irishmen among townsmen socially above the working classes added to feelings of anti-Catholicism in Stockport. Police superintendent Barrett probably expressed the view of many civic authorities in the following statement made to the Commission on the State of the Irish Poor in Great Britain in 1835: 'The Irish are the most violent and troublesome set of people we have to deal with, in consequence of so many living in a house, and the manner in which they support one another; whole crowds will turn out at a minute's notice and will set out on the first person they meet and maltreat him cruelly, in order to revenge themselves.'[69] Though Barrett and Samuel Gaskill, a surgeon at the Stockport Infirmary, went on to describe the horrible living conditions of the Irish, few positive comments were made about their general behaviour. The famous anti-Catholic riot of 1852 was supposedly rooted in religious controversy, but it was much more the product of social tensions between the English working class and the Irish, inflamed by religious and racial bigotry.

Since the Papal Aggression crisis erupted nationally, the question of the ceremonial activities of Roman Catholics was significant. In Stockport it had been the custom for some time for Catholic students and friends to form up in processions on one Sunday each year. A mere seven days after the passage of the Ecclesiastical Titles Act forbidding such public displays of 'Popery,' the Catholics, chose to go ahead with the annual event. Though Sunday saw little violence, by the following Tuesday, 29 June 1852, the inevitable fights had broken out between Irish and English. The final outcome was an unprecedented amount of damage to Irish Catholic homes in Rock Row and Carr Green, the destruction of two Catholic churches, scores of injuries, and one death. H. Heginbotham reported that many Irish actually fled the town for weeks, sleeping in fields, afraid to return.[70] Special constables and the military were necessary to restore a normal routine to the town.

The Nonconformist and Anglican elites were not directly involved in these developments. Of course, they shared in the general prejudice of the times against Catholics, but had no special animosity towards them. The Tory-Anglican elite sometimes did engage in Orange rhetoric for political purposes, but this was not unusual in these northern towns – Tory-Orange activity was not noticeably higher in Stockport than in Bolton, Preston, or Blackburn. The Stockport Anglican-Tory elite, however, through their Orange rhetoric, may have acted on occasion as a catalyst for violence in a tense situation among the working classes.

The Nonconformist and Anglican elites in Stockport did ultimately benefit from the conflict between English and Irish workers. The elites were based largely on the wealth resulting from the new industrial order of the late eighteenth century. As we have seen, sectarianism reinforced this social pattern. An outright conflict between propertied and propertyless – between industrial elites and workers – would have disturbed this pattern. Anti-Catholicism among the English working classes was another way in which sectarianism worked to preserve the industrial social order. Anti-Catholic and anti-Irish activity (almost synonymous in the case of Stockport) on the part of the English working classes poured much social antagonism into popular sectarian agitation. In Stockport, as has been seen, the difficulties between owners and employees could lead to serious conflict. Anti-Catholicism tended to draw off working-class energies and to divide the working class. It therefore assisted indirectly in maintaining the position of the elites. After 1850 religious hatred between Irish and English was the most important area of tension for the town's work force.

The various forms of local administration in Stockport were in the control of the propertied interests in the community, both before and after municipal reform. Millowners enjoyed greatest prestige among the propertied. By the early nineteenth century industrial wealth assumed a great importance in town society, reflected in the social composition of the membership of local governmental bodies. In 1833, for example, almost all of the sixteen aldermen of the town were millowners.[71] Proud of its ancient traditions, and still far from the time when the town would be virtually swallowed in the sprawl of modern Manchester, Stockport local government leaders longed for more control of their own affairs before municipal reform. The confusion of powers between the Court Leet and police commissioners, accelerated by the necessity for expansion of governmental activities, made the need fo reform acute.[72] A.G. Wilkinson and T. Hogg concluded in their report to the Municipal Corporation Commission in the 1830s: 'It would not be easy to select a town that is better suited for the experiment, should it ever be deemed expedient, to grant to any borough a well-devised scheme of government.'

The state of industrial relations in the town also prompted a reform of local government in the interest of the protection of property. Important legal questions were exclusively reserved to the county magistracy. This meant that in times of violent disorders, the Court Leet would have to wait upon the county magistrates, most of them local gentry, for action in the matter. This was not only degrading for the town leaders but also dangerous. A memorial sent to the Privy Council in 1833,[73] signed by the mayor, aldermen, and principal burgesses, pointed to the fact that the interests of the rural magistracy were not those of the propertied townsmen. It further asserted that the appointment of prominent townsmen to the magistracy would not solve their problem: 'It has been said that, although the gentry withdraw from the smoky vicinity of far-spreading towns, those who have enriched themselves there linger on the spot, and that they, being made county magistrates, will rule the towns like corporate officers, and will have a great regard for their fellow-townsmen. It is always a sage caution to beware of counterfeits, the retired tradesmen and the quondam attorney will think only of aping the justices, to whose society they have lately been introduced, and will forsake their old friends, with heads turned by the sudden change, for new ones.' The solution, the memorial suggested, was some better form of local government where 'the prosperous timber-merchant, the master manufacturer, the corn-dealer, the wine-merchant, are honoured by the acceptance of corporate authority.'

An underlying problem in this pre-Reform situation was the antipathy between country gentry and town industrialists. Though, as the municipal commissioners noted, the gentry had largely withdrawn from the vicinity of the town by 1833, in the three decades before that date there was considerable friction between gentry and manufacturers. The town's growth depended on the growth of industries. This made for a great many nuisances to the local gentry, who preferred a more well-ordered, tranquil state of affairs. The localism and the politics of many townsmen, especially businessmen, developed in a spirit of opposition to the gentry.

Municipal reform was encouraged both by those who feared the temper of the working classes and wanted better ways to control it and by those who wished to expand their social power. Members of the Dissenting elite were among the most prominent advocates of municipal reform. There is certainly no evidence that they were excluded from participation in pre-Reform government. As early as

1721 Stockport is recorded as having a Quaker mayor.[74] Many Dissenters served later in the police commission. Nevertheless, Courts Leet, select vestry, and other similar ancient local government bodies were usually not characterized by large numbers of Dissenters in their general membership. Though wealthy Nonconformist millowners must have rejoiced that their occupation was no bar to public office, they would be angered that religion could be, in some cases. Henry Coppock, Henry Marsland, and other Nonconformist leaders pressed for new local governmental structures to increase their representation.

The denominational groups had a vital interest in local politics from the inception of the reformed town council. 'Every town,' Henry Marsland, the great Liberal Nonconformist millowner, proclaimed in 1845, 'should be known by the politics of its corporation.'[75] Marsland felt that the dominant group in the corporation should represent the dominant or most prominent interest group in Stockport. This is why he and most other leading Nonconformists became the backbone of the local Liberal party. The basis of the party was sectarian affiliation. The same was true of the commitment of Anglicans and their allies to the Tory party.

The first municipal election held under the provisions of the Municipal Corporations Act took place on 26 December 1835. It was a very active election. Meetings on the Reform side were held from September and were riddled with the sectarian spirit. Prominent Dissenters such as Henry Coppock and the Unitarian minister, W. Smith, in particular, took leading parts in these meetings. The Reformist speeches seemed to be especially directed toward the lower orders in town – both electors and non-electors. Such actions on the part of the Liberals stimulated the Tories, in turn, toward efforts at arousing mass support. An Operative Conservative Association was formed against the 'Socinian' Reformers.

The new town council held its first meeting on 31 December 1835. The council was certainly dominated by Liberals, only one of the forty-two councillors being a Tory. Phyllis Giles has even asserted that all members of the new council were Nonconformists.[76] The Liberal slate of candidates, as a whole, had triumphed over the Conservative slate by a substantial majority of votes. The first order of business at this meeting was to elect the new aldermen of the town – the men who would be placed in a higher position of respect on council. It is interesting to note the occupations of these twelve new aldermen: one solicitor, one surgeon, three manufacturers, two shopkeepers, one draper, one flour dealer, one grocer, one leather dealer, and one tailor.[77] The tradesman and shopkeeper classes, well represented here, of course, were most associated in the popular mind with Dissent. In fact, the social structure of the Liberal-dominated council closely

93 Stockport and the 'Dark Satanic Mills'

resembled the social structure of the Nonconformist chapels, with the exception that no lower working-class people were present in the corporation.

The sectarian quality of this Liberal regime appeared more openly at the next meeting of council on 1 January 1836. Though some continuity with old institutions were preserved in the election as mayor of Thomas Steele, Sr, one of the old burgess aldermen, the overall atmosphere of the meeting was one devoted to the establishment of a new order. Symbolizing the emergence of this new order was Henry Coppock, elected as town clerk by a vote of 19 to 9.[78] Coppock was a zealous sectarian and was identified as the leader of the Liberal interest in town. The Liberal regime was swift in organizing and utilizing corporation powers to the fullest extent. In March 1836 the powers of the police commissioners were transferred to the council. In the same month salaries were instituted for town clerk and mayor. With the emasculation of an old institution and the creation of a new salaried professional group of administrators, the Liberals hoped that the council would become a focus for talented people interested in improving the town.

Other areas of local administration saw less dramatic political developments. The first meeting of the Stockport Poor Law Union took place on 8 February 1837. The union represented an amalgamation of sixteen parishes with twenty-one guardians. The politics of the union was reflected in the election of Henry Coppock as clerk to the guardians without a single dissenting vote.[79] Either the board was fairly apolitical or it was almost completely Liberal-dominated.[80] The former may have been the case, as there were few contested elections for guardians or overseers in the following three decades. The predominance of Liberals on the town council undoubtedly influenced their choice of borough magistrates. Coppock was also made clerk to the 'Russell magistrates.'[81] Major Coppock seemed to symbolize Liberal domination of local government at every point. He was simultaneously town clerk, clerk to the borough magistrates, clerk to the board of guardians, and even clerk to the police commissioners. His intense and aggressive Nonconformity singled him out as the arch-villain to most town Tories. Friend and foe alike acknowledged him as 'King of Stockport.'

In the late 1830s the corporation continued to streamline local government. In 1837 an Improvement Act was sought for the borough that would greatly enlarge the powers of the corporation and allow it, for example, to purchase the local gas works. This was the first local Act of parliament dealing with specific powers of local administration in Stockport since the old Police Act. Final estimates of the cost of securing the Act ranged from £1634 to £1800.[82] There is no question that the town council, through such undertakings as securing a new Improvement Act, had made local government more expensive than it had ever been. Tory criticism of increased expenditure became progressively more savage. The Tory *Stockport Advertiser* stated on 18 March 1837: 'We suppose, then, that the town council was created for the same reason that the locusts of Egypt were created, in order to give that virtuous and disinterested reformer, the town clerk, a salary of £500 per annum, and £500 or £1,000 more for soliciting the improvement bill; that it was created in order that one or two ambitious busybodies might govern the town in the name of the town council. It was created to make the inhabitants regret more bitterly the tranquil and economic government of the old police commissioners, those halcyon days, when every man who wished to be one, if he possessed the moderate qualifications required by the act, became one of their body without pledging himself to the wild and impractical folleries of reform; without any inquisition into his political opinions; and when those who pay the taxes control the expenditure of them.'

The increased expenditure of the corporation meant progressively increasing borough rates – a charge felt most keenly by the wealthy. The Tories, therefore, began increasingly to criticize the Liberal regime for not considering the interests of the wealthy citizens of the borough. Though not a few of the wealthy inhabitants were both Liberal and Nonconformist, the Tory press made a definite attempt to court the vote of the well-to-do. Tory propaganda attempted to portray the Liberals as a group composed mainly of lowly Dissenters and tradesmen. Many in the Liberal ranks in council were Nonconformists, drawn from the lower middle class, but some, such as the Unitarians Kershaw and Coppock, were decidedly in the upper stratum of society in both wealth and prestige. The *Stockport Advertiser* chose to identify all the Nonconformists in council with small property-owning and labouring class sectarians in town. The paper commented, as early as 25 November 1836: 'Perhaps, as dissent is now all the fashion, and several influential members of the corporation belong to the new Methodists, they would have no objection to the Mount Tabor Chapel bell being run on the Saturday nights instead of the *expensive* clapper of the St. Mary's Church, which has actually cost the town 40 shillings during the past year.' On 18 March 1837 it stated concerning the Liberal majority in council: 'Many of them are in very low stations in life; of no education; some of them of equivocal character; of small property; and chosen for no other earthly qualification than their rabid Radical politics.' The council did not have the confidence of the burgesses of the town, and, the *Advertiser* noted, a large meeting of ratepayers (undoubtedly sponsored by the Tories) had voted by 1000 to 3 that the town corporation should never spend more than £200 a year on improvements. Thus

95 Stockport and the 'Dark Satanic Mills'

TABLE XXII

Thirty Liberal town councillors, of 'Trifling Assessment,' 1836–7

Name	Occupation	Assessment	Ward
John Ashe	Shopkeeper	£12.10.0.	Portwood
James Beard	Carrier	£15.10.0.	Heaton Norris
William Blake	Shopkeeper	£12.10.0.	Heaton Norris
Thomas Booth	Tailor	£ 3.10.0.	Edgeley
William Brierley	Yeoman	£ 6. 0.0.	Edgeley
John Caine	Shoemaker and other occupation	£18. 0.0.	Middle
W. Charlesworth	Shawl manufacturer	£ 7.10.0.	St Thomas
Alderman T. Cheetham	Surgeon	£ 8.15.0.	St Thomas
G.B. Cheetham	Cotton spinner	£ 9.10.0.	Heaton Norris
S.H. Cheetham	Surgeon	£ 9.10.0.	Middle
L. Cheetham	Attorney	£16. 5.0.	Middle
William Clarkson	Silk Weaver	£ 5. 0.0.	St Thomas
Alderman L. Doran	Shopkeeper	£ 8. 0.0.	Edgeley
William Gordon	Yeoman	£ 8. 0.0.	St Thomas
James Hampson	Hatter	£16.10.0.	Middle
James Higginbottom	Grocer	£16. 0.0.	St Mary's
John Holland	Yeoman	£ 6. 0.0.	St Mary's
Thomas Holland	Yeoman	£ 7.10.0.	St Thomas
Thomas Kenyon	Grocer	£18. 0.0.	Middle
George Oldfield	Rent Agent	£ 5. 0.0.	Middle
James Otterenshaw	Waste dealer	£12. 0.0.	Middle
Isaac Moss	Tailor	£15. 0.0.	St Mary's
Thomas Robertson	Publican	£12. 0.0.	St Mary's
Edward Sanderson	Shoemaker	£ 7.10.0.	Middle
George Smith	Overlooker in factory	£ 4. 0.0.	Heaton Norris
Ellis Shawcross	Publican	£14. 0.0.	Heaton Norris
Thomas Stilfol	Yeoman	£13. 0.0.	Edgeley
Daniel Tym	Draper	£16.15.0.	St Mary's
John Wardle	Cheesemonger	£ 3. 0.0.	St Thomas
Thomas Worsley	Draper	£15.10.0.	Edgeley

Stockport Advertiser, 24 March 1839

the article inferred that the Liberal councillors, not being large property owners or gentlemen, were irresponsible.

On 24 March 1839 the *Stockport Advertiser* devoted an article to the council and the new Improvement bill, questioning how far the members of council 'represent the property and respectability of the borough.' It cited 'the startling fact that out of fifty-six individuals comprising the Town Council, there are not

96 The Sectarian Spirit

above ten or a dozen of the class of heavy ratepayers,' and alleged that 'nearly all the great millowners and ratepayers are carefully excluded from office.' It listed thirty 'obstructive' Liberal town councillors, together with their occupations and 'trifling assessments'[83] (Table XXII), as evidence of the numerical dominance of the tradesman and shopkeeper classes in the Liberal ranks at this time.

Tory propaganda also tried to extend the accusation of social baseness to other parts of local government touched by Liberal influence. So it was that the *Advertiser* tersely pointed out on 25 July 1839 that 'the present government has brought too many tradesmen to the Bench.' The claim was ostensibly made against the Whig administration at Westminster, but it was well known that borough justices were usually appointed on the recommendation of the town council.

Effective Conservative criticism, however, had to wait for burdensome and imprudent measures on the part of the Liberal regime. Though it was recognized by Tories that Dissent formed a very important element in the Liberal ranks, the Liberals engaged in few overtly sectarian acts in council. There were some instances of the Nonconformist conscience at work: in the spring of 1837, for example, a certain Mr Parish was said to have been forced to leave town because the council disapproved of his theatre.[84] Apart from this sort of trivia, however, usually reported in the *Advertiser*, the corporation appeared to initiate little or no sectarian action. In the 1840s the Liberal regime brought fresh and promising opportunities for Tory criticism in the handling of municipal affairs. In 1841 and 1847 two more Improvement bills were sought by the council at a cost of not less than £2566. The Improvement Act of 1847 was an example of early 'municipal socialism,' allowing the corporation to purchase and define the manorial and market rights of the town, together with the right to establish public parks, lease or purchase water works, build bridges, and make or improve other types of communication links within the borough. The Tories, naturally, charged that these Acts were unpopular, expensive to secure, and politically motivated.

The political motives behind these Acts, however, were not easy to prove. It was clear that the transfer of manorial and market rights from the Court Leet to the corporation would make the former institution completely redundant. The animosity of some members of the corporation toward this body was well known. As a self-elected remnant of the pre-Reform order of government, it was, undoubtedly, in principle repellent to the fervent reformer. Yet an argument could also be made against the practical obstructiveness of the Court Leet. That ancient body still claimed authority over market affairs, appointment of constables, and the legal position and privileges of its burgesses. Such authority was potentially annoying to the zealous municipal

97 Stockport and the 'Dark Satanic Mills'

legislator. There was also a question of money involved. Thus, a committee of the council was appointed to look into the subject, particularly manorial tolls, in 1845. This led to the Improvement Act of 1847, after much money was spent in negotiations with Lord Vernon, his agent, Mr White, and with the lawyers and agents involved in securing the passage.of the bill. The bill included other provisions for the future expansion of corporation powers.

According to J.H. Hanham,[85] the Improvement Act of 1847 was an important factor in the downfall of the Liberal regime a year later. Its cost, and the way it was introduced and procured, resulted in great bitterness being turned against the Liberals. Yet the Liberals were determined to put it into law. The dynamic element behind the Liberal regime was Dissent. Dissent was localist-minded and added a special determination to Liberal actions. What better way for Dissent and the Liberal regime, in general, to get things done than by building up one institution (the town council) with authority over all other bodies. Thomas Eskrigge, a Liberal councillor and Independent, stated that in his party's push for the 1847 Improvement Act they were working for 'the principle of local government there.'[86] The influence of Coppock, Kershaw, and other prominent Nonconformists in the Liberal leadership in council or, as the Tory press called them, 'the *imperium in imperio* of the council,' was fundamentally denominational. This denominationalism had a positive side – the desire to implement the uniquely progressive ideas of Unitarians on civic improvement. But much of the motivation was essentially negative in the direction of expanding the power of the new corporation, at the expense of the remnants of the ancient Anglican-dominated organs of government (centred around the Court Leet). It was in reference to this important element in the Liberal leadership elite that the *Stockport Advertiser* asserted, on many occasions, that the Improvement Act of 1847 was the work of Dissenting ministers and millowners, in league with Liberal members of the town council.

The Liberals in local government were more intensively localist than were the Conservatives. This may have been tied to sectarianism. The Nonconformist elite in Stockport found its power enhanced and reinforced by local government autonomy, as they did with local chapel autonomy. The particular national political issues that were taken up locally can reveal much. In general, the willingness of Tories to seize on anti-Catholicism, especially after 1850, illustrates their somewhat greater national orientation. The fact that local political machines were already in place, of course, made the dissemination of national political views much easier. Cardinal Newman was correct in his well-known observation that the wave of anti-Catholicism in 1850 originated in London. Tories exhibited the universalist mentality of members of the Church, on such occasions, in their reception of these issues. Liberals, in contrast, displayed the opposite tendency. Their reputation as 'spenders' and municipal socialists, when in power, was totally different from the laissez-faire image of the national leaders. This, of course, may have reflected to a certain extent the lower social background of many of their number compared with the Tories.[87]

Professor Hanham's assertion that intense local party feeling among the masses in Stockport in the nineteenth century was largely 'whipped up' over very specific issues, such as the Manorial Tolls bill of 1846,[88] is only partially correct. Specific issues could spark intense political activity by the two parties in local government, but politics was already quite alive without any important local issues upon which to focus. There also seems to have been no possibility of special parties being built on entirely local issues. The Nonconformist and Anglican elites were the backbones of the Liberal and Conservative parties, respectively. Their denominational animosity toward one another ensured that politics would be vital. Important specific issues were simply the frosting on a political cake that was already dominating the concerns of those in local government. The local political story was a much longer and more complicated business than Hanham implies.

Given the Liberal-Nonconformist interest in town council affairs, it was only natural that many Liberals took their politics extremely seriously. Factionalism is often a by-product of intense politics, and factionalism within the Liberal ranks was very evident in the 1840s.[89] Schisms within the Liberal group and defections to the Tories greatly assisted the latter group to power. On the other side of politics, the actions of the Conservative party in the mid and late 1840s showed a new willingness to try a variety of techniques to achieve power. Their steady gains in council seats from the late 1830s onward were depicted as victories of the respectable element in local society over the tradesmen. The *Stockport Advertiser* described the change in the character of the council that had occurred between January 1836 and the fall of 1843: 'But it [the Council] is now very different; by the assiduity of Conservative zeal, some of the largest capitalists, and most intelligent men in the borough, have been sent to the Council; and we think that when the proper time arrives, the corporate body should be so composed that they will not appoint the petty tradesmen or barely qualified councilman, to the dignities and distinctions which ought to be held by the respectable, responsible, and influential gentlemen to whom we have referred.'[90]

In Stockport, unlike Bolton, as the forces of Toryism and Liberalism became almost evenly balanced in council, bitterness greatly increased between the two factions. This was due both to the very thrusting nature of Stockport's Nonconformist elite and to political fanatics of a very aggressive

Stockport and the 'Dark Satanic Mills'

nature on both sides. The Tories had used the Workmen's Ratepayers' Association as a means of creating fear among the electors and non-electors concerning increased rates by the Liberal regime. This attempt by an elitist-directed political party to organize working-class support was not new to Stockport. An informal alliance had existed between the Liberals and the Chartist Working Men's Association from 1836 to 1839. The break-up of that alliance caused many a Chartist to look to the Tories for protection. James Mitchell, for example, an old Chartist leader, was one of the organizers of the Workingmen's Ratepayers' Association. In the ensuing hostility between the two elite parties each group accused the other of having Chartist sympathies. The Liberals organized the Protection to Voters Society, ostensibly to challenge the Tory beerbarrel and hooligan gangs at election time. The Tory *Advertiser*, however, described it as a group of men 'hired for the purpose of knocking out the brains of every man who did not think that Alderman Kershaw was as pure as a saint.'[91]

The municipal elections of November 1848 assured the Tories of complete ascendancy in council. Conservatives swept the seats in five wards, with rumours that Tory millowners had brought special pressure to bear.[92] Tory efforts to sway the poorer ratepayers and the Irish may also have been successful.[93] The Tory strength in council was immediately used to strike at the patriarch of the Liberal cause in local government, Henry Coppock. The motion of William Bradley 'that Henry Coppock, Esquire, be no longer Town Clerk of the Borough of Stockport' was carried by a vote of 24 to 21, with seven members neutral and four absent.[94] It should be noted that all seven Liberal aldermen voted against the motion. Coppock's removal signified the end of the first reform era in the history of Stockport local government.

The period in council of what the *Stockport Mercury* called 'rampant Healdism'[95] now began. The Tories not only set their own style to local government but tried to allocate Tories to positions of strength on certain committees – particularly the Watch Committee. The governing committee of the gasworks also came under Tory direction on the pretext of Liberal mismanagement. In spite of Tory claims in the past of bringing gentlemen, millowners, and other men of substance into local government, it appears that the Tories also embraced large numbers of shopkeepers and tradesmen within their ranks in council. The occupational statistics of the Conservative-dominated town council of 1848-9 reveal that at least half of the members could be described as lower middle class. As Table XXIII reveals, the Conservatives in the 1852-3 council had more representatives from these classes than did the Liberals. It is not surprising that Tory propaganda began to ignore the social background of their Liberal opponents about this time.

The Sectarian Spirit

TABLE XXIII

Stockport Town Council, 1852-3, occupational composition

	Liberal	Conservative
Aldermen		
Gentlemen	1	1
Cotton manufacturers		3
Solicitors	1	1
Surgeons		2
Coal merchant		1
Stationer		1
Bleachers		2
Wright		1
Councillors		
Gentlemen	1	1
Cotton manufacturer	9	4
Physician		2
Surgeon	2	
Cotton dealer		1
Waste dealer	1	
Candlewick manufacturer	1	
Gingham manufacturer	1	
Provision dealer	2	1
Grocer	1	1
Coal merchant	1	
Timber dealer	1	
Paper dealer		1
Hardware dealer		1
Corn dealer		1
Spirit dealer		1
Brewer		1
Hotel keeper		1
Druggist		1
Calico printer		1
Woollen draper		1
Draper	1	
File cutter		1
Clog and shoemaker	1	

Compiled from *Whellan's Classified Directory of Manchester and Salford for 1853*, together with local newspapers

The question of social and occupational background of councillors may be an important clue in the explanation of the Conservative victory of 1848. Tory propaganda against Liberal financial extravagance must have had an effect on

101 Stockport and the 'Dark Satanic Mills'

the ratepayers in the shopkeeper and tradesman classes. Even the hard-core political Dissenters must have been swayed by the argument for economy and frugality. There were Conservative shopkeepers and tradesmen who supported the Tory interest, but few of them sat in council before the late 1840s. While significant tradesman, shopkeeper, and even factory workers' support for the Conservative cause probably dates from the 1840s, it was then of an impermanent kind. The switching of their allegiance back to the Liberals in considerable numbers might explain the rapid reinstatement of Liberal rule in 1852. Tradesmen, shopkeepers, and some industrial workers, after all, identified with the Nonconformists and with the Liberals.

The Tory regime from 1848 to November 1852 was short-lived. Undoubtedly one of the reasons for the Tory decline by 1851 was council expenditure. The Conservatives, once the staunch critics of costly local improvements, now embarked on a few of their own. They passed a resolution ordering the corporation to begin financing and building a huge market hall for the town; the projected costs naturally made ratepayers worry about their taxes. The Liberals took full advantage of this situation and hotly debated the question of the market hall both inside and outside the council chambers. The project for bridges at Chestergate and Park had to be postponed in the fall of 1852 until the costs of these projects could be fully ascertained. Conservatives, by this time, were probably afraid of an adverse reaction among the ratepayers.

The style of corporation life under the new Conservative mayor was another source of strife between the two political factions. The banquet, or annual major's dinner, was initiated in January 1848. The display of elegance, wine, and even the use of cooks from Manchester made it reminiscent of pre-Reform days. The Liberal response to this new style revealed a growing sectarian bitterness against the Tories. The Liberal *Stockport Mercury* stated on 3 February 1848: 'First – the Banquet, as it is called, has become a mere manifestation of political party. Secondly – it will become a means of corrupting the corporation – of weaning them from the strict discharge of their attention to the influences of wealth and station. Thirdly – it takes from the trade of our town a considerable sum of money, and where is that money – in Manchester.' The Teetotal, Nonconformist, and localist underpinnings of this Liberal criticism are self-evident.

The loss of support for the Tories among the lower orders of ratepayers was related to the disappearance in 1850 of the Tory-inspired Workingmen's Ratepayers' Association. The *Stockport Mercury* exclaimed at the time: 'Honour to the shopkeepers and the workingmen who made so resolute a stand against the domination of the great Tory millowners.'[96] This apparent loss of the working-class vote probably inspired renewed Tory efforts to consolidate support from the upper ranks of society. As the Conservative *Stockport Advertiser* stated on 6

November 1851: 'There is an influence arising from superior position and information, which might and ought to be exerted by every Conservative millowner.' The paper did caution, however, against Tory manufacturers turning their factories into 'political clubhouses.'

Along with possible changes in allegiance of certain social groups within the two parties, there was a marked increase in overt denominationalism in politics from 1850 onwards. This increase was apparent on both the Liberal-Nonconformist and Tory-Church sides. The Papal Aggression controversy assisted in the growth of sectarian feeling in general. The tension between English and Irish Catholic workers was an established fact by 1850, encouraging the formation of Orange lodges. The Orange lodge provided a new political organization for the Tories that could reach into the lower orders of town society. Rule Two of the Protestant Association of Stockport, formed in 1850, stated: 'It will be an *especial* object of this society to return to the *Municipal Council* and to Parliament men who represent the opinions of this society.'[97] Invariably, those who best represented their opinions were Tories, though even Liberal candidates were occasionally approached.[98]

Not only were the Tories noted for their Orange propaganda in the press and on the platform in the 1850s, but also for their ultra-Protestant actions. In 1851 the Tory-dominated council dismissed two gas works employees on short notice, apparently because the men were Irish Catholics and Liberal supporters.[99] There were, however, limits to the Conservatives' Orange crusade. Clearly, sectarianism could gain some political supporters for the Tory party among the working classes. Too much sectarianism among the lower orders, on the other hand, was not of benefit to any political group. Such sectarian zeal could be translated into violence, as in the 1852 riots, causing only destruction – both physical and social – to the town. The political parties were, after all, still dominated by social elites that, above all, demanded public order and social stability in the town. At the height of anti-Catholic feeling in 1868 the main point of the Tory campaign was the importance of economy in local government. E.D. Steele has noted that the Irish (Catholic) issue usually touched Leeds politics when it was inspired nationally.[100] The same was true of Stockport, but the much larger Irish Catholic population was also less subdued and predictable in its reactions. While engaging in sporadic Orange sympathies in the 1850s and 60s, the Tories clearly felt that they had more to lose than to gain from outright sectarian warfare among the lower classes of Stockport.

Overt sectarian actions by the Liberals appear to have gradually increased in the 1850s. In the early years of that decade the Liberal press, for example, began to attack individual members of the Conservative regime in council on religious grounds. In 1850, for instance, the *Mercury* criticized Councillor Bradley, a

103 Stockport and the 'Dark Satanic Mills'

devout Wesleyan, who had recently chaired a Methodist meeting opposed to authoritarianism in the conference. The newspaper sarcastically wondered if this might eventually lead Bradley to revolt against 'the despotism and intolerance of Toryism and High Churchism in Parliament.'[101]

The renewed ascendancy of Liberals in council after 1852 actually increased their sectarian actions. They reached their height in the Grammar School question of 1859–60. As has been seen in the area of direct denominational conflict, however, by the early 1860s the Liberal regime was more concerned with civic matters than sectarianism, a result in part of the Cotton Famine. In a town with a volatile working class, governmental actions could not stray far from essentials. The District Waterworks Act and the Public Libraries Act were well received by the public. The Local Government Act was passed by a vote of 31 to 2 (4 neutral) in August 1863. This Act, making the town council unquestionably sovereign in local governmental affairs, was enthusiastically adopted by the Liberals and allowed the council to authorize more public works. The Liberal regime could, of course, be over-zealous in its local enterprises at times. In 1867 the council took steps to secure a local Act of parliament in order to build its own waterworks. The enterprise failed and the council simply became empowered to buy the existing privately-owned waterworks. The waste of money in lawyers' fees and other expenses gave the Tories some fuel for their renewed criticism of Liberal extravagance.

As the Liberal regime grew in confidence in the 1860s and extended its impressive list of accomplishments in local improvements, sectarian animosity seemed to lessen. The successful consolidation of power instilled a sense of social ease among the Nonconformists. Their well-to-do members had reached at least a social equality with the Anglican elite in town, though they were occasionally guilty of betraying their special tastes. For example, in 1865 the Public Closing Act was adopted in council by a majority of 31 to 5. In 1856 Henry Coppock claimed openly that a burial board would discriminate against Protestant Nonconformists and Roman Catholics.[102] They were, however, less and less guilty of open sectarian bitterness. No doubt Coppock at the time of his death in 1870 felt satisfied that Nonconformists now formed as established an elite as the Anglicans. Certainly the leadership of Liberal Dissent in town politics formed as much a propertied elite as did the Tory Anglican leaders.

Parliamentary politics at the constituency level was shaped and influenced by the sectarian situation in Stockport. However, being less relevant to local society than local politics, national political activity was a less important area of expression for sectarian conflict. The Liberal cause and the Conservative cause, nevertheless, were associated with the town's Nonconformist and Anglican elites, respectively. The first parliamentary election in 1832 illustrated this fact graphically. The main Liberal candidate in the election, Henry Marsland, the wealthy Unitarian millowner, was eagerly supported in his campaign by Henry Coppock and other prominent members of the local Nonconformist elite. The Anglican elite in town seemed to be closely identified with the Tory candidate, the Anglican Major Thomas Marsland, who was also a cotton manufacturer. The riots that resulted after the election of the Tory candidates gave the impression that the Liberal candidates were more popular with the non-electors[103] than their Tory opponents.

Squibs, speeches, and pamphlets all emphasized the involvement of sectarianism in national politics in Stockport. Typical of the political tracts published in the town in 1833 was one allegedly written by 'A Dissenter,' *A Few Reasons why I Vote for a Conservative Member*, which urged Nonconformists to vote for Conservative candidates at parliamentary elections. The alternative was to follow the lead of a clique of Liberals in returning 'infidels and scoffers to the legislature.' These infidels, it was argued, would then try to change the Established Church, to the detriment of both Anglicans and Dissenters alike.

The Nonconformist-Liberal elite made inroads among the masses in the 1830s. By the end of the decade a close liaison developed between the Liberal elite and part of the Chartist movement. The alliance was felt to be an unnatural one at the time by some members of both groups. In November 1837 J.R. Stephens, on a visit to the town, attacked the alliance, claiming that it was a way of enslaving the working classes to Whiggery, Malthusian economics, and the hypocrisy of conscientious dissent. The alliance, nevertheless, survived until 1839, to the great benefit of the Liberals.[104] Liberal influence spread among the voters and non-voters of the town, aided by Chartists. The breakdown of the alliance in that year revealed the tensions that were always present in this odd association, and marked the beginning of a period of conflict between the working classes and the Liberal-Nonconformist elite. Henry Coppock and his prominent Unitarian associates were held to be responsible, reinforced by the Unitarian elite's treatment of social inferiors in their own chapel. Indeed, the majority of Tory slurs against the Nonconformist-Liberal elite were directed against the Unitarian congregation of Stockport. The Unitarian chapel was a key institution for the Liberal party in the area, both in membership and in organization, and James Coppock, 'the organizer of Liberalism' nationally, was a member of the chapel in his youth.

The powerful Nonconformist chapels, especially the Unitarian, were most certainly responsible for the success of many political campaigns in the town. They were political organizations in themselves, before the advent of the modern party machinery of the late 1860s. From the correspondence of Richard Cobden, for example, it is clear that this venerable politician left most of the political

105 Stockport and the 'Dark Satanic Mills'

management of the borough to Henry Coppock and other members of the Nonconformist elite. Cobden, who personally disliked much of the practical side of local electioneering, appears to have had profound confidence in Coppock and his associates. As he wrote: 'For a man who wishes to be free to work at a great national question, there is not, I believe, another seat like mine ...'[105] J.B. Smith and his Liberal friends a decade later were less inclined to accept Coppock's bossism in parliamentary politics.[106]

Even before the 1860s the chapels were key political institutions for Liberalism. Between elections small registration societies seemed to be the only secular political organizations. The life expectancy of pro-Liberal newspapers was discouraging. Though the *North Cheshire Reformer* published for twelve years, the *Stockport Free Press*, the *Stockport Guardian*, and the *Stockport Mercury* lasted but a few months each. The last-named newspaper was the only one to have the services of a capable editor, John Baxter Langley.[107] As the *Stockport Advertiser* said of the declining *North Cheshire Reformer*, 'neither the monies of the Secret Service Fund in Downing Street, nor the patronage of a Reformed Municipal Corporation in Stockport ... can procure for it sufficient favour in the eyes of either a reading or an advertizing public.'[108]

The Tories, for their part, rallied the forces of the Church party behind them. So involved were the Conservatives with the Church party that there was a debate in 1835 as to whether the new Stockport Conservative Association should not be called the Stockport Protestant Association.[109] Orange propaganda was useful to both the Church elite and general Tory interest in town, providing them with a means of inspiring support among the English (especially unskilled) working classes in town. The other means for securing better public relations was the *Stockport Advertiser*, which had a large circulation[110] and was considered one of the most successful newspapers in the northwest. The first editor, James Lomax, was strongly attached to the Church and Tory interest in town. Under his direction the paper prospered for forty-six years.

The balance between the two elites was maintained throughout most of the period. In spite of the assertions of the Tory press concerning the transient influence of the Liberals and Free Traders in town, it was obvious that the two political groups were fairly evenly matched in economic controlling power. The Liberal cause did, of course, gain the adherance of the Roman Catholics by the election of 1852. Blaming the Conservatives for much of the Orange agitation in 1850 and thereafter, Father Frith supported the Liberal candidates in that election.[111] This pattern of Catholic support may well have become permanent in the decades after the election. The Catholic vote for the Liberal interest, especially after 1868, balanced the specific Orange vote for the Tory interest. Evidence from one pollbook in existence[112] indicates, as with Bolton, that

106 The Sectarian Spirit

Liberal and Conservative voters were roughly the same in social and economic background. The other differences – religion being among the chief of these – were not recorded.

Sectarianism, then, seemed to function in Stockport society in much the same way as it had in Bolton, ensuring that the primary clash in industrial society would be between social elites rather than between classes. Again, the main channel for this conflict would be in the area of local politics. Local political stances were, initially at least, defined in relation to personal association with one elite or another. Most of the continuous tension and ill feeling in Stockport politics (both local and parliamentary) throughout the period were rooted in sectarianism. Stockport, also, from time to time, displayed serious tensions arising from class divisions. The working classes had a bent toward industrial violence, and when the two denominational elites failed to attract them to their banners, cruder forms of sectarianism often did. After 1850 the two types of sectarian conflict, the elite-organized variety and the unorganized type (principally in the area of popular anti-Catholicism), both worked to lessen the importance of class division in Stockport. The result was a social order perhaps somewhat less disturbed than that of Preston, at least in class terms, but none the less volatile.

5
Blackburn: an Archetypal Cotton Town

The sectarian situation in Blackburn was in many ways half-way between that of Bolton and Stockport on the one hand and Preston on the other – a position deriving from the comparative weakness of Blackburn's Nonconformist elite. Though Blackburn, as opposed to Preston, had a sufficiently large elite of wealthy Nonconformists, this elite seemed to practice somewhat more restraint and political quietism than did its counterparts in Bolton and Stockport, probably because of its weaker numbers and financial resources. Political Dissent, nevertheless, was reasonably active in Blackburn throughout the Victorian years, relying initially on the small shopkeepers, tradesmen, and other labouring classes within Nonconformity for direction. At times the conflict with the Tory-Anglican elite resembled the sectarian clashes of Preston, which reinforced the lines of class tension. However, the presence of a Nonconformist elite of some substance ultimately ensured that sectarianism would divide society vertically, crossing class boundaries.

The explanation for the small size of the Nonconformist elite lies in the nature of Blackburn's industrialization. The backbone of the eighteenth-century Anglican oligarchy were merchant 'barons' of King street. These families, together with other Anglicans, dominated the new forms of manufacturing which appeared at the end of the century. Nonconformists therefore did not have the opportunity to congregate in large numbers among the new industrialist class. These commercial factors were of the greatest importance in this cotton town. Unlike Preston, the other north Lancashire town, Blackburn had relied upon the textile industry since the reign of Elizabeth. Originally the centre of textile handicraft industry, in the Interregnum period it also achieved fame for its 'checks' or 'greys' – the weaving of linen, woollen, and mixed cloths. As the popularity of Blackburn greys grew, the handloom weavers and other cloth workers fell increasingly under the influence of the great cloth merchants or gentlemen clothiers. The clothiers acted as middle men between district workers and the Manchester and London markets. Calico printing also absorbed the energies of such merchant families as the Liveseys and Swainsons.

The factory system was a natural progression for many merchants. They simply associated more closely with their weavers in a gradual transition from weaving shed to factory. The Hornby family, for example, which ended up with great factories, began as one of the largest handloom-weaving firms in Lancashire.[1] Blackburn was also a pioneer area in spinning. Hargreaves's spinning jenny was invented there about 1765, and within two years several jennies had been placed in Peel's new spinning mill at Brookside. Unfortunately, all the new carding and spinning machines in the spinning mill at Wensley Fold were destroyed by a mob in 1789, a fate similar to that of Hargreaves's earlier workshop. As one writer observed in 1834: 'Of this folly Blackburn became the victim. Perhaps no place in the whole County of Lancaster was so admirably adapted as was Blackburn for cotton spinning. But the outrages of the Wensleyfold mob banished cotton spinning from Blackburn. At Burton-upon-Trent, Tamworth, Stockport, Matlock, and in other peaceable districts large mills were speedily built, and fitted up on the most approved principles.'[2]

Nothing in the social background of the cotton spinning manufacturers indicates that 'newcomers' were attracted to this branch of the industry. Members of old mercantile families – Shorrock, Eccles, Livesey, Turner, and Thorp – dominated the scene.[3] Yet cotton spinning was eventually bound to grow with the general growth of cotton manufacturing in Blackburn. Weaving and, in the earliest decades of the nineteenth century, calico printing stimulated some spinning. By 1825 there were 100,000 spindles in the town, though only four firms were exclusively in cotton spinning.[4] Double mills became popular in north Lancashire by the mid nineteenth century, again encouraging spinning. Six such mills were built in Blackburn between 1839 and 1841 alone.[5] By 1850 there were over one million spindles in the town. However, there was still a disproportionate specialization in weaving, a situation which prevailed until 1870.

Great merchant families such as Turner, Hornby, Hutchinson, Dugdale, Baynes, and Feilden became important cotton manufacturers in nineteenth-century Blackburn, in the process perpetuating their influence over town life. As in the other towns under consideration, a number of resident cotton manufacturers (approximately eighty owning fifty firms at mid century[6]) directly controlled the fortunes of almost half the adult male population,[7] though variations in the number of workers employed by manufacturers could be considerable.[8] Professional men and gentlemen of independent means, being even smaller in number than in the other cotton towns, offered no rivalry to the manufacturers in social

Blackburn: an Archetypal Cotton Town

influence. The hegemony of the cotton magnates was even greater in the industrial suburbs, where there was an opportunity for them to provide a complete social setting, including housing and public utilities, for their employees. These colonized areas – Brookhouse, Nova Scotia, and Grimshaw Park – commanded the services by the mid nineteenth century of about one-third of the Blackburn area's operatives.[9] The influence which the Hornby family in Brookhouse, the Eccles family in Nova Scotia, or the Pilkingtons in Grimshaw Park exerted over their employees was considerable. Some nineteenth-century millowners such as James Pilkington and William Eccles were Nonconformists, but Anglicanism was still decidedly in the ascendancy.

Patrick Joyce[10] has emphasized the social significance of the great millowners in many aspects of later nineteenth-century Blackburn society and, in particular, in the area of politics. He believes employer influence, whether Liberal or Tory, was extremely important in directing the lives of mill workers, including their religious activities in churches and schools. Though Joyce contends that churches, chapels and their related institutions were supported by the great millowners in an effort to extend their political influence, their motive was one of paternalism rather than a general cultural encroachment by the propertied middle class (embourgeoisement). Factors such as sectarianism occupy a subordinate role to factory paternalism, he claims, in determining the course of political and social development by the 1860s. The view presented here, while conceding the importance of factory paternalism, sees sectarianism as a broader and more crucial factor in determining political and social alignments, at least in the early and middle decades of the century. Joyce's argument is one way of explaining the social mechanism by which Blackburn factory workers gave their support to the two political banners (most convincingly on the Tory side) in the 1860s and thereafter, but it fails to explain the allegiance of other elements in the labouring masses to particular political causes. Joyce also ignores the social independence of artisan-led Blackburn Radicalism of earlier decades and the adherence of some factory workers to it.

Even in this typical cotton town the classes involved in other occupations outside the mill were reasonably numerous. As in the other northern towns, their numbers kept pace with the general population increase (Table XXIV). The tradesmen and small shopkeepers, according to Peter Whittle, were not highly regarded in mid-century Blackburn society. 'Could society exist without the shopkeeper, and all the rest? No; not for a week. Yet many scorn these men on account of their trade, as being low and vulgar.'[11] Tradesmen and shopkeepers were assigned a social status close to that of workingmen, and this class relationship was reflected in politics. George Dewhurst, the famous Radical reedmaker, made his earliest political speeches to local handloom weavers.[12] It is clear that

TABLE XXIV

Males twenty years old and over in retail trade and handicrafts

1831	1552
1851	2379
1871	5899

Census Reports, PP, 1833, XXXVI; 1852-3, LXXXVIII.II; 1873, LXXXII

men like Dewhurst considered themselves, in economic interest-group terms, to be much closer to the proletariat than to the propertied class.

Lines of tension between the propertied and propertyless were drawn well before 1832 and continued to be important through the mid-Victorian period. Working-class violence had been a powerful factor in town life since the late eighteenth century. The employers had acted cautiously in these circumstances – spinning and power-loom machinery being introduced very late. Nevertheless, serious riots of handloom weavers occurred, often causing great damage as in 1826 when the 'Dandy factory,' the most mechanized in town, was destroyed. The driving force behind the unrest was both economic and social. The Reverend Thomas Greenwood, in a letter to the Rev. Mr Whittaker, attempted to correct the vicar's idea that politics was behind the industrial strife of the 1820s: 'If plots there are it is against powerlooms and hunger, not against King, parliament, rotten boroughs or unpaid magistrates.'[13] Luddism as an organized movement was never strong in the neighbourhood. The unrest among Blackburn's factory hands also lay in the confused price and pay-scale situation. In the year of the great industrial disorders of 1826 the *Blackburn Mail* strongly advocated a minimum wage, noting that 'there are *almost as many different prices paid in this town for weaving the same description of cloth as there are manufacturers...*'[14] Just as Bolton manufacturers avoided much industrial strife by the Bolton List, Blackburn manufacturers encouraged it by not having any price or wage agreements. The cost was high. The disorders of 1826 cost the Hundred of Blackburn an estimated £13,960.50. in damages.[15]

Though meetings of handloom weavers persisted into the mid 1830s, the numbers of such workers had greatly diminished by that time.[16] The burden of class strife had already shifted to the numerous factory operatives. On the whole, however, class tensions failed to live up to this promise of continued, overt conflict between 1832 and 1870. There were certainly demonstrations of serious division in the industrial community. In 1836 there was an important spinners' strike. In the same year Richard Oastler allegedly said that he would teach children how to destroy mill machines with knitting needles in the cause of Ten Hours.[17] Chartist activities were also impressive, particularly the plug-drawing

111 Blackburn: an Archetypal Cotton Town

riots of August 1842 (the 'turn-out mania allegedly beginning in Preston) when almost all of the mills in town were attacked by mobs. The mobs, which were reportedly composed mostly of strangers, eventually forced authorities to bring in troops. The riots at the Jubilee Cotton Works witnessed the spectacle of the 72nd Highlanders firing over the heads of rioters.[18] Smaller strikes and disturbances took place in the 1850s. Class conflict, however, did not seem to dominate people's lives in a continuous way. Large-scale workers' organizations, in particular, came late to the Blackburn cotton industry.

There were a number of factors contributing to this industrial peace. A certain caution has already been noted in the employers' handling of workers. Payment of weavers by piece rather than time, which was adopted with the factory system in Blackburn, seemed a fair way to encourage good work. The lack of a universal price scale continued to plague industrial relations to some extent,[19] causing serious strikes at Messrs Hopwoods's mill in 1847 and in 1848 at Walsh's mill in Darwen. Finally, in 1852 a committee chosen by masters and operatives was formed to agree upon an average town price for weaving and spinning; the resulting 'Blackburn List' was adhered to until 1869. Though officially accepted only by the Blackburn Cotton Spinners and Manufacturers Association (and not by the weavers' association formed one year later), it seemed to be a good *modus vivendi* in industrial relations.[20]

Industrial relations were not worsened by the Cotton Famine in the early 1860s. As Mary Ellison[21] has demonstrated, the economic distress caused by this devastating event overshadowed other concerns, including divisions arising from social, political, or ethnic divisions. Blackburn was hit even more severely by the Cotton Famine than the other three cotton towns,[22] and its effects cannot be minimized.

Class tension in Blackburn was also tempered by the continuing operations of sectarian conflict, as in Bolton and Stockport. The most important riots between 1832 and 1870 were those inspired by sectarian hatred during the elections of 1868. A Mrs Whittaker wrote to her husband in 1829 concerning renewed industrial unrest in the area at the outset of this period: 'It is very fortunate that the Catholic Bill had passed previous to these tumults, or they could most likely have joined and mixed religious animosity with personal suffering and what the consequences might have been it is impossible to predict.'[23] This unorganized sectarian conflict, as in the other towns, was less important at least for politics than that organized and maintained by the influential in the community. Other social classes, however, particularly in the ranks of Nonconformity, were to contribute more heavily to sectarian conflict than in Stockport or Bolton.

The religious censuses of 1829 and 1851 (Tables XXV and XXVI) give a good idea of the relative numerical strength and growth pattern of the different

112 The Sectarian Spirit

TABLE XXV

Places of worship not of the Church of England, 1829, Township of Blackburn
(population 1831: 27,091)

Sect	Number of chapels	Number in each sect or persuasion
Independents	1	1500
Particular Baptists	1	260
Quakers	1	46
Roman Catholics	1	3400
Primitive Methodists	1	80
Wesleyan Methodists	1	800
Presbyterians	1	240
Total	7	6326

Records of the Clerk of the Peace, QDV/9, LRO

denominations and sects. Following these statistics, chapel records and other materials can supply the historian with a picture of exactly how these groups fitted into local society. While the general social background of chapels and societies is important, it must be pointed out again that the existence of one wealthy patron could heavily influence the course of events in a particular denomination.

The Church in Blackburn was a classic case of 'parochial centralization.' In 1850 twenty-one churches were alleged by Chamberlain[24] to be under the patronage of the vicar of Blackburn. There was also, he said, a close alliance between the propertied elements and the principal clergymen in town. Archdeacon Rushton's papers note the large number of local benefactors for Church enterprises.[25] Six new churches were in fact consecrated between 1821 and 1865. The vicar, the Reverend John Whittaker, writing to the national Society on 9 August 1843, explained that the parish could not contribute to the National Fund because 'at present all of our considerable families are at the seaside, an invariable practice at this season.' The majority of 'considerable' families in the town were those connected with the cotton industry.[26] As George Miller remarked, a walk through St John's churchyard reveals the tombs of many of the greatest cotton manufacturers – the Hornbys, Bayneses, Coddingtons, Hopwoods, Jacksons, Listers, Turners, 'and many others whose names were once linked with power in the closeknit community.'[27] The Thwaites family of brewers were also Anglican and Tory. Daniel Thwaites (1817–1885), the family patriarch, was buried in the family vault in Mellor church yard, his wealth assessed at £465,000 at the time of his death. It is interesting to note that his

113 Blackburn: an Archetypal Cotton Town

TABLE XXVI

Religious census of 1851, Municipal Borough of Blackburn (population: 46,536)

	Church	Others
Percentage of sittings to population	19.1	20.6
Percentage of sittings to total number of sittings	47.1	52.9
Estimated percentage of population at divine service	19.1	

Denomination	Number of places of worship	Number of sittings		Total attendances Census Sunday
		Free	Appropriated	
Church	7	3429	5104	7784
United Presbyterian	1	210	590	1095
Independents	4	865	1928	2416
Particular Baptist	3	310	704	674
Baptists	1			20
Friends	2	600		101
Wesleyan Methodists	1	250	660	482
Primitive Methodists	1	300	460	1050
Wesleyan Association	1	150	500	620
Wesleyan Reformers	1	400	300	735
New Church	1	97	57	418
Roman Catholics	2	226	1000	1900
Latter Day Saints	1	100		240

'The returns omit to state the number of sittings in one place of worship belonging to the Church of England, attended by a maximum of 150 persons at a service, and in one place belonging to the Baptists (not otherwise defined), attended by a maximum of 20 at a service. The number for attendants is not given for two places of worship belonging to the Roman Catholics.' *Census of Religious Worship, 1851*, ccliii

personal estate far surpassed that of the great millowner, William Henry Hornby (worth approximately £250,638).[28]

This close alliance between many of the wealthy cotton magnates and the Church did not appear to hold true for all districts of Blackburn. The town was divided into seven school districts by the mid nineteenth century. In one of these, St Matthew's, the vicar, writing in 1889, stated that only two of twelve employers in the district were Churchmen. However, he went on to note that 'the larger half of the working population are Church people.'²⁹ A similar picture was apparent in Saint Thomas's school district. The Reverend Henry Wescoe, incumbent, stated in October 1867 that the Church could expect little financial aid for its school endeavours. In his section of the parish, though there were twenty-eight mills, few could be depended on for financial assistance. Many mills changed hands two or three times in a five-year period, leaving them with new men with little or no capital. Wescoe also noted that 'several are dissenters, do not feel called upon to contribute to Church schools, and of the two largest Church employers one, during the last eight months, lost over £9,000.' Consequently, the school programme was 'without the moral help of a single resident manufacturer.'³⁰ The situation in Lower Darwen, where the rival Nonconformist elite was more in evidence, appears to have been even worse for the Church. The Reverend Charles Hunt wrote to the National Society on 11 May 1837: 'The leading manufacturers who are wealthy and influential are decided enemies to our venerable establishment and it would be tedious to enumerate the methods they make use of to compel their work people to go to dissenting meeting houses. They are now busily engaged in endeavouring to erect a chapel and unless we counteract their efforts by a school, which the bulk of the people have been anxiously desiring for several years, the consequences may be serious.'³¹

The fact that some members of the working class – weavers, spinners, labourers, and other low income groups – were affiliated with the Church in Blackburn can only be partially verified by such documents as a sampling of the parish church marriage registers in the nineteenth century (Table XVII). The church functioned as an informal registration agency, a situation as likely to attract sporadic participation as a sense of commitment to Anglicanism among the working classes.³² There is no sign that the Anglican elite attempted to develop a good relationship with these working-class people, though popular Toryism may have assisted its appeal.

Other propertied groups in Blackburn were also aligned with the Church; for example, William Carr and Thomas Clough, wealthy lawyers, and William Dickinson, owner of the Phoenix Iron Works, as well as the Thwaites family already mentioned. The clergy, on the whole, remained closely aligned with the propertied class. In 1820 the Reverend Thomas Whitaker, vicar of Blackburn, preached a sermon in aid of poor relief.³³ While pointing to the need for more food and clothing for the lower classes, he took the opportunity to attack 'the lying and impudent vagabonds' inciting the people to attack property and their social superiors. There was a slightly positive note to Whitaker's sermon when he noted that the Christian charity of the well-to-do Blackburnians would provide the working classes with clear evidence that they were 'their real friends.' The same antagonistic attitude toward the working classes was evident in

115 Blackburn: an Archetypal Cotton Town

TABLE XXVII

Male occupations from Blackburn Parish Marriage Registers

Dates	Male weavers, spinners, labourers	Total number of marriages
Jan.–June 1838	98	202
July–Dec. 1853	156	337
Jan.–June 1871	12	34

Registers in Blackburn Library on loan from Blackburn Cathedral

Thomas Whitaker's successor, the Reverend J.W. Whittaker. In a famous sermon to Chartists in the parish church on 4 August 1839[34] the vicar stated that, according to James v: 1–16, Christ 'was put to death not exactly by the rich but rather by a tumult of the poorer and lower classes ...' Whittaker drew further derogatory parallels with the 'irreverent assembly' then occupying his church.

Not all of the propertied classes of the town were Churchmen. As the National Society correspondence indicates, there was a Nonconformist elite. It can also be seen from the census data that Dissenters were as numerous as Churchmen in Blackburn. This was characteristic of a town edging toward the eastern section of the county, close to the Pennine Mountains.[35] The largest single group of Dissenters, the Congregationalists, were particularly blessed in Blackburn. In 1816 the town became the site of the famous Blackburn Academy, which supplied Congregational ministers to the whole county. The planned removal of the academy to Manchester gave some concern to local ministers as early as 1827. D.T. Carnson of Preston feared the consequences of removing the academy from 'the centre of the county – from districts whose thin population and whose religious indifference render them both unable and unwilling to procure the means of grace at much expense ...'[36] The transfer of the academy in 1830 did not adversely effect Independency in the area, as advanced education under Congregationalist supervision was supplied by Hoole's Academy on King Street.

Direct information on the social background of Congregationalists in Blackburn is rather scant, but there are indications that the denomination was composed chiefly of tradesmen and shopkeepers. Some of these classes had an important role to play in chapel business. The original trust deed of their first chapel in 1788 lists seventeen trustees, of whom sixteen were smaller chapmen and one was a merchant.[37] The congregation must also have included a considerable number of weavers in certain periods. It is said that a special sermon given by Mr Fletcher, an earlier minister, in October 1817 did much to suppress embezzling of factory goods.

TABLE XXVIII

Growth in Congregational chapel facilities, 1851–78

	Number of chapels	Sittings
1851	4	2793
1878	6	5683

Figures compiled from *Census of Religious Worship, 1851*; list of Congregational churches for Oct. 1878 in W.A. Abram, *A Century of Independency in Blackburn*

The growth of the denomination in both facilities and membership was tremendous in the nineteenth century. The James Street Chapel, for example, had twenty-nine members in 1841, two years after opening, and 148 by 1848. Table XXVIII clearly shows the growth in chapel facilities. In 1878 there were also ten schools with a total of 5333 sittings, 4353 Sunday teachers and scholars, and 3650 day pupils. This expansion was greatly assisted by the generosity of a few wealthy patrons in the denomination. Joseph Eccles, the cotton manufacturer, donated a site for a new chapel in 1859 and at the same time gave £800 to the building fund. Park Road school was built entirely on the £6000 donation of the Pilkingtons – another great cotton magnate family. Patrick Joyce feels that under the Pilkington brothers' leadership Park Road Congregational Chapel and school were also important to the political life of the town, being the 'unofficial H.Q. of Blackburn liberalism'[38] from the 1850s to the 1870s. Richard Cunliffe, a banker, had helped to finance the Blackburn Academy as well as the chapels. Considerable support for Congregationalism, however, came from the general membership. Fund drives and collections were usually quite successful. One of the deacons of the Chapel Street Chapel, W.H. Ainsworth, is said to have remarked to a prospective minister in 1865 that 'we are a go-ahead sort of people in Blackburn.'[39]

The Presbyterian congregation in Blackburn dates well back into the seventeenth century. Its exact origin is vague, but the denomination was clearly associated with Scottish immigrants living in the town. The Presbyterians were closely linked with the Independents and worshipped with them in the old Chapel Street Chapel until 1809. The vicar's census for 1804, however, is said to have revealed separate figures for the two groups: 1490 Presbyterians and 396 Independents.[40]

A schism in the Chapel Street congregation in 1809 eventually resulted in the formation of a separate Presbyterian congregation in Mount Street. The chapel became known as the Scotch Church, having been acquired by the United Secession Church of Scotland on the congregation's behalf. The congregation flourished under the capable leadership of Francis Skinner, pastor from 1829 to

1866. Proof of Skinner's popularity is reflected in church attendance. In 1852, though there were only 151 members, the average number at chapel on Sunday was four hundred. Skinner was able to found numerous organizations, from an anti-slavery society to one devoted to total abstinence,[41] mostly of working-class membership. It is interesting to note that the Mount Street Chapel was the only congregation that was able to maintain its own young men's improvement classes, without outside assistance, during the Cotton Famine.

Skinner and other members of the Presbyterian chapel were often referred to as Unitarians by the Tory press. However, it is clear that the congregation must have been Trinitarian in theology. George Dewhurst, the famous Radical reed-maker, stated at a vestry meeting in 1832[42] that as a Unitarian he had no place of worship in Blackburn. From the newspapers of the time it is impossible to know who was actually a Presbyterian or a Unitarian. All that can be said is that conscientious Unitarians were probably not members of the Mount Street Chapel. They may, occasionally, have worshipped at the Unitarian Chapel in Accrington. Blackburn, then, was quite different from Bolton or Stockport in not possessing a clearly-defined wealthy and influential Unitarian congregation.

Very little is known about the background and activities of Baptists in Blackburn. A trust deed surviving for the Blackburn Calvinistic Baptist congregation in 1842[43] lists fourteen trustees – all non-residents. The occupations of the trustees were as follows: a gentleman (Joseph Leese of Pilkington), a manufacturer, a cotton broker, a coal merchant, a schoolmaster, two goldsmiths, a wool stapler, three mercers, and three calico printers. J. Lea asserts that some of the Baptist churches in Blackburn, as in certain other cotton towns, were predominantly working-class.[44]

The Methodists remain something of a mystery. According to the various censuses of Dissenters, Methodists were numerous in Blackburn. Little information seems to be available concerning the Wesleyans. One source of information on the social background of the membership does survive for the Primitive Methodists, and the baptismal registers show that a considerable portion of their adherents were industrial working class; of the 480 baptisms registered between January 1825 and May 1837, 226 record the occupation of the father as that of weaver.[45] This pattern of strong working-class representation is confirmed in later samplings.[46] Only one cotton manufacturer in Blackburn, J.H. Horrocks, besides the Hamer family, was known to have been a Methodist.

Dissenting factory owners in Blackburn, though not numerous, were enough to provide an elite group within the Nonconformist community. This is obvious even from the records of the National Society. Their wealth and prestige enabled Dissenters to sponsor some social and political attacks upon the Anglican elite, especially after 1850. That most Nonconformist chapelgoers were shopkeepers, tradesmen, artisans, and even factory workers was by no means a disadvantage to the cause of Nonconformity. Because these worker groups were members of the same chapels as their more prosperous co-religionists, there was a real chance that this link could be exploited for aggressive denominational purposes. The Nonconformist cause could gain in strength through the cohesion of social groups in chapel. The upper strata of working men, the small shopkeepers and tradesmen, were a very important element in chapel, acting not only as emissaries from the elite to the proletariat (perhaps through the Liberal party) but also as important working-class leaders in their own right. Nonconformity's strength as a popular force in Blackburn society largely depended on these aristocrats of labour, especially in the first half of the nineteenth century.

Roman Catholicism in Blackburn grew in direct proportion to the growth of the Irish community in the town. At the time of the religious census of 1851 there were 2505 Irish-born inhabitants in Blackburn. Clearly, from the religious census itself, many of these Irish people were not attending Mass on Census Sunday. Nevertheless, the Catholic church in Blackburn must have rested to a great extent on their support. The original English Catholic group in the town was very small. Therefore, Blackburn was typical of those towns which, the Catholic Poor School Committee once stated, had 'no resident Catholic population whose capital and industry might have grown with their growth ...'[47] and the expansion of church and school facilities was a great financial burden upon the Catholics of the town.

The new sects which were present in the other three northern towns were also to be found in Blackburn. The figures given in the religious census of 1851 indicate the number of adherents for the Mormons and the Swedenborgians at mid century. The *Millennial Star* reveals that Blackburn already had about fifteen members and one priest in the local Mormon chapel by 1840.[48] Little is known about the New Church congregation in Blackburn, though Jonathan Bayley in nearby Accrington was a leader of British Swedenborgians.[49] It can be assumed that the New Church chapel and the Mormon chapel had a fairly large proportion of working-class people in their numbers, as in the other three northern towns. A deed for the New Jerusalem Temple in Blackburn in 1860,[50] however, indicates a more varied background among the trustees of the chapel, which included three cotton manufacturers (all residing outside the town), a justice of the peace, a brush manufacturer, a bookseller, a painter, a reedmaker, two tailors, two grocers, a power-loom weaver, a cloth sooter, a drawer-in, and a joiner. The fact that persons above the cotton hands on the social scale belonged to a sect-type congregation is significant. It could mean that a few prominent people had in fact withdrawn from certain temporal and combative issues of Blackburn society. Some Nonconformist shopkeepers and even industrialists

119 Blackburn: an Archetypal Cotton Town

may have been tempted to leave the quest for social rivalry and find fulfilment in new 'otherworldly' sects.

In Blackburn the local Secularist Society was formed in 1852, along with similar societies in Over Darwen, Burnley, and Colne. It started with a reasonably large following – sixty-four paying members. The numbers immediately adhering to the call of 'free thought' strongly indicate that the society rested on the sympathy of older groups already in town – Socialist, Paineites, and splinter Radical groups. In 1856, for example, *The Reasoner*[51] reported a great celebration in Blackburn for Thomas Paine's birthday sponsored by the Secularists. Even George Dewhurst, the great Nonconformist Radical leader, appears to have had some association with the society. This association was rather strange, as Dewhurst's Radicals and the Secularists had in essence different objectives. The former were willing to accept old Liberal leadership, provided Radical aims were realized; the latter group aimed at new directions in political and social thought for the common people.

Harold Baker's newspaper shop appears to have been the centre for Secularist activities through most of the 1850s. Under his watchful eye not only *The Reasoner* but other newspapers of a similar viewpoint were freely discussed and sold. William Billington, the poet, and Thomas Stephenson, a future working-class newspaperman,[52] were seen meeting frequently at the shop. At one point in the 1850s Baker published his own periodical, the *Blackburn Pioneer*. His shop was a meeting place for all sorts of groups interested in change in Blackburn society, and was obviously an important institution as one of two shops distributing newspapers in the town until well into the 1860s.

Blackburn appears to have had its share of ritualistic friendly societies. According to the *Blackburn Standard* of 21 May 1844[53] no fewer than sixteen societies marched through the streets of the town on Whit Sunday. The Orange Lodge, ostensibly a friendly society in mid century, was well represented in Blackburn. By 1835 it had been issued five warrants and had ninety-five members. The assistance of Orangemen[54] to the Tories in political and denominational conflict in Blackburn may well have been crucial.

As in the other towns pure sectarian issues stimulated some conflict between sectarian groups. The vehicle or circumstances of each confrontation might have been different but the motivating factors were usually the same. On the question of the position and privileges of the Church in Blackburn, however, Professor Ward's hypothesis of sectarian conflict reflecting class division may be applicable, especially in the first third of the nineteenth century.

Compared with Rochdale,[55] the Blackburn 'Church question' peaked rather early. Scarcely had the new parish church been completed in 1826, at the price of £15,000 in church rates, than the vicar and trustees decided upon the necessity of

120 The Sectarian Spirit

an additional rate to gas light the impressive edifice. As has been seen, 1826 was not a good year for industrial relations in this community. The appearance of a new church rate was not taken kindly by the working classes in general as well as by Dissenters and Roman Catholics. It is indeed revealing that in an early vestry meeting on the subject one of the leading opponents of the measure was Edward Hammond, an operative spinner. He argued that it was unfair both to non-Anglican Christians in the parish and to the working classes in their present circumstances.[56] Like other opponents of the rate, Hammond was influenced by developments in connection with church rates controversies at Leeds and nearby Chorley. The church rate question lasted roughly for twelve months between September 1826 and September 1827. On 10 September 1827 an extraordinary parish meeting was convened on the subject, which soon adjourned because of disorders, leading the pro-Church *Blackburn Mail* to comment: 'We cannot but regret that the apathy of Churchmen should on this occasion have afforded the enemies of the Establishment even an *apparent* triumph. We may say the enemies of the Establishment but we might have said the enemies of *Protestantism*; for we will venture to affirm without fear of contradiction that two-thirds of the persons present at the meetings, were Papists, Socinians and Atheists – and these, too, the lowest of the low – the vilest of the vile – the scum and off-scouring of the town.'[57] The fact that many Nonconformists and Roman Catholics were tradesmen or industrial workers undoubtedly contributed to this statement. The tension between Church leaders (clerical and lay) and many Nonconformists was therefore social as much as sectarian. The Church party's higher social prestige can be readily seen by an analysis of the 102 leypayers who signed a pro-rate memorial in 1827.[58]

The ill-will caused by the passage of the church rate (by means of a public poll) in 1827 was not forgotten. When the issue was once again raised between 1832 and 1834 the bitter fight was resumed, generating more interest than the spinners strike of 1836 and as much squib writing[59] as the parliamentary election of 1832. The successful attack upon the church rate was led by the Radical tradesman, George Dewhurst.

If conflict over the financing of the Church was not important after the disappearance of the church rate in 1834, education remained a source of trouble between Churchmen and Nonconformists throughout the century.[60] From the primary school to the university, Nonconformists and Churchmen engaged in creating rival institutions of learning. Blackburn was no exception to this rule. Church schools and chapel schools, a Mechanics' Institute and a Church institute – each type of educational facility had variations and counterparts in the institutions of Church and Dissent alike. Sectarian animosity in educational matters was possible at any time; even during the Cotton Famine it reared its head. Roman Catholic girls had been in the habit of attending Church-sponsored sewing classes in the Mechanics' Institute early in the Famine. In July 1862, however, the Church clergy, under the direction of Vicar Rushton, moved to limit these classes to Anglicans only, resulting in cries from Roman Catholics and Nonconformists alike. The Roman Catholics, in particular, had argued for classes 'on what is called a broader basis,'[61] since they felt their resources were insufficient to look after their own. In the end, however, this is precisely what happened – each denomination did look after its own. The 'Non-Sectarian' class was established only for those without any denominational affiliation. This decision closely paralleled the sectarian spirit exhibited in other areas during the crisis.[62]

In the course of developments over the Education Act of 1870 Blackburn proved itself capable of compromise. The Conservative Anglican majority on town council was initially hostile toward the Act. However, recognition of the inadequate school facilities, combined with the diligent efforts of two aldermen, finally secured a board in 1871. This was possible, however, only through the acceptance of a representation formula for the board by the denominations. The ratio worked out was seven seats to Churchmen (one being a Broad Churchman of Liberal political views), four seats to Nonconformists (including Methodists), and two to Roman Catholics.[63] The representation was roughly proportional to the numerical size of each denomination. It is surprising that a town which had experienced severe political and religious riots as late as 1868 could arrange such a rational compromise. The proximity of the school board question to the 1868 riots may have encouraged those who argued that moderation must prevail. In any case, denominational school systems continued to hold sway after 1870.

Other denominational-related cultural institutions were not exploited as direct avenues of conflict in the cotton towns, first and foremost because there were so few of them. Nothing comparable to a cultural enterprise like the Lunar Society of Birmingham existed in the four northern towns. Alderman Baynes's intensely proud speech at the Blackburn Mechanics' Institute in 1857 thus appears odd: 'The creation of large towns is undoubtedly one of the missions of the cotton trade. It brings together men professing various arts, working together and aiding and assisting each other, as only men so situated are able to do; and its further development is essential to the progress of society. There is an interchange of thought, mind is brought into conflict with kindred mind, and made brighter and sharper by the friction. It is according to the order of society, everywhere and in all ages, that the growth of large towns should be co-incident with progress and the development of intellectual superiority.'[64] In these same northern towns the farther the institution was removed from direct denominational affiliation within the locale, the less it figured in sectarian conflict. A case in point was the attitude toward the rights of Dissenters at Oxford and Cambridge. Clearly, local society bore a minimal relationship to these institutions, and only occasionally was attention directed to the religious tests by members of the Nonconformist elites and their press.

Anti-Catholicism was apparent in the Tory newspaper press from the beginning of the century. From the time of Catholic Emancipation onwards, press attacks usually corresponded to the trend in national events – such as Papal Aggression. However, one of the few local initiatives did take place in 1829 when the vicar, speaking for the British Society, challenged the priests of nearby Stonyhurst College to meet him in debate.[65] The wording of Whittaker's challenge led to an unpleasant exchange of letters between the vicar and the Roman Catholic clergy of the town and college. The end result was simply an increase in bad feelings between Churchmen and Catholics. The existence of an active Orange group added to the tension. It found its final expression in the riots of November 1868.

Politics in Blackburn, as in the other towns, was a much more important arena for the playing out of sectarian conflict than overt denominational rivalry. Here cultural apartheid was impossible. Unlike Bolton or Stockport, Blackburn's smaller Nonconformist elite would have had difficulties in challenging the Anglican elite alone. Those lower on the social scale in Dissent, however, were peculiarly dynamic in Blackburn and men like George Dewhurst were able to involve shopkeepers, tradesmen, and even working-class people in Radical political causes which ultimately profited Dissent. Politics once again assisted as an active partner in the strengthening of sectarianism. These Nonconformist groups had a reasonably good relationship with the more Whiggish Nonconformist elite and with the leaders of town Liberalism – which included men of many religions. Their assault on the Anglican elite was just as aggressive as those of their wealthier co-religionists in the other northern towns and the working-class Teetotallers of Preston. In Blackburn the smaller Liberal Nonconformist elite co-operated with the tradesmen and artisan Nonconformists before 1850. The end result, as in Bolton and Stockport, was to involve the people, both voters and non-voters, in conflicts which reflected sectarian tensions rather than the tensions between propertied and unpropertied groups in local society. In the short run, however, it often appeared that the Dissenting leaders of the working classes were assisting class conflict. Perhaps in this activity they almost subconsciously reflected their class feelings.

There can be little doubt that the Anglican elite dominated local government before the Reform era. The county quarter sessions, the Court Leet, and the select vestry were almost exclusively Anglican, as were the first improvement commissions. The provisions of the Act setting up the commission specified that

Blackburn: an Archetypal Cotton Town

the trustees were the vicar and eleven other men named 'for the time being – these eleven men to meet each year in April to select candidates to fill vacancies on the Board of Trustees.'[66] The terms of the 1803 Act, therefore, virtually acknowledged Anglican connection with this statutory body. In practical terms the vicar, together with important Anglican families such as the Feildens and the Hornbys, ran local government in the early nineteenth century. The Reverend Thomas Whitaker, vicar and county magistrate, for example, established a position of almost dictatorial authority over the townspeople in the early decades of the century. He did so, of course, with the aid of the leading members of the Anglican-Tory establishment in town. The result was also ineffective local administration. The first report of the Blackburn National and Sunday Schools in 1828 notes:

The town of Blackburn is at present, with a population of nearly 30,000 inhabitants, without a resident magistrate, and completely destitute of any efficient police, so that no civil authority is at hand to check disorder, to punish vice, or to enforce respect to the Sabbath. Its very streets at night are unlighted; so that they who love darkness rather than light, can practise their deeds not only with impunity, but without dread of exposure. In this lack of legislative provision, or executive diligence in public bodies, it becomes a duty on the public at large, and on all who fear God and love their country, to step forward and stem the torrent of vice and profligacy which threatens to overwhelm us. The fear of the law is wanting – let us give to those who are in danger of being misled by vice a *moral* restraint; a *fear of offending*. Let us impart to them by education in youth, a love of order, regularity and decency; an early respect for religion, and a devout reverence of that awful Being who knows their thoughts, views their actions, and will bring them to judgment for both. So, and so only, can we repair the evil which legislative supineness, and municipal negligence, have brought upon our town; and learn to apply a powerful corrective of a calamity which in its origin is beyond our reach.[67]

Without adequate local government, the direct influence of millowners and other propertied persons on the lives of townspeople was possibly greater than it otherwise would have been.

If the personnel and manner of administration in Court Leet and board of improvement commissioners were sources of dissatisfaction to many people in Blackburn, the old administration of poor relief offered little more to admire. A certain Thomas Ainsworth, in his correspondence with the new poor law commissioners in 1834, painted a picture of indifference on the part of many of the ruling class for the poorer citizenry. Some of the clergy, being incumbents of chapels of ease at small salaries, had little to do with the poor.[68] In some adjoining parishes, such as Clayton-le-Dale, where there were heavy concentrations of workers and fewer upper- and middle-class people, ratepayers found the burden of poor relief too great. The introduction of the salaried assistant overseer was regarded by these ratepayers as only a further way of running the townspeople into debt.

The New Poor Law brought the first of the reforms to Blackburn's local administrative structure. The new union was to contain some twenty-three parishes with twenty-nine guardians, Blackburn town itself having five. All the Blackburn representatives on the first board were cotton manufacturers,[69] and two were also Congregationalists – Bannister Eccles and James Pilkington. The old Anglican elite, however, was well represented in the union as a whole, Joseph Feilden being elected as the first union chairman. The tradesman and shopkeeper classes do not appear at all, at least in the 1830s, an absence perhaps connected with the plural voting allowed the propertied classes.[70] There was little serious denominational division of opinion among the members of the union in its early years, though there was disagreement over the selection of the board's clerk. Twenty guardians voted for Peter Ellingthorpe and nine for Richard Wilding,[71] the former being elected as the choice of the old Anglican Tory clique in town. Few divisions between Tory-Anglicans and Liberal-Nonconformists occurred thereafter, the only arguments in the 40s, 50s and 60s were over the secular issue of expenditure – principally over the size of salaries given to relieving officers.

Organized opposition to the New Poor Law was not in evidence on the Blackburn board. Part of the reason was that many of the guardians had originally been assistant overseers of the various parishes, who ran the system of rates and relief under the new law just as they had under the old. They saw that the new law could be even more economical than the old. The expenditure for the year ending in 1839 was £7911 compared with the yearly average of £8440 under the Old Poor Law for the various parishes combined. Inspector Power wrote to the poor law commissioners concerning the reception of the New Poor Law: 'The Blackburn guardians, however, and some of the neighbouring gentlemen, including Mr. Fielding [Feilden], the chairman, are wholly friendly, and the prospect of success is by no means diminished.'[72] The New Poor Law seemed to work out well financially and to cause little division between political parties in the area. As Power noted in a letter to the commissioners in February 1840, the Blackburn board was 'not political.'[73]

Though the administration of poor relief was more effective by the late 1830s in Blackburn, the other local government bodies, especially the police commissioners, proved progressively less capable. The example of other towns with

125 Blackburn: an Archetypal Cotton Town

reformed corporations must have been a factor influencing Blackburn's civic leaders towards further reforms. In 1841 and 1847 two Improvement Acts were passed, setting up a new improvement commission with more than usual power; the new body was empowered to erect a town hall, repair and build new bridges, and improve the sewage system. The commissioners were also given reserved powers for the future, including the right to manufacture and sell gas to the town. These acts were clearly a concession on the part of the town's old Anglican elite to the working people – especially the tradesmen and small shopkeepers. The franchise was considerably widened,[74] and the qualifications for commissioners themselves became virtually identical with those of the voters, making it possible for tradesmen or shopkeepers to qualify for both. While there is no evidence that the old improvement commissioners set up under the 1803 Act did not include Dissenters or Reformers, such persons were much more in evidence among the new commissioners. William Hoole, a prominent Congregationalist teacher, was chairman for many years and James Boyle, a small confectioner and well-known Nonconformist and Radical, was also a member. The two elements in Blackburn Nonconformity – elitist and that upper stratum of toilers, the shopkeeper / craftsmen class (to use Derek Fraser's term) – were therefore represented.

The Improvement Acts also seemed to be aimed at removing unnecessary vestiges of Blackburn's archaic institutions. The 1841 Act removed any lingering powers granted to the old manor of Blackburn. These archaic powers and privileges were undoubtedly associated in the public mind with the old Anglican order of previous centuries. It was, therefore, in the interest of the present ruling classes – now both Anglican and non-Anglican – to appear more progressive by disposing of such unnecessary privileges.

The improvement commissioners of the 1840s were probably more important to most Blackburnians than any previous body of administrators. Not only were they more representative, but they were responsible for a few progressive innovations. In January 1848 the first market hall was opened – an important milestone in the economic growth of the town. Yet it was obvious that Blackburn was less well governed than incorporated towns. Economic, social, and political progress, as well as sheer local pride, dictated that Blackburn must be incorporated.

When incorporation finally came to the town in 1851, no resistance was offered. There was no petition war and other forms of resistance, as there had been in Bolton between 1838 and 1842. There seems to have been a general acceptance of the measure as one long needed for the progress of the town. Many members of the improvement commissioners joined the town council in due course. Baynes, who joined the corporation, expressed his view of the importance of the new council in 1857: 'A Town Council is a miniature parliament, a representative of the national government; and is an excellent training school to fit men for the higher and more responsible office of representing any constituency in the Imperial legislature. It is opposed to that principle of centralization, which is the bane of continental governments. It fosters freedom. It teaches the people to rely upon their own exertions, to think and act for themselves; and that is the characteristic of a free people.'[75] Although the formal transfer of powers from improvement commissioners to town council was not complete until 1854, the real transfer was already well under way in 1851. The very existence of a town council made the commissioners appear superfluous. In the first election for council in November 1851 William Hoole, chairman of the commissioners, acted as the general returning officer, and John Hargreaves, clerk to the commissioners, became the first town clerk. The transition to corporation government was a very smooth operation, including the adjustment to thousands of new municipal voters.

The first municipal election saw the appearance of local political parties. This was not surprising as the Nonconformists and Anglicans, as in other places, had identified with the Liberal and Conservative causes, respectively, for quite some time. The election results gave the Tory party a substantial majority, eleven of the twelve new aldermen being Tories. Symbolizing the Tory-Anglican elite's triumph, W.H. Hornby was elected the first mayor. Some Reformers, however, sat in the new town council. Among these were Radical tradesmen such as George Dewhurst and Miles Baron, and Liberal free traders including the cotton magnate James Pilkington. Most corporation reformers were clearly Dissenters, whatever their social background. In contrast, the character of the Tory party town council was decidedly elitist. Approximately thirty-two of the forty-eight members of the corporation (including all twelve aldermen) were classified as gentlemen in the town directory,[76] most of them members of wealthy commercial families.

The Tory majority in town council did not restrict appointments to the borough bench to particular occupational groups. The first twelve appointees on 19 July 1852 included seven merchants, one physician, one wine merchant, one grocer, and one rope manufacturer. The list of borough magistrates eight years later reflected much the same social composition, with merchants still very well represented.[77] The identification of the Anglican Tory clique with the old mercantile group continued. Even as the Tory regime in the new corporation made moves to strengthen local government, at the expense of certain ancient privileges of the Church, it also gave indications of its special association with the Church. In May 1852 two new committees of council were organized – the

127 Blackburn: an Archetypal Cotton Town

grammar school committee and the parish church procession committee. The first body was set up to look into the future management of a school dominated by Anglicans. The second was to investigate the provision of special pews for members of the corporation at Sunday service or special occasions such as the formal installation of a new mayor.

It was a combination of both sectarian suspicions and social antagonism that encouraged the Radical Liberals to political action in the last months of 1853. Their efforts were also being turned away from national to local politics at this time. The general character of the dominant group in town council – elitist and Anglican-inclined – made many Radical Liberals restless about this body that was supposed to represent all interest groups. In November 1853 a fierce campaign was launched by the Liberals in every ward of the town. Their swift and well-organized move met with Tory opposition only in St Peter's Ward, where the 'friends' of Messrs Hebert and Forrest, the Tory candidates, stood in front of the hotel which was the polling station. The Liberals took this as being direct interference with the electoral process. At 11 AM on 1 November Messrs Eccles and Company, a Nonconformist-owned cotton concern, released their operatives with instructions to 'dispossess the Hornbyites of their point of advantage.'[78] The Liberal-Nonconformist elite therefore gave powerful direction in this political effort that embraced many classes. A riot ensued, in which the Tory supporters were driven away. The Liberals then took up a similar position in front of the hotel, accompanying their street victory with the smashing of Mr Hornby's town house windows.[79]

The result of the Liberal electoral activity in November 1853 may be summarized by the Tory *Blackburn Standard* for 16 November 1853:

The government of the town of Blackburn has passed into the hands of the radical faction. It was the wont of this faction to decry the monopoly of power which they falsely attributed to the conservatives. But monopoly is only wrong when it is not in the hands of the 'liberals.' We confess that we never willingly applied the term which we have just quoted to the radical party, for a more *illiberal* set never breathed the air of heaven. This self-styled 'liberal' party claims to itself the sole right of administering our local affairs – municipal as well as parochial. It does not signify that considerably more than one-half of the public rates are paid by conservatives; the latter must not have any voice whatever in the government of the town. It does not signify that the conservatives notoriously pay more than one-half the gross amount of wages paid in Blackburn, they must not even presume to ask the suffrage of their own work people. It does not signify that more than one-half of the people of Blackburn are members of the Church of England; they must content themselves with a Town Council composed (excluding the aldermen) of a majority of Romanists and dissenters – a majority which will ere long be still further augmented. All this is very exclusive and one-sided, but it is quite in keeping with the true principles of modern liberalism.

History was a powerful determining factor in the course of sectarianism and politics. Traditionally, Dissent was a vital force in Blackburn, although it did not fare as well with the growth of the cotton industry as it did in Bolton or Stockport. It was in large measure the religion of the shopkeeper and tradesman. The sense of powerlessness among these latter groups only added to religious and social hatred for the Anglican elite. Since the seventeenth century this hatred had been an important factor in Blackburn society. In local government the exclusiveness of old self-elected corporations did not apply to Blackburn before 1835 because it was not incorporated. As in other towns, the improvement commissioners (the most important organ of local government) showed no evidence of official restrictions against Dissenters becoming members; indeed, in the 1840s it could have appeared to some that Dissenters were on their way to dominating that institution.[80] When Tory interests rallied to the call of municipal politics after incorporation, however, this in turn stimulated Liberal activity in corporation affairs. Eventually, Radical tradesmen and shopkeepers within the ranks of Liberal Nonconformity found themselves deeply involved in council politics, Blackburn lacking the more genteel Unitarian municipal politicians often found among the first wave of reformed corporation leaders elsewhere.

Dissent helped to organize swift and effective Liberal action in municipal politics. In the 1853 municipal election the Liberals had overcome the small Tory majority in council and had provided a new opportunity for some members of a lower social strata to allay their feelings of political inferiority. The power ambition of the tradesman and shopkeeper groups had been helped by the chapel and also by the Nonconformist elite. In so doing, the rhetoric and actions of these groups, having been reinforced with success, became even more linked with sectarianism. Most of their leaders were zealous Dissenters – above all George Dewhurst. It is misleading for political historians to focus on well-to-do Nonconformists when describing the contribution of Dissent to Liberal leadership in Lancashire.[81]

The initial indication of just how sectarian the new Liberal regime was occurred at the first meeting of the council after the elections. James Boyle, exhibiting a zealous Nonconformist conscience, raised an objection to the 'inconvenience' of the mayor and council conferring at the mayor's home before the installation ceremonies in the parish church;[82] he objected most strenuously to their drinking glasses of wine with the mayor as part of the festivities. A Tory jokingly took exception to Boyle's remarks at the time, but this warning

129 Blackburn: an Archetypal Cotton Town

presaged a new moral standard for the town. According to W.A. Abram, a Nonconformist historian, the town government of Blackburn passed under a Puritan dictatorship for the next few years:

For eight of those years, from 1853 to 1861, Blackburn may be said to have been under the sway of the Puritans. Puritans were its Mayors and acting Magistrates; Puritans mainly its Aldermen and Councillors; Puritans a number of its officials. Messrs. Hoole, William Pilkington, Shaw, Arthur senior, and Ashburn were Congregationalists; Mr. Shackleton, a Quaker; Messrs. Miles Baron and Thomas Thwaites, Baptists; Messrs. Turnbull, Rutherford, Boyle and Johnston, Presbyterians; Messrs. Grime and Hirst, Methodists; Mr. George Dewhurst, Unitarian; and others, whom I forget. Even the Police took to reading religious tracts in their spare moments at the Police Office, given to them by Mr. Hoole, who also looked in at the Town Hall, on Sunday afternoons, to see that the Town Hall keeper and his family and any police officers or men in attendance, were seriously engaged. I do not say that all the 'ruling elders' of the civic body, in these years, were equally strait-laced in their Puritanism.[83]

Along with initiating a 'Puritan' regime, the Liberal majority in council represented to a great extent the tradesmen and shopkeeper classes. At least eleven of the fifteen persons mentioned by Abram were drawn from these occupations. The Reformers in the 1861 town council had a wide diversity of such occupations and in religion were almost always Dissenters. The Conservatives, in contrast, were drawn almost entirely from the gentleman, professional, and cotton magnate classes, and were, with few exceptions, Churchmen. Though the statistics in Table XXIX are from the period immediately after the so-called Puritan regime, they show clearly the background of the two factions in council. Many of the most prominent men described by Abram managed to survive in the elections of November 1861.

The Liberal-dominated council from 1853 to 1861 was extremely busy, but whether this activity was constructive is open to question. Much of the stigma attached to the regime was associated with the Watch Committee. The so-called Liberal-Puritan clique probably established its influence on this body even before 1853. Alderman William Hoole, the stern Congregationalist schoolmaster and perhaps the best-known representative of the entire Puritan regime, was appointed permanent chairman of the Watch Committee on 22 November 1852. As time passed and he gathered like-minded men on the committee, Hoole and his associates were able to root out vice, as they saw it, within the ranks of the police and the population at large. On 6 December 1852 Constable Henry J. Bray was reprimanded by the committee for 'the use of unbecoming language in the police station to a prisoner named Joseph Harrison whilst taking him to the

130 The Sectarian Spirit

TABLE XXIX

Blackburn Town Council, 1861-2

Name	Occupation	Politics	Religion
ALDERMEN			
Thomas Thwaites	Gentleman	Liberal	Baptist
James Cunningham	Brewer	Conservative	Churchman
H.A. Grime	Surgeon	Liberal	Methodist
J. Turnbull	Travelling draper	Liberal	Independent
R. Wilding	Solicitor	Liberal	R. Catholic
Miles Baron	Tailor	Liberal	Baptist
Peter Johnston	Tea merchant	Liberal	Independent
John Baynes	Spinner	Liberal	Churchman
William Johnson	Cheese dealer	Liberal	Baptist
William Hoole	Gentleman	Liberal	Independent
James Boyle	Confectioner	Liberal	Independent
Robert Railton	Ironfounder	Liberal	R. Catholic
COUNCILLORS			
St Mary's Ward			
John Dugdale	Ironfounder	Liberal	Churchman
Thomas Duckworth	Gentleman	Conservative	Churchman
John Dean	Coal Merchant	Conservative	Churchman
Christopher Alston	Spinner	Conservative	Churchman
Ellis Duckworth	Builder	Conservative	Churchman
Edward Holroyd	Sizer	Liberal	Independent
St John's Ward			
R. Duckworth	Gentleman	Conservative	Churchman
Thomas Clough	Solicitor	Conservative	Churchman
Charles Tiplady	Printer	Conservative	Churchman
James Caughey	Gentleman	Conservative	Churchman
Henry Pemberton	Manufacturer	Conservative	Churchman
William Stones	Builder	Conservative	Churchman
Trinity Ward			
Thomas Lund	Commission agent	Conservative	Churchman
William Yates	Cotton spinner	Conservative	Churchman
William Forrest	Cotton spinner	Conservative	Churchman
James Lewis	Cotton spinner	Conservative	Churchman
Thomas Walmsley	Manufacturer	Conservative	Churchman
Thomas Lewis	Cotton spinner	Conservative	Churchman
Park Ward			
Joseph Harrison	Gentleman	Conservative	Churchman
Daniel Mills	Ironfounder	Conservative	Churchman

131 Blackburn: an Archetypal Cotton Town

TABLE XXIX continued

Blackburn Town Council, 1861–2

Name	Occupation	Politics	Religion
R.H. Hutchinson	Cotton spinner	Conservative	Churchman
A.W. Paterson	Manufacturer	Conservative	Churchman
W.D. Coddington	Cotton spinner	Conservative	Churchman
Richard Shackleton	Miller	Liberal	Quaker
St Peter's Ward			
Richard Thompson	Gentleman	Conservative	Churchman
John Pickop	Solicitor	Conservative	Churchman
William Dickinson	Cotton spinner	Conservative	Churchman
W.H. Cartwright	Gold thread maker	Conservative	Churchman
John Ratcliffe	Cotton spinner	Conservative	Churchman
T.H. Pickup	Druggist	Conservative	Churchman
St Paul's Ward			
Francis Johnston	Manufacturer	Liberal	Independent
John Smith	Quarryman	Liberal	Churchman
Thomas Gillibrand	Manufacturer	Conservative	Churchman
William Hopwood	Land surveyor	Conservative	Churchman
J. Murray	Agent	Liberal	Independent
William Arthur	Currier	Liberal	Independent

Blackburn Standard, 6 Nov. 1861

police cell...'[84] Yet the number of reprimands and dismissals was not noticeably higher than in other towns in the period. A reprimand, for example, against a constable attending an Irish wake, or one for being seen in the company of a prostitute, were typical products of the general value system of the times. The numerous charges of drunkenness might have been excessive. In 1854, during the first official year of the regime, there were nine reprimands against constables for drinking. In the same year new regulations were also issued against innkeepers and beersellers supplying constables with drink on duty. However, drinking may well have been a very real problem among police in the northern towns. The 'Puritanism' or Nonconformist conscience exemplified by the committee may not have been excessive for the times.[85]

The Liberal majority in council from 1853 to 1861 initiated few measures for the benefit of the community as a whole. The regime's attention was drawn to itself – on its new-found position of authority and on the reaffirmation of its sectarian and political values. Some action, of course, had to be taken on urgent issues perplexing the town. In 1856, for example, the town council authorized drainage works to be constructed to deal with the problems of sewage. Little real attention, however, was paid to the project and eventually a major pollution problem resulted from this mismanagement. In 1865 legal proceedings were even taken against the corporation under the health acts. There was much to do. Civic enterprise, however, did not seem to appeal to the tastes of the Liberal-Radical councillors.[86] This Liberal regime was essentially a tradesman group stimulated by vague Radical political idealism, blessed by the town's Nonconformist elite but not given much direction by them.

The Tory party had initially fared reasonably well in the new electoral arena of municipal politics after 1851. It was no accident that W.H. Hornby, the great Tory millowner, was elected Blackburn's first mayor. His appeal amongst voters and non-voters was considerable. His mill at Brookhouse was a model of working conditions and in 1841 he (along with W. Kenworthy) presented a playground, 'Brookhouse Gymnasium,' to the people of the district.[87] He was also a staunch advocate of the Ten Hours bill. J.C. Lowe points to the considerable political influence of Hornby and other millowners in harnessing the forces of popular Toryism[88] in alliance with the drink interest and militant Anglicanism. Even members of the tradesmen and shopkeeping classes could be attracted to the Hornby banner as demonstrated, for example, in the well-known career of councillor Thomas Mullineaux, the Tory butcher.[89] This was somewhat different from the situation described by J.R. Vincent in Rochdale, where the Tory party survived on little more than the prestige of a few leading families, the drink interest, and electoral corruption.[90]

As time passed the Liberal-Nonconformist elite began to enlarge its influence over the Radical lower middle-class Nonconformists, and the Tory-Anglican elite cultivated its popular following. From the late 1850s sectarian conflict was progressively more of an inhibitor than an initiator of class conflict. The working classes were at last given some direction by the largest property owners in the two political parties, a situation which, by 1868, resembled that described by Patrick Joyce in *Work, Society and Politics*.

The municipal elections of 1861 marked the end of the Liberal-Puritan supremacy in council; the Conservatives captured nine of the twelve vacant seats, making their over-all number in council thirty-one compared with the Liberal's eighteen.[91] Despite Abram's implication of a sudden change in the political climate in that year, the Liberals still had a predominance in aldermanic seats and certain committees, though this would pass. This divided situation on council made for confusion in the selection of those to fill vacancies on the borough bench after November 1861. On 11 December 1861 James Pilkington sent a letter to the Duchy Office in London containing a memorial 'from a certain portion of aldermen, councillors and other inhabitants of the town.'[92] The memorial suggested a list of candidates quite different from that submitted

133 Blackburn: an Archetypal Cotton Town

earlier by the Conservative mayor. Pilkington's letter objected to the mayor's list on two grounds – first, that 'the Conservatives having already a majority on the bench' were not entitled to all six places, and second, 'I may just say that the Conservatives acquired a majority in the corporation at the last election in consequence of their having objected to the names of every Liberal on the burgess list.' Pilkington suggested a compromise of three Liberals and three Conservatives drawn from the two lists.

The position of the labouring masses was of some importance to the two rival political groups in the 1860s. As has been pointed out, the working classes through the cotton industry did possess the potential for working-class solidarity and organization in Blackburn. It was also obvious by 1860 that the old Radical, Nonconformist, lower middle-class leadership of the labouring classes of the town was declining. George Dewhurst died in 1857. This 'Radical of Radicals' had inspired working men in Blackburn from the time of his famous address to handloom weavers near Burnley in 1815 to his participation in Liberal municipal politics in the 1850s. Samuel Salter, a chairmaker and later proprietor of 'Radical Corner,'[93] also died in the same year. Most of the other Radical and Nonconformist artisan leaders of the working classes either died or effectively disappeared from the scene in the decade of the 50s. This vacuum in political leadership was then filled by the propertied elites – especially the cotton manufactures in this period.

The Secularists, led by Henry Baker, and other groups had some opportunity to lead the working classes in new directions by the 1860s. Liberal fears concerning the growth of Secularism among the masses can be seen in the action of Hoole, as chairman of the improvement commissioners in 1852. As one of their last acts, the commissioners refused in March 1852 to allow the Secularists to use the sessions room to hear a speech by Holyoake.[94] Not all persons belonging to the old denominations on the commission concurred with the Hoole-led decision. The Tory-Anglican Feilden, at the annual meeting of the commissioners in 1852, stated that he felt his colleagues had acted disgracefully in refusing Holyoake's application.

Concerted political activity by the working classes, prompted by Secularists, against both the Anglican-Tory elite and the wealthier Liberals might have been a possibility by the early 1860s had it not been for distracting social developments, by-products of the Cotton Famine. Blackburn was very much a cotton town, dependent on American supplies of raw cotton. It therefore suffered a complete breakdown in its economy, which forced the working classes into feelings of both helplessness and bitterness. Unorganized violence by the masses may also have become a more common occurrence in the 60s. In November 1862, for example, the town was engulfed in a battle between the county constabulary and a mob over the trial of eight local poachers. The Riot Act was read and cavalry was sent in from Preston. The Watch Committee then took elaborate precautions to prevent possible violence on all public occasions.[95]

This changed social climate made the possible evolution of a well-formed and concerted working-class political initiative extremely difficult. Established institutions had a new lease on life, as the old denominations and the Church provided good relief to the distressed in the Famine. Occasionally, of course, the churches might have been deceived as to the public's real attitude to their efforts. Ellen Barlee reported that on a trip through industrial Lancashire in 1862 she had heard of 'one man who professing to belong to five different church denominations was living off the fat of the land in idle luxury.'[96] However, the Blackburn Relief Committee was extremely active right from the beginning of the Famine. Instead of waiting for the approval of town hall, the committee convened its own first meeting and summoned the mayor to come and hear the deliberations. Its liaison with the poor law guardians was superb. The most prominent member of this committee was James Boyle, the old Radical 'Puritan' confectioner. Hungry people can be grateful people. The politico-religious groups also chose their areas of conflict more carefully. When Richard Cobden decided to visit the town during the height of the Famine, Boyle managed to arrange a small demonstration in his honour[97] and the town Tories raised no objection.

A serious political force having failed to emerge from the working classes, it was possible for the old pattern of sectarian politics to be resumed after the Famine had ended in 1865. In 1866 and 1867 the Liberals began to organize ambitious campaigns in some wards, with the special financial help of J. Gerald Potter,[98] and overt sectarian issues were raised as a means of aiding the Liberal cause. In January 1866 the Liberals organized a petition against the necessity of the mayoral procession to the parish church. In February 1866 the Liberal *Blackburn Times* attacked the imposition of the oath not to harm the Church of England, administered on taking any municipal office. Yet working-class political consciousness was not completely dead. As the second Reform bill approached the *Blackburn Times* noted a certain breach between the 'capitalist Liberals' and 'operative Liberals.'[99] Though no full-fledged political movement of industrial workers had emerged, the materials were, nevertheless, still at hand. It was a question of how long the turmoil of the 1860s could overcloud the basic division between working classes on the one hand and the large property-owning classes on the other.

Even after the second Reform Act the sectarian spirit, among other factors, appeared to overshadow thoughts of concerted, independent political activity on the part of the working classes. Working-class frustrations and bitterness also

135 Blackburn: an Archetypal Cotton Town

had an immediate outlet in such events as the election of 1868. The Irish Church question dominated issues in municipal politics as much as parliamentary politics at that time – one example of the 'nationalization of local politics.' The Tory interest was able to receive new English working-class support by firmly adhering to Orange rhetoric, helped by the visit of orator Murphy to Blackburn. Irish Roman Catholic workers looked to the Liberal party as their protector. The result was unprecedented violence. On 2 November 1868, municipal election day in Blackburn, riots broke out in almost every ward of the town. The precautions of the Watch Committee to prevent hooliganism at pooling booths were insufficient. Eventually, the Riot Act was read in various parts of town, and county constables and dragoons were used to disperse the mobs. As if this were not enough, the triumphal march of Orange supporters through the Irish quarter after the Tory victory produced fresh riots. Many of the Tory-Orange supporters were still known as the Brookhouse lads, based on the allegiance the Hornby family could still command from their workers in their old industrial suburb of Brookhouse in St John's Ward.[100]

A similar picture to that of corporation politics was revealed in parliamentary electoral activity in Blackburn. Radicalism was a political creed peculiarly suited to the world of the Nonconformist shopkeeper and tradesman, but, as the century progressed, less suited to the cotton operative. This distinction was not readily perceived by the early leaders of Radicalism. Dewhurst launched himself into politics in 1816 with the agitation of cottage weavers against the corn tax, and in 1819 he was arrested for organizing a meeting of handloom weavers and colliers in Burnley. After a short exile in America, he was back in Lancashire involving himself again in causes broadly concerned with the ills affecting the lowest element in wage-earning society.[101] The first parliamentary election in 1832 saw the Nonconformist Radical forces rally behind the Liberal candidate, Dr John Bowring, a London Unitarian. Dewhurst, Miles Baron, the Durham brothers, and most of the key Nonconformist-Radical leaders campaigned vigorously on his behalf. Such a hard campaign, however, was not enough to defeat the forces working for the Tory and Whig candidates. Most of the respectable, old, wealthy Whig families – the Pilkingtons, the Eccles, the Turners, and the Houghtons – feared the Radicals and Bowring almost as much as they disliked the Tory candidate. Bowring was thought to have been a very dangerous man politically. He was even attacked in the press by William Cobbett for his extremism. Dewhurst, in turn, accused the Whigs and the Tories of an electoral compact after the news of Bowring's defeat.

Whig opposition to the cause of Radicalism in Blackburn, however, was not completely intransigent. A libel case brought against Dewhurst in 1832 for his accusation of ill-treatment of women paupers in Mellor workhouse caused the wealthy Dissenter James Pilkington to rally to the defendant's side. Other well-known Whig-Liberals, such as John Burrell, editor of the *Blackburn Gazette*, supported Dewhurst. The *Gazette* tried to refute the Tory press charges of Bowring's unbelief during the 1832 election. Undoubtedly, the ties of Dissent encouraged members of the Nonconformist elite to begin to support Dewhurst's Radicals in the 1830s.

In spite of the aid given to the Radicals by a few wealthy Nonconformist and moderate Anglican Whig-Liberals, the Tories still retained great influence at election time. Their economic and social power in this mill town was formidable. It has been estimated that well over half of the millowners (including most of the large employers) were strongly Tory.[102] The Radical hope lay primarily in the small manufacturers and more prosperous shopkeepers and tradesmen. The Liberal *Blackburn Gazette* realized this fact in an editorial in 1835: 'If the Tories are more wealthy than we are *individually*, they are not so *collectively*, and we need only to concentrate our resources to show that the *silver* of the many will do more than the *gold* of the few.'[103]

The Tory-Anglican elite in town could also marshal their political power between elections. In 1833, for example, they sent a petition with over one hundred signatures to parliament protesting against Irish Church reform. The Liberal press called this the work of 'hole-and-corner gentry with two or three parsons at their head.'[104] The Tory elite was aware of the various means of securing political advantage. Between elections the Tory press schooled the electorate in the wider objectives of the party for the nation as a whole. The *Blackburn Standard* was a particularly successful newspaper, as is borne out in its many years of existence after its foundation in 1835.[105] James Walkden, the proprietor, was accepted into the highest Tory social circles, 'his newspaper office became a sort of polite lounge for the beau monde of the town.'[106] His friends included the leading Tories in both local and parliamentary politics in the town. It appears that Walkden was a true Tory gentleman, even taking snuff from the surface of a sovereign in order to avoid soiling his fingers.

The old methods of electioneering – bribery in its various forms – appear to have been employed by the Tories (and on occasion by Whigs) in this period. Following the second defeat of Dr Bowring in 1835, Gilbert Wardlow of the Blackburn Academy wrote to George Hadfield of Manchester concerning this Radical-Nonconformist defeat in the town:

No terms can be too strong in reprobation of the conduct of the tory party here, and, in fact, of the Committees of both the returned candidates, which coalesced in opposition to Dr. Bowring. The town has been deluged with immorality for the last three weeks. Four or five persons have died of intoxication in consequence of the free drinking

137 Blackburn: an Archetypal Cotton Town

system to which both Turner and Feilden had recourse from the first. It has been in consequence of the most unprincipled corruption that the majority against Dr. Bowring was gained by Feilden. Fifty men pledged to vote for the former have broken their words, many of them had stood firm till the last night – an additional night, gained by the Tories by the illegal manœuvre of shutting up two booths when there was no disturbance at either, certainly not at one of them. One of the deputy returning officers (in the tory interest) acknowledged that the majority (13), small as it was, would have been reduced to eight by a scrutiny of votes. And it is equally certain that but for the closing of the booths, Dr. B. would have gained. Would that some strong and faithful pictures of the details of such elections as ours could be held up to the same men who do wickedness and tempt others to it with such unprincipled recklessness as has been the case in Blackburn![107]

There seemed to be many persons, both voters and non-voters, in the town who were greatly displeased with the election results. The patriarch of town Tories, W.H. Hornby, was seized by a pro-Bowring crowd and flung over the parapet of the old Salford bridge.

By the late 1830s the Radicals were seemingly willing to throw their weight behind moderate Liberal candidates supported by the Nonconformist elite. Political lines hardened on sectarian lines more than ever before. In the 1837 election, and in the elections of the 1840s and early 1850s, no separate Radical candidates appeared. William Turner and later James Pilkington, great mill-owners, acted on behalf of the Radical Nonconformist interest as well as their own, advocating the abolition of the church rate, economy in government spending, and free trade. The political groups were increasingly based on denominational allegiance and less on class. Methodists, it appears, occupied a central position supporting the Tory-Anglican group at first, then gradually coming over to the Liberal side in the second half of the century. The Liberal press made an assessment of these allegiances, including the Toryism of some Wesleyans, in 1865:

With respect to the Wesleyans, they have with only few exceptions gone the 'whole hog' for the Tories. Surely, they have forgotten their predecessors preached in barns, and fields, and on hill tops, when Church and King mobs dispersed them with besoms, sticks and threshing flails and pelted them with rotten eggs, vowing that they would not let a Methodist live in the parish. The United Free Methodists have done better, but even they have acted with one accord. The Primitive Methodists, whose founder, Hugh Bourne, had a thoroughly democratic mind, have not as a body done much better than their ancient friends the Wesleyans. The Independents and Baptists have, as a whole, voted consistently; but amongst them some old ones have broken away from the flock, while the selfish policy of plumping has been a little too prevalent among others ... with regard to mother Church, her dignitaries have been all of one way of thinking, nestling closely and fast to the bosom of Toryism, and denouncing everything of an opposite tendency with the pain of eternal death.[108]

In this period the chapel ties between the Nonconformist elite and Nonconformist tradesmen and artisans had helped in blending both groups into one in the cause of fighting Toryism. The result in chapel was to blur the lines between the elite's Whig tendencies and the more extreme Radical tendencies of the tradesmen. One effect was an upswing in popular, moderate Liberalism in town as a sort of blend of the two viewpoints. The Tories, for their part, continued to rely on the Anglican elite, though some efforts were made to secure more popular support through such groups as the Operative Conservative Association.[109] Clergymen such as the Reverend E.A. Verity could also be helpful in this task at times.[110] Interest in national political affairs by town Radicals occurred only sporadically by the late 1850s. This was again due in large measure to the disappearance of old Radical leaders such as Dewhurst. Renewed efforts under the separate banner of Radicalism were frequently the work of people associated with Secularism. In 1859, for example, John Patrick Murrough of London was put forth as 'an advanced Liberal'[111] candidate against the two older party candidates. His showing in votes was quite respectable considering the circumstances.

The 1868 election, however, seemed to indicate that sectarian hatred and the power of the propertied elites was going to be the most vital factor in Blackburn politics for some time to come, regardless of the extension of the franchise. The 1 November municipal elections witnessed such a bloody clash between Tory and Catholic mobs that authorities were forced to take all kinds of precautions for the parliamentary election. On polling day, 16 November, a strong wooden wall was erected to separate Tory and Liberal supporters. Troops arrived in the middle of the proceedings to keep a special watch on the crowd of some 80,000. The Liberal John Gerald Potter, in addressing the crowd following his defeat by the two Tory candidates, stated that the Conservative victory was the work of 'the screw put on by the Tory employer of labour.'[112] Patrick Joyce has given us ample evidence of the electoral power of millowners. But the workings of sectarianism were also significant. J.C. Lowe's interpretation of the Tory victory of 1868 as the result of popular Conservatism over popular Liberalism captures the emotions of the moment as conveyed in press accounts. Deference was part of the group loyalty of the crowds, but so was the brash enthusiasm engendered by sectarianism. Both explanations seem closer to the reality of the situation than Professor Vincent's stress upon the importance of the electoral preferences of the newly-included townships of Little Harwood, Witton, and Livesey.[113]

139 Blackburn: an Archetypal Cotton Town

The Tory-Anglican elite and the Liberal-Nonconformist interests in town had managed to survive the expansion of the electorate in 1868. They continued to rule the political processes of local and national government in Blackburn for some time to come. They did so, however, only in an atmosphere of violence and social fragmentation. In Blackburn the working classes had failed to achieve solidarity and independent political consciousness for a variety of reasons. Though in many ways the factory workers, being mostly weavers, had as much chance as those in any of the four northern towns to achieve such solidarity, they did not. Circumstances, some deep-rooted and some temporary, prevented such a development. One very important factor, however, was the character of Dissent in the town. Dissent provided a powerful assist for the radically-inclined lower middle classes to challenge and even partially overcome the Tory-Anglican elite – an elite with both old status and new wealth early in the century. Dissent was a dynamic element in this challenge, providing leadership, organization, and goals to power-deprived groups in society. Some of this dynamism, in the form of men like Dewhurst, brought many in the working classes under its spell. With the failure of Radicalism, however, the working classes, especially in the early 1860s, had few political options beyond succumbing to the influence of the propertied political-sectarian elites. Working-class solidarity and independent political consciousness never really had a chance in this period of Blackburn's history.

Another form of sectarian conflict also triumphed in the late 1860s. The new working-class voters and their unenfranchised companions were to be swayed by violent, overt sectarianism, which drew the lines of political conflict in a way that diminished specific working-class aims and consciousness. This may have been beneficial in maintaining some form of social cohesion, but the costs of extreme denominational strife were lamented by at least one newspaper in 1869: 'The tides of sectarian and political feeling run exceptionally high in Blackburn. In one sense that fact is not discreditable; it is at least proof of the intense zeal and sincerity of men of every persuasion. But it often leads to melancholy results as, for example, when it affects the complete alienation of old acquaintances and friends; still more, when it induces men to work each other every possible injury in business or in reputation. The hatreds engendered by the deadly conflicts of faction by which our English and especially our Lancashire society is marked, are most difficult to allay.'[114]

6
Wider Perspectives

Geoffrey Best, R.J. Helmstadter,[1] and others have recently pointed to the lack of a well-defined set of questions and methodology in historians' investigations of the various social roles of Victorian religion. This is no less true for Victorian sectarianism. Many areas, especially of popular and unorganized sectarianism, remain to be explored. Here the work of sociologists such as Oxford's Bryan Wilson might be particularly useful.

Even in the more structured area of politics and 'organized' sectarianism there is much that could be investigated by changing the social setting. Stephan Thernstrom[2] has noted for nineteenth-century American urban life that the differences between large and small cities were of kind as well as of scale. The 'worlds' of the four largest Victorian cities – London, Liverpool, Manchester, and Birmingham – could well have produced a different pattern of sectarianism from that observed in medium-sized towns such as those examined here.

In London the immense size, social fragmentation, and low church attendances may have worked against sectarianism as they did against religion, making it something less than a strong force in that locale as a whole. In any case a great deal of research must be done on the framework of London municipal politics as well as religion before much can be said about sectarianism and politics there.

Liverpool and Manchester, both in Lancashire, seem to conform somewhat to the pattern found in the cotton towns. There was a close affinity between politics and sectarianism in Lancashire, as Bishop Fraser of Manchester pointed out on numerous occasions. In Liverpool, however, the old mercantile oligarchy had survived the period of the Industrial Revolution and remained the most powerful propertied class in the city.[3] The numerous Tory-Church merchants were then allied to a strong Evangelical Anglicanism which brought many rank-and-file supporters into their camp. The small Nonconformist elite, mostly composed of Unitarian merchants, was not buttressed by successful 'self-made businessmen who elsewhere financed Nonconformity,' as noted by Ian Sellers.[4]

Nonconformity relied more on Irish Roman Catholics as rank-and-file supporters of Liberalism. This in turn helped the Orange cause of Liverpool Toryism, attracting support from some Nonconformists, including perhaps Irish Presbyterian immigrants. These facts may explain the unusual popular vitality of sectarianism in Liverpool as well as the Tory success at both municipal and parliamentary elections throughout the period. The different course of political events in Manchester may be attributed to an impressive Nonconformist elite, among other factors.[5]

Victorian Birmingham has been the subject of some excellent urban studies by Asa Briggs, Conrad Gill, and E.P. Hennock.[6] The results of these and other research efforts have generally reaffirmed the importance of religion in the evolution of an urban culture in this great Midlands town. In particular, the key role of Dissent from the development of the Lunar Society to the gospel of municipal reform has been well documented.

In Birmingham orthodox Dissenters and Unitarians co-operated in dominating much of the local political life from the 1840s to the 1880s. Unitarian and Quaker families controlled most of the great businesses of the town, exerting a specially powerful influence over all facets of social life. Their desire to build up civic institutions reflected both their social pride and the unusual unleashing of localist impulses found deep within the structure and perhaps even theology of Nonconformist denominations. The town's diversified industrial scene and widespread social mobility did not lend itself to working-class estrangement from these developments. Instead, large sections of the working class co-operated with the various endeavours of Nonconformists – many of which involved direct improvements in their physical environment. With a weak Tory-Church faction and social factors inhibiting class conflict, the social role of sectarianism was obviously different from that in the cotton towns. The social hegemony of Nonconformity and the historically high degree of class co-operation in the town provided the leaders of Dissent with a unique opportunity at positive, creative efforts within the environs of Birmingham.

Hugh McLeod in his important book *Class and Religion in the Late Victorian City* (1974) has noted a number of factors, including size, which might affect the religious character of nineteenth-century English towns. The character of local industry as well as the proportion of rural migrants, the pastoral efforts of the churches, and the 'regional factor' are listed.[7] In reference to sectarianism, the character of local industry and the 'regional factor' might be worth further investigation, as we have already seen in relation to the four greatest cities of Victorian England.

In urban Yorkshire there was a diversity of industrial pursuits with the woollen and worsted trade in Leeds, Bradford, Huddersfield, and Halifax, shipping at Hull, and iron, steel, and cutlery production in Sheffield. The various forms of industrial occupation were not alone in making the social situation different from the cotton towns on the other side of the Pennines. Nonconformity, especially Methodism, was numerically stronger, in general surpassing Anglicanism. The Leeds Nonconformists who, according to E.P. Hennock, also derived wealth from the 'new' industry of the late eighteenth and early nineteenth centuries, were an important reason for the Liberal-Reformist strength in the first half of the century.[8] The match was an unequal one for the Anglican Tories who understandably were not particularly combative. The most famous Leeds Anglican was their High Church vicar, W.F. Hook, an outstanding urban pastor.

In Bradford the Tory Churchmen fought harder to retain their pre-Reform position. Ultimately, however, the Tory-Church forces were defeated here,[9] as in Halifax, Huddersfield, Sheffield, and many smaller towns. Anti-Catholicism was noticeable but less important in the Yorkshire press than in the cotton towns. With fewer Catholic Irish present it was harder for Tories to play the Orange card.

In the Midlands, diversity in patterns of sectarianism paralleled to some extent the rich diversity of social and economic situations to be found in each town. Leicester, according to Temple Patterson's *Radical Leicester*, appears to have had a mechanism for sectarianism and politics not unlike that of Bolton, Stockport, and Blackburn. There were differences, however, in working-class attitudes toward the sectarian-political struggle. In Coventry, as John Prest has pointed out, there was neither much working-class militancy nor a vital political Dissent.[10] There were many social, historical, and political reasons given by Prest for Coventry being 'a city apart.'

In the west of England, where church attendances were generally higher according to the religious census of 1851, diversity again appeared to be the rule, with sectarianism playing a major role in the political and social life of Bristol[11] and a minor one in the case of Bath.[12] In Exeter, according to Robert Newton, the Anglican social clique was never seriously challenged by the fairly numerous Nonconformists, and this may help to explain the general Tory domination of local politics in the Victorian era.[13]

In the rest of England, whatever the region, there was a variety of medium-sized towns, commercial and industrial, such as Crewe, Southampton, Newcastle-upon-Tyne, that exhibited varying degrees of sectarianism. There were also smaller-sized towns, cathedral and university towns, spa towns and industrial 'regions' such as the towns and hamlets of western Wiltshire, that usually displayed some degree of sectarian animosity in their political and social life. The suspicion here is that sectarianism declined appreciably with the smaller-sized, less dynamic industrial (or non-industrial) centres.[14] However, more research will have to be done on these and other factors before firm conclusions can be drawn.

One observation that might be made for the cotton towns and for much of urban England as a whole is that sectarianism may well have prevented local politics from becoming too 'parochial' in the nineteenth century. H.J. Hanham has noted that municipal politics in Manchester and some of the largest towns rarely focused on local questions as 'an issue between the parties.'[15] Conrad Gill has also observed in the case of Birmingham that local political parties developed on similar lines to those at the national level.[16] The best known political cleavage throughout urban England was between Liberal-Nonconformists and Tory-Churchmen. It was an important and ready-made constant in which some towns served as models for other towns. This situation, sometimes taken for granted by historians, is an important aspect of political life in Victorian England as a whole.

In recent years there has been some interest expressed by historians and political scientists in the so-called nationalization of local politics. In the process of their investigations it has been revealed that national issues came to dominate the local hustings during parliamentary elections in the last two decades of the nineteenth century.[17] Donald Read[18] has also noted the increasing centralization of power and decision-making in the Liberal and Conservative organizations. Even more relevant to the concerns of this book, it appears that national political leaders began to see the utility of aligning municipal and parliamentary party activities by the end of the century.[19] In Edwardian London, in particular, there were obvious advantages to such acts of mutual reinforcement. It is arguable that such developments were only a further step in a process begun much earlier. Whatever the local issues, firm lines of party loyalty patterned much of English urban politics by mid century. Sectarianism had played a major role in the development of local Liberal and Conservative organizations as well as voters' 'partisan self-image.'[20] It was an easy matter for national trends to begin to appear in municipal election results, with advancing communications and democracy later in the century. This was also linked to the effort on the part of political strategists to exploit and direct such trends for national purposes.[21]

The importance of the propertied classes in sectarian-political strife has been emphasized in this book. J.R. Vincent has noted the elitist character of urban Lancashire Dissent in *The Formation of the Liberal Party*.[22] What perhaps has been forgotten was the continuing existence of Anglican elites in the cotton towns after the early Reform era. They were one powerful reason why Tory-Anglican forces made such a hard fight, including many victories along the way. They were assisted in this by both popular support for the Church and anti-Catholicism which brought many an English workingman to the Tory banner.

144 The Sectarian Spirit

Temple Patterson's description of Victorian Leicester indicated a much more politically triumphant Dissent.

The significant role exercised by the lower middle class-upper stratum of workingmen, particularly within Nonconformity, must also be obvious in this study. Often they acted as faithful lieutenants of the propertied interests inside and outside chapel in their struggle with the Tory-Church party. In Blackburn they were particularly important given the smaller number of wealthy Dissenters. In Preston they were central to the general opposition to the Tory-Church party. These classes were often prominent in the ranks of quasi-sects such as Teetotalism and in the new sects such as the New Church and Secularism. Again their response to the social and political environment varied with group and town situation.

The role of sectarianism in class relations, part of the same story viewed from a different perspective, has also been discussed. The conclusions in this complex area of investigation must of necessity be drawn somewhat more tentatively. In the area of politics, however, it is possible to conclude with more certainty that sectarianism occupied a key position in the determination of men's thoughts and actions in the cotton towns.

Appendix

I Church and chapel expansion in the cotton towns, 1851-71

	Increase in population	Churches and chapels erected				Increase in sittings
		Church	Nonconformist	Catholic	Others	
Bolton	21,683 (35.4%)	2	10	2	3	12,870 (66.4%)
Preston	15,886 (22.8%)	6	7	3		12,148 (49.3%)
Stockport	834 (1.5%)		loss of 1	3	1	-904 (-4.1%)
Blackburn*	36,390 (78.2%)	3	9	1	1	10,546 (63.3%)

Taken from the *Nonconformist*, supplement, 6 Nov. 1872
* Parliamentary borough

II Increase in sittings and chapels of the Nonconformists, 1851-71

	Bolton	Preston	Stockport	Blackburn
Presbyterians	300 (1)			1100 (1)
Congregationalists	2250 (3)	1070 (1)	514 (2)	2242 (2)
Baptists	600	1124 (1)	decline of 170 (2)	200
Friends		22	150 (1)	
Unitarians	550 (1)	55	50	
Wesleyan Methodist	2980 (4)	1837 (3)	decline of 1081 (3)	800 (2)
United Methodist		410 (1)		1250 (2)
New Connexion	100		21	300 (1)
Primitive Methodist		100 (1)	138 (1)	700 (2)
Other Methodist	400 (1)			

Number of chapels in parentheses follow figures for sittings

Notes

ABBREVIATIONS

BM British (Museum) Library
CRO Cheshire Record Office
HO Home Office records kept at PRO
LRO Lancashire Record Office
PP Parliamentary Sessional Papers, House of Commons; HL for House of Lords
PRO Public Record Office, London

CHAPTER ONE: INTRODUCTION

1 For an analysis of Fraser's role in diminishing sectarian strife see my essay, 'James Fraser, Bishop of All the Denominations,' in *The View from the Pulpit: Victorian Ministers and Society*, ed. P.T. Phillips (Toronto 1978), 87–115.
2 For a clear set of sociological definitions see Ernest Troeltsch, *The Social Teachings of the Christian Churches* (London 1931). Also useful is Bryan R. Wilson, 'An Analysis of Sect Development,' in *Patterns of Sectarianism* (London 1967), 22–45.
3 P.F. Clarke, *Lancashire and the New Liberalism* (Cambridge 1971), chap. III. More recently A.J. Ainsworth, like Clarke, has stressed the importance of religion in the political and social life of late nineteenth-century Lancashire – in this case amongst the working classes. See Ainsworth, 'Religion in the Working Class Community and the Evolution Socialism in Late Nineteenth Century Lancashire: a Case of Working Class Consciousness,' *Histoire sociale / Social History*, X, 1977, 354–80.

4 A.D. Gilbert, *Religion and Society in Industrial England: Church, Chapel and Social Change, 1740–1914* (London 1976), 51
5 W.A. Abram, 'Social Condition and Political Prospects of the Lancashire Workmen,' *Fortnightly Review*, IV, 1868, 436
6 G. Kitson Clark, *The Making of Victorian England* (London 1962), 162
7 G. Kitson Clark, *The Making of Victorian England; The English Inheritance* (London 1950); and *Churchmen and the Condition of England, 1832–1885* (London 1973); Desmond Bowen, *The Idea of the Victorian Church* (Montreal 1968); Owen Chadwick, *The Victorian Church*, Parts I and II (London 1969 and 1970)
8 K.S. Inglis, *Churches and the Working Classes in Victorian England* (London 1963); E.R. Wickham, *Church and Society in an Industrial City* (London 1957); Standish Meacham, 'The Church in the Victorian City,' *Victorian Studies*, XI, 1968, 359–78; Gilbert, *Religion and Society in Industrial England*; W.R. Ward, *Religion and Society in England, 1790–1850* (London 1972)
9 See K.S. Inglis, 'Patterns of Religious Worship in 1851,' *Journal of Ecclesiastical History*, II, 1960, 74–86.
10 W. Cooke Taylor, *Notes of a Tour in the Manufacturing Districts of Lancashire* (London 1842); Andrew Ure, *The Philosophy of Manufactures* (London 1835); Henry Ashworth, *The Preston Strike* (Manchester 1858) and 'A Citizen of the World,' *Manchester and the Manchester People* (Manchester 1843)
11 H.J. Perkin, 'The Development of Modern Glossop,' in *Small Town Politics: a Study of Political Life in Glossop*, ed. A.H. Birch (Oxford 1959), 8–33
12 Ibid., 21–2. Perkin has also developed the concept of sectarian religion acting as the 'midwife of class' in early nineteenth-century England as a whole. Here Perkin believes it served three main purposes in (i) giving expression to emancipation from the old order of dependency before the new class system had solidified, (ii) serving as a model for class organization, and (iii) nudging emerging class conflict in the direction of non-violence. See H. Perkin, *The Origins of Modern English Society 1780–1880* (London and Toronto 1969), 196–208, 347–64.
13 J.C. Lowe, 'The Tory Triumph of 1868 in Blackburn and in Lancashire,' *Historical Journal*, XVI, 1973, 742
14 Since initial completion of my manuscript, Foster's views have generated a largely unresolved debate on important aspects of working-class consciousness in Oldham – see D.S. Gadian, 'Class Consciousness in Oldham and Other North-West Industrial Towns 1830–1850,' *Historical Journal*, XXI, 1978, 161–72, and R.A. Sykes, 'Some Aspects of Working-Class Consciousness in Oldham, 1830–1842,' *Historical Journal*, XXIII, 1980, 167–79.
15 See H.B. Rodgers, 'The Lancashire Cotton Industry in 1840,' *Institute of British Geographers Transactions and Papers*, XXVIII, 1960, 135–53, and A.J. Taylor, 'Concentration and Specialization in the Lancashire Cotton Industry,

Notes for pages 7–11

1825–1850,' *Economic History Review*, 2nd ser., I, 1948–9, 114–22. In the late nineteenth century the situation appears to have changed, weaving becoming more important in Preston and very much less important in Stockport. See Henry Pelling, *The Social Geography of British Elections* (London 1967), chap. XII.
16 See Sidney Pollard, *The Genesis of Modern Management: a Study of the Industrial Revolution in Great Britain* (London 1965), 91.
17 For the complexities of defining class see Aubrey Weinberg and Frank Lyons, 'Class Theory and Practice,' *British Journal of Sociology*, XXIII, 1972, 51–65. For a fresh analysis of the class structure in early nineteenth-century England see R.S. Neale, *Class and Ideology in the Nineteenth Century* (London 1972), chap. I. R.J. Morris, *Class and Class Consciousness in the Industrial Revolution, 1780–1850* (London 1979), provides a good survey of existing literature on the subject. On the theory of the labour aristocracy see Eric Hobsbawm, 'The Labour Aristocracy in Nineteenth Century Britain,' in *Labouring Men* (London 1964), 272–315; Henry Pelling, 'The Concept of the Labour Aristocracy,' in *Popular Politics and Society in Late Victorian Britain* (London 1968), 37–61; Michael J. Piva, 'The Aristocracy of the English Working Class: Help for an Historical Debate in Difficulties,' *Histoire sociale / Social History*, VII, 1974, 270–92; Geoffrey Crossick, *An Artisan Elite in Victorian Society: Kentish London 1840–1880* (London and Totowa, NJ 1978), and A.E. Musson and John Foster, 'Discussion: Class Struggle and the Labour Aristocracy, 1830–60,' *Social History*, III, 1976, 355–66. See also chapter 2 of this book, note 13.
18 Crossick, *An Artisan Elite in Victorian Society*, and Trygve R. Tholfsen, *Working Class Radicalism in Mid-Victorian England* (London 1976)
19 For a general sociological discussion of elites see T.B. Bottomore, *Elites and Society* (London 1964). See also chapter 2, note 4. Again in the use of such terms I have tried to opt for simple, conventional, working definitions best seen in the context of this study.

CHAPTER TWO: BOLTON: THE GENEVA OF LANCASHIRE

1 W. Cooke Taylor, *Notes of a Tour in the Manufacturing Districts of Lancashire* (London 1842), 7. Bolton's population, like that of other cotton towns, showed a remarkable increase in the late eighteenth and nineteenth centuries. In 1700 the town itself had about 500 inhabitants, in 1791 there were 11,000, and the census figures after 1800 reveal the enormous growth in the Victorian years.
2 Anon., 'Bolton-le-Moors,' *St. James's Magazine*, Nov. 1869, 225
3 Gathered from individual returns for Bolton in the Census of Religious Worship, 1851, HO 129 / 468

4 In the past there may have been some reluctance in using the word elite in reference to the English provinces. This has been effectively laid to rest by George Kitson Clark's recent essay, 'The Leeds Elite,' in *University of Leeds Review*, XVII, 1975, 232-58.
5 E. Whitehead, *The Duty of Bearing One Another's Burdens* (Manchester 1774)
6 Chamberlain was a great opponent of the Anti-Corn Law League which claimed Bolton as one of its centres.
7 John Lyons to the National Society, Bolton file, 28 Oct. 1843
8 Neville Jones to the National Society, Bolton file, 28 Dec. 1868
9 *Bolton Chronicle*, 12 April 1862
10 Statement of J.J. Bradshaw, quoted in *Bank Street Chapel: Bicentenary Commemorative* (Manchester and London 1896), 96
11 Adherence of these great families to Bank Street is confirmed in the various trustee lists. See ibid., appendix.
12 *Census of Religious Worship*, 1851, PP, 1852-3, LXXXIX, ccliii
13 The distinction between tradesmen (craftsmen, independent artisans) and shopkeepers is not a sharp one — some tradesmen such as shoemakers having their own shops. I have tended to include under the term shopkeeper those given that direct designation as well as those clearly in retail service such as grocers. The size of a shop, obviously important in determining the status of an individual, is usually impossible to ascertain from lists. For further information on the problem of categories, even in census data, see Michael B. Katz, 'Occupational Classification in History,' *Journal of Interdisciplinary History*, III, 1972, 63-88.
14 The terms 'spinner' and 'weaver' could be used by both operatives and employers in some towns. Owners of weaving establishments usually called themselves manufacturers.
15 'The Circle' was a special society made up primarily of influential and intellectual Bank Street members. Fourteen people first met in October 1867 and new members were co-opted by the society thereafter (the number never to exceed fifteen). A list of the papers read to the society, found amongst the chapel records, reveals a special concern for the major social and political problems facing the nation. Raymond V. Holt's book, *The Unitarian Contribution to Social Progress in England* (London 1938), gives some idea of the general intellectualism of Unitarians and their interest in social questions. R.K. Webb's forthcoming book on Unitarianism will undoubtedly supply a more complete picture.
16 The working-class element among chapel attenders can be discovered by going beyond the membership (or seat-holders) list to other sources. For example, a marriage register kept at the chapel indicates that of thirty-seven men married between 29 January 1865 and 19 October 1868, seventeen were tradesmen and small shopkeepers and fifteen were workmen. Other samples taken from the

Notes for pages 13–16

register (which runs up to 5 June 1895) indicates a similar, though not quite so heavy, concentration of labouring people.
17 Franklin Baker, *The Moral Tone of the Factory System Defended* (London 1850)
18 Henry Ashworth (1794–1880) was a leader of the Anti-Corn Law League, an industrialist, and a Quaker. For an idea of the breadth of Ashworth's religious views embracing both formal Quakerism and outside influences see Rhodes Boyson, *The Ashworth Cotton Enterprise: the Rise and Fall of a Family Firm, 1818–1880* (Oxford 1970), chap. 13. Philanthropy was one area in which Evangelicalism had a particularly strong impact on Ashworth and other Quakers. For remarks on the impact of Evangelicalism upon English Quakerism see Elizabeth Isichei, *Victorian Quakers* (London 1970), xxi, xxv, and chap. I, esp. 3–16.
19 Ashworth believed that great upward mobility from operative to factory owner was still possible in the industry at mid century. It was certainly possible for small spinning sheds to be opened even at that time with little capital. These small, short-lived operations, however, were a far cry from the Ashworth mills or those of other well-known manufacturers in Bolton. See Henry Ashworth, *Statistical Illustrations of the Past and Present State of Lancashire and more particularly the Hundred of Salford* (Manchester 1842).
20 Henry Ashworth, *The Preston Strike, an Enquiry into its Causes and Consequences* (Manchester 1858), 35
21 See *Reports of the British and Foreign Schools Society*, 1837.
22 Edgworth and Bolton Preparative Meeting Minutes, Vol. I (17 Nov. 1776–14 Dec. 1828), Vol. II (1 April 1832–29 June 1845), and Vol. III (3 May 1857–1 Jan. 1871), FRM 11 / 1, 2–6, LRO; MS *Recollections Relating to the Members and Other Attenders of the Religious Meetings of the Society of Friends Constituting the Preparative Meeting of Edgworth and Bolton, Commencing About the Year 1800*, FRM 2 / 7, LRO; Digest of Marriages, Friends House Library, Euston Rd, London. Ashworth appears to have been a member of the Quaker Conference on Tithes held in London, 28 and 29 November 1850. He may well have been the recorder of the original MS minutes of the conference held at Friends House Library, London.
23 Baptismal register of Duke's Alley Independent Chapel, Bolton RG 4 / 4365, PRO
24 Found in F.W. Peaples, *History of St. George's Road Congregational Church* (Bolton 1913), 69–70
25 John Foster, *Class Struggle and the Industrial Revolution* (London 1974), 214–15
26 R.B. Walker, 'The Growth of Wesleyan Methodism in Victorian England and Wales,' *Journal of Ecclesiastical History*, XXIV, 1973, 270
27 Professor W.R. Ward points to the schism within the Bolton Sunday school with 200 members seceding over the imposition of Conference discipline in 1833. *Religion and Society in England, 1790–1850* (London 1972), 172

28 Geoffrey Best, *Mid-Victorian Britain, 1851–75* (London 1971)
29 *The Revivalist*, VI, 4, 1860, 'Revival Intelligence' section
30 See James Clegg, *A Chronological History of Bolton* (Bolton 1875), 25, especially 21 December 1859 and January 1860.
31 See the annual reports of the Bolton Mechanics' Institution, especially the first one published in Bolton in 1826. The object of the institution, in spite of the great influence of Dissent, was not to encourage sectarian conflict. See J.H. Arrowsmith, *Essay on Mechanics' Institutes, with a Particular Relation to the Institute Recently Established in Bolton* (Bolton 1825).
32 *Second Annual Report of the Catholic Poor School Committee*
33 Timothy Grimshaw, *The Cognitions and Opinions of Timothy Grimshaw* (Bolton 1838), 12
34 W. Cooke Taylor, *Notes of a Tour in the Manufacturing Districts of Lancashire* (London 1842)
35 *Millennial Star*, I, 1, May 1840
36 The general remarks on Mormons are in the introduction to the *Census of Religious Worship*, 1851. See also chapter III for the section on Mormonism.
37 Of the thirty-five baptisms registered at the New Jerusalem Chapel, Little Bolton, between 1828 and 1837, the occupations of fathers were as follows: 21 weavers, 7 spinners, 2 labourers, 2 bleachers, 1 painter, 1 nailer, and 1 boatswain.
38 Most of the early leaders seem to have been Primitive Methodists such as James Raper. Vicar Slade, however, was also very active in the society.
39 Two articles have explored the 'religious' aspect of Secularism – Susan Budd, 'The Loss of Faith,' *Past and Present*, XXXVI, 1967, 106–25, and F.B. Smith, 'The Atheist Mission,' *Ideas and Institutions of Victorian Britain* (London 1967), ed. R. Robson, 205–35. See also Edward Royle, *Victorian Infidels* (Manchester 1974).
40 Robert Owen's papers held at Co-operative Union Library, Holyoake House, Manchester, contains some correspondence with Bolton Socialists – see nos 800, 823, 825, 1201.
41 Most of the reference material on the Secularists in these four northern towns derived from the *Reasoner*, and was supplied to me by Dr Edward Royle, formerly of Selwyn College, Cambridge, now of the University of York.
42 F.W. Peaples, *History of the Great and Little Bolton Co-operative Society* (Bolton 1909)
43 One exception was Thomas Thomasson, who even invited Holyoake to stay with him while the Secularist leader lectured in Bolton. Thomas Thomasson to G.J. Holyoake, 24 Sept. 1867, G.J. Holyoake letters, no 1742, Co-operative Union Library, Manchester
44 The workingmen's candidates were Isaac Barrow, a building surveyor, Caleb Ritson, a provision dealer, and John Bramwell, a clerk. Barrow and Bramwell

Notes for pages 19-26

were Unitarians and Liberals. Ritson was a Wesleyan and a Tory in politics. It is not clear exactly what groups did sponsor these candidates. *Bolton Chronicle*, 26 Nov. 1870
45 See A.A. MacLaren, *Religion and Social Class: the Disruptive Years in Aberdeen* (London and Boston 1974).
46 Patrick Joyce, 'The Factory Politics of Lancashire in the Later Nineteenth Century,' *Historical Journal*, XVIII, 1975, esp. 547-8. Also see chap. V, passim. Joyce's book, *Work, Society and Politics* (Brighton 1980), covering Lancashire and Yorkshire, appeared when the final revision of this book was completed.
47 W.G. Rimmer, *Marshalls of Leeds: Flax-spinners 1788-1886* (Cambridge 1966), 66
48 *Liberator*, 1 Oct. 1865
49 *Census of Population*, PP, 1852-3, LXXXVIII-II
50 Baker, *The Moral Tone of the Factory System Defended*, 29. Baker's fellow Bolton Nonconformist, Henry Ashworth, supplied much of the information on northern factory owners.
51 A novel was written by one Boltonian on the insecurities of employment in the mills: Thomas Greenhalgh, *Lancashire Life, Or the Vicissitudes of Commerce: a Tale* (Liverpool 1854).
52 Bolton appears to have been the most active Luddite centre in Lancashire. The principal source of information on Luddism was the corespondence of the local magistrates with the Home Office. Bolton had two exceptionally reactionary magistrates at that time – the Reverend Thomas Bancroft and Colonel Ralph Fletcher. Fletcher used two spies, Bent and Stones, as *agents provocateur*. The spectre of revolution was possibly used as an excuse for further political repression. E.P. Thompson in *The Making of the English Working Class* (London 1963), 491, is not sure that the extremes of Bolton Luddism were the result of a truly revolutionary situation. The reported situation may indeed have been the contrivance of magistrates. Malcolm Thomis, *The Luddites* (London 1972), 83, 90-2, generally supports the latter view.
53 This term is used by Derek Fraser in *Urban Politics in Victorian England* (Leicester 1976), 259.
54 For an interesting discussion of these alignments see ibid., 196.
55 Thomas Laqueur, *Religion and Respectability: Sunday Schools and Working Class Culture, 1780-1850* (New Haven 1976), 124
56 The presidential addresses of E. Ferguson in 1867 and 1870, for example, made a strong plea for Disestablishment. 'Papers of the Bolton Hesperus Literary and Christian Association,' Bolton Public Library
57 The following figures in the paper were taken to be Nonconformist propaganda by the Tory-Anglican press: *Sunday School Facilities in Bolton*: 2014 scholars in 4

154 Notes for pages 26–7

schools connected with the Church Establishment; 1085 scholars in 1 Roman Catholic school; 6768 scholars in 16 schools belonging to various classes of Dissenters. Mr Ian Cowan is currently at work on a Lancaster University thesis concerning education and industry in nineteenth-century Bolton.

58 Among the 18 Conservative candidates there were 11 Churchmen, 5 Wesleyans, 1 Free Churchman, and 1 Roman Catholic. Among the 12 Liberal candidates there were 2 Independents, 2 Unitarians, 2 Wesleyans, 2 Churchmen, 3 Roman Catholics, and 1 Quaker. *Bolton Chronicle*, 26 Nov. 1870

59 E.A. Verity, *Church Reform: the Ecclesiastical Problem of the Age or, The Prayer-Book – The Parochial System – And the Common People* (London 1854), 5

60 Canon Carter was rector of Saints Peter and Paul Catholic Church from 1847 to 1875. Carter was a leading member of the Relief Committee during the Cotton Famine. He was also elected to the poor law union and the school board.

61 This was generally true in the northern industrial areas, though in the country as a whole the parliamentary electorate was larger. 'The Small Tenements Act' of 1850 (13 and 14 Vic., c 99), an act passed to simplify the collection of rates, also inadvertently gave the municipal vote to many tenants, and was the subject of enquiry by a select committee of the House of Lords (1859, Session I, Vol. XII). As the Hammonds point out, the municipal electorate in Bolton increased from 2539 to 7107 as a result of the adoption of the act in that borough. See J.L. and B. Hammond, *The Age of the Chartists, 1832–1854* (London 1930), chap. V, and Bryan Keith-Lucas, *The English Local Government Franchise: a Short History* (Oxford 1952), chap. III. The act was in fact adopted in stages in Bolton – Great Bolton in 1850, Little Bolton in 1855, and not at all in Haulgh at the time of the Lords' investigation.

62 The Liberal party, of course, had the support of many moderate Churchmen. Only a very few Nonconformists, however, would have been Tories before 1868. In 1868, as a result of intense waves of anti-Catholicism, some Nonconformists became temporarily aligned to Tory groups in the northern towns. A great many obituaries of prominent Liberals in the northern towns note this phenomenon. See biographical sketches in such books as A. Hewitson, *Preston Town Council* (Preston 1872).

63 Bolton (incorporated in 1838) was the second town in England to be incorporated under the Municipal Reform Act of 1835.

64 This speech is paraphrased in J.C. Scholes, *The History of Bolton* (Bolton 1892), 478.

65 MS transcript of the proceedings of the Court Leet (and Court Baron) of Little Bolton, 1791–1841 (Bolton Library). Millowners and other manufacturers had ample representation.

Notes for pages 27–32

66 Scholes, *History of Bolton*, 482
67 Ibid., 484–5
68 Paving, lighting, cleansing, and watching the streets were the usual activities of improvement trustees. The boards were somewhat exclusive in their property qualifications for members even for the eighteenth century – under the original 1792 Act, £1000 for Great Bolton trustees, £500 for those of Little Bolton. In 1830, however, the qualifications for both trustees and voters were made much wider for Little Bolton.
69 The Courts Leet, for example, maintained their own police in opposition to the will of the corporation. Many Tories also refused to pay the borough rate and therefore had no municipal vote.
70 Thomas Teal on 20 July 1849 stated before the Commons Committee on the Sale of Beer that the Bolton bench contained vigorous Teetotallers among their number. PP, 1850, XVIII
71 See Bolton Biographical Newspaper Cuttings, B1, 44–72, Bolton Public Library.
72 Lord Lyndhurst in Parliament and many people outside Parliament criticized Darbishire for his delay in ordering troops into the town. The implication in much of this criticism was that Darbishire was pro-Chartist.
73 The society was founded in 1841 by a few philanthropists including Canon Slade and the Unitarian millowner, Robert Heywood. See R. Heywood, Bolton Biographical Cuttings, B1, 429.
74 *Bolton Chronicle*, 18 Nov. 1862
75 Derek Fraser noted this fact about the rival groups within 'the elite contesting power in the great cities,' *Urban Politics in Victorian England*, 195.
76 Heywood's rather uninteresting diaries cover the period 1818–68 and are kept in the Bolton Public Library.
77 *Bolton Free Press*, 13 June 1840
78 The Conservatives were responsible for the local Act of Parliament 10 and 11 Vic., c 17, transferring the privately-owned waterworks company to the corporation at a cost of £112,500.
79 The parliamentary and municipal franchise were made the same by the Second Reform Act. The number of voters in the borough in 1869 was 12,585 (PP, HC 1871, LVI). In 1865–6 the total number of parliamentary electors was 2293. *Parliamentary Representation Returns*, PP, 1866, LVII
80 *Bolton Chronicle*, 12 Nov. 1853
81 Ibid.
82 C.J. Darbishire supported the Chartist 'Six Points.' Thomasson felt Repeal of the Corn Law came before all else. However, he was favourable to the Chartists and opposed the use of troops in 1842. Thomasson even approved of female suffrage.

156 Notes for pages 32–4

83 The local Fenian disturbances in January 1868, and the subsequent tense relations between English and Irish, probably attracted Murphy to Bolton. After Murphy's Orange meetings led to further disturbances the borough magistrates bound the orator over to be of good behaviour for twelve months.
84 *Bolton Chronicle*, 11 Feb. 1837
85 Nonconformists, often being confirmed localists, were perhaps more apt to downgrade parliamentary politics. Derek Fraser notes their reluctance to realize the importance of this area of politics in urban England as a whole. Fraser, *Urban Politics in Victorian England*, 267
86 Corruption was prevalent in parliamentary politics in all four Northern towns. It may have been another reason for the lesser degree of interest in this type of politics. John Taylor, in his *Autobiography of a Lancashire Lawyer* (Bolton 1881), says of the Bolton parliamentary election of December 1832: 'For many months previously the town had been canvassed. Potato pie suppers and free drink could be had at different public houses. A great deal of money was spent, and no secret made of it' (41). Stories and litigation over the use of the beer barrel and intimidation by employers at election time were quite common until the 1870s.
87 Jones had originally supported Catholic Emancipation and his change of heart was interpreted by many as a product of coercion exercised by influential Anglican-Tory interests and by his father-in-law who was violently anti-Catholic. W. Brimelow, *Political and Parliamentary History of Bolton*, I, 65–6
88 According to the parliamentary committee investigating Orangeism in 1834 (PP, 1835, XVII.I), seven warrants were issued for separate lodges in the Bolton area. This was an indication of considerable Orange strength at the time.
89 *Bolton Chronicle*, 19 March 1831
90 This is clearly revealed by a fairly rudimentary inspection of newspaper accounts, pamphlets, squibs, that survive for the period. Other issues, of course, such as the question of free trade, did come up. These concerns, however, never displaced the position of denominational issues as the chief source of political debate throughout the period.
91 The debate on Popery dominated political rhetoric in Bolton throughout the 1850s.
92 This was brought about chiefly by the reduction of governmental restrictions on newspapers throughout the country in the early and mid-nineteenth century. The number of master printers in Bolton increased enormously between 1830 and 1860. See J.C. Scholes, *Bolton Bibliography* (Manchester 1886), passim, for background on the Bolton press in general.
93 According to the official return on newspaper stamps issued, the average yearly circulation of the *Chronicle* in the 1830s and 40s was 35,000 (PP, 1851, XVII). This was much higher than any competitor. Tory newspapers usually did better than

157 Notes for pages 34-8

Liberal newspapers in the northern towns. It is difficult to discover why. Even the record of government stamps issued, as the *Bolton Chronicle* pointed out, was not an infallible way of gauging the actual circulation of a paper (22 April 1854).

94 Franklin Baker, the Unitarian minister, actively campaigned for the Radical candidates in 1832. Vicar Slade and the Reverend John Lyons openly worked for the Tories in the elections of 1837 and 1841, respectively. See Franklin Baker, *A Letter to the Rev. John Lyons* (London 1841). Baker is quick to point out in this pamphlet the close liaison between the Anglican clergy and the Conservatives but overlooks his own strong attachment to the Liberals.

95 All prominent members of the Bank Street Unitarian Chapel, for example, who could be located in the 1835 pollbook, voted for the Whig and Liberal candidates.

96 Normally in northern pollbooks 'weaver' and 'spinner' referred to operatives, as opposed to cotton weaver and cotton spinner which referred to millowners. This rule, however, is not a hard and fast one.

97 Thomas Thomasson to G.J. Holyoake, 22 Jan. 1868, no 1757, Holyoake Letters, Co-operative Union Library, Manchester

98 P.F. Clarke, *Lancashire and the New Liberalism* (Cambridge 1971), 33

CHAPTER THREE: PROUD PRESTON

1 Preston was first recorded as a borough in 1183. The date of its first charter of definite municipal privileges was 1154.

2 In 1837 a joint-stock company was formed to improve navigation of the Ribble River. In 1841 the company was given money by the corporation to deepen the channels and build docks. By the late 1850s there was a steady increase in tonnage and revenues. It was not until the twentieth century, however, that Preston once again reached importance as a port. Charles Hardwick, *History of the Borough of Preston* (Preston 1857), 308, 391-400

3 The name applied to the town for centuries.

4 Preston's population growth followed the same general pattern for the other northern towns, as is revealed by the following census figures:

1801	1831	1851	1871
11,887	33,112	69,542	85,427

5 Food prices were quite reasonable for Preston workers, undoubtedly because of the proximity of the agricultural estates of the Flyde.

6 John Horrocks (1768-1804) was born in the village of Edgeworth near Bolton. In 1768 he erected a cotton spinning mill in Preston. Thereafter, he built a number of mills in conjunction with his brother Samuel and an associate named

158 Notes for pages 38-9

Cooper. Employing some power-looms, he was also one of the largest muslin manufacturers in the county.

7 This was generally true of north Lancashire. See Duncan Bythell, *The Handloom Weavers: a Study in the English Cotton Industry During the Industrial Revolution* (Cambridge 1969), passim.

8 Between 1839 and 1841, for example, combined mills were built with a total of 187 hp, compared with 80 hp for weaving mills and 40 hp for spinning mills built in the same period. Reports of the Inspectors of Factories, PP, 1842, XXII

9 See H.B. Rodgers, 'The Lancashire Cotton Industry in 1840,' *Institute of British Geographers, Transactions and Papers*, XXVIII, 1960, 151, also A.J. Taylor, 'Concentration and Specialization in the Lancashire Cotton Industry, 1825-1850,' *Economic History Review*, 2nd ser., I, 1948-9, 114-22. There were no detailed statistics for Preston or Blackburn, as for Bolton and Stockport, in the 1834 Factory Inquiry Commission Report. PP, 1834, XIX

10 The very early (and somewhat ruthless) introduction and specialization in power-loom weaving in Stockport, for example, must certainly have contributed to working-class unrest in that town. For a picture of the impact of industrial life on the family in Preston see Michael Anderson, *Family Structure in Nineteenth Century Lancashire* (Cambridge 1971).

11 Franklin Baker, *The Moral Tone of the Factory System Defended* (London 1850), 29. Thirty-two per cent of all males and 13 per cent of all females twenty years old and over were cotton workers. The impression of a somewhat disproportionate number of males to females presented in these figures is modified by the figures for the entire population – 26 per cent of all males and 21 per cent of all females. There must have been a considerable number of female operatives under twenty years of age. *Census of Population, 1851*, PP, 1852-3, LXXXVIII.I

12 Preston was the first town outside London to receive gas light. The town's footpaths were flagged, water-pipes laid, police force increased, and burial ground extended for the use of the growing population before 1835. D. Duckworth, *The Story of a Church* (Preston nd), 1-2

13 See Reports of the Reverend John Clay, QGR/2, LRO, and the Rev. Walter L. Clay, *The Prison Chaplain* (London 1861).

14 See Edward Baines, *History of the Country Palatine and Duchy of Lancaster*, II (London 1836), for an idea of their county-wide importance. Baines was born in the town and educated at the local grammar school.

15 Most of the information on the old corporation's struggles comes from the various works of William Dobson, especially *History of the Parliamentary Representation of Preston* (Preston 1868).

16 A similar situation existed in Nottingham after 1835. See Charlotte Erickson, *British Industrialists: Steel and Hosiery, 1850-1950* (Cambridge 1959), 89.

Notes for pages 39–43

17 Horrocks was the son of a Bolton Quaker. However, his name appeared in the Preston Quaker Monthly Minutes between 1832 and 1870, LRO.
18 A. Temple Patterson, *Radical Leicester* (London 1954), passim.
19 From the Preston pollbook for the 1835 parliamentary election
20 Edward George Stanley and John Horrocks were elected, without contest, in the 1802 parliamentary election as a result of this compromise.
21 Roads were greatly improved around 1812. Eighty-one coaches passed through the town every week by 1830. Besides canals, four railway lines ran through the town by 1840.
22 The house was razed as a symbol of the family's abandonment of the town. It had been used only sporadically, usually around the racing season, though in 1829 it provided food and shelter for the poor during an industrial depression. Hardwick, *History of the Borough of Preston*, 225, 430
23 *Census of Population, 1851*, PP, 1852–3, LXXXVIII.1
24 Ibid.
25 Professor H.J. Hanham notes that the Duke of Devonshire and Lord Sefton were backed in their Liberalism by a considerable number of millowners set up as landed gentlemen in North Lancashire. *Elections and Party Management: Politics in the Time of Disraeli and Gladstone* (London 1959), 287, n 2
26 The year in which the mill was constructed is uncertain. It was most probably during the first decade of the nineteenth century. Professor Vincent feels that the gentry continued to have a strong influence on Lancashire urban politics even into the late 1860s. See J.R. Vincent, 'The Effect of the Second Reform Act in Lancashire,' *Historical Journal*, XI, 1, 1968, 88.
27 Archdeacon's Visitation Book, Sept. 1839, PR 1439, LRO
28 The Report on the Religious Census of 1851 noted for Preston that 'the number of attendants is not given for seven places of worship belonging to the Church of England and for one place belonging to the Roman Catholics' (cclxvii). Other sources do not clarify the actual number of churches in the town itself. Archdeacon Rushton's notebook, for example, says there were nine in 'Preston and vicinity' in 1841. Notebooks of the Rev. John Rushton, English Manuscripts no 706, John Rylands Library, Manchester
29 The Reverend Owen Parr, however, did indicate a paternal concern for workers on many occasions. For example, he attended a 'Short-time Festival' to celebrate the reduction of work hours from 12 to 11 at R. Gardner's mill in 1845. See *Place Collection of Newspaper Cuttings*, vol. 53, sect. E, 276.
30 *Preston Chronicle*, 18 Feb. 1854
31 All Saints' Church on Elizabeth Street begun in 1846 was often known as the 'Poor Man's Church.' It was said that some of the contributors were operatives. Charles Hardwick, *History of the Borough of Preston*, 478

160 Notes for pages 43–9

32 The articles were reprinted by the *Chronicle*, also in 1869, in pamphlet form entitled *Our Churches and Chapels, Their Parsons, Priests and Congregations, Being a Critical and Historical Account of Every Place of Worship in Preston*. References are to this pamphlet. A modified version of the pamphlet, with much valuable material deleted, appeared in Hewitson's *History of Preston* (Preston 1883), 452–541.
33 Hewitson, *Our Churches and Chapels*, 9
34 Ibid., 37
35 Ibid., 62
36 Ibid., 92
37 Ibid., 145
38 Bairstow's will also reveals a long list of bequests to national religious organizations (approx. £52,000) including £16,000 to the governors of Queen Anne's Bounty alone. Will for John Bairstow of Preston, proved at Lancaster, 31 Dec. 1868, Somerset House, London
39 Hewitson, *Our Churches and Chapels*, 200
40 Ibid., 212
41 Ibid., 172, 129, 207, respectively
42 Ibid., 156
43 Ibid., 107
44 H.W. Clemesha, *A History of Preston in Amounderness* (Manchester 1912), 322–3
45 Minute book, Unitarian Chapel, Preston
46 Ibid., 11 March 1827
47 Ibid., 28 April 1844
48 The words of the *Preston Guardian* on the occasion. Reprinted in *The Centenary Celebrations of the Fishergate Baptist Church* (Preston 1958), 12
49 Livesey appears to have left the congregation in the late 1830s. According to the *Blackburn Times* (11 Aug. 1932) he severed his connection with the chapel after being shocked at the festivities during a minister's ordination. This seems more of an excuse than a reason.
50 Fishergate Congregational Minute Book, 26 Oct. 1820
51 HO 129 / 1693, PRO
52 Samuel P. Antliff, *Independency in Preston* (Preston 1880), 25
53 Preston Register of Sufferers 1795–1856, FRP 1 / 10, LRO
54 FRP 5 / 7, LRO. The number of Quakers must have grown considerably in the early nineteenth century. The Lancashire Quarterly Meeting held in April 1807 had contemplated joining Preston to another meeting because of its weakness. FRP 17 / 37, LRO
55 W. Pilkington, *The Makers of Wesleyan Methodism in Preston* (Preston 1890)

Notes for pages 49–54

56 List of trustees for Marsham Wesleyan Church (1872) and Midge Hall Chapel (1867) held at Preston Lane St and Orchard Circuit chapels.
57 HO 129/1062, PRO
58 Sir George Head, *A Home Tour Through the Manufacturing Districts of England* (London 1836), chapter XXVIII, 417
59 Hume's pamphlet was written in response to a series of letters on 'Dissent in the Poor Populous Districts,' written by Herbert S. Skeates to the *Nonconformist* in 1861. Skeates's favourable interpretation of urban Dissent's role amongst the poor was never in agreement with Hume's view.
60 A. Hume, *The Church of England: the Home Missionary to the Poor*, 22
61 Hewitson, *Our Churches and Chapels* 30
62 Ibid., 145
63 Hume, *The Church of England*, 21
64 Hewitson, *Our Churches and Chapels*, 30
65 Ibid., 192
66 Ibid., 68
67 Ibid., 136
68 Ibid., 73, 103
69 Ibid., 25
70 Ibid., 95, 160, 176, 179, respectively
71 'The Preston Mission, S.J.,' 327. *Letters and Notices*, IX, Jesuit Archives, London. Catholics also supported the Stuart cause in the early eighteenth century.
72 *The Catholic Directory* for 1819 states that there were 6000 in the town. *The Catholic Diocesan Visitation Papers* put the number at about 9000 in 1855. Other estimates can be found in 'The Preston Mission, S.J.'
73 B.F. Page, *The First Catholic Charitable Society of Preston* (Preston 1923), Appendix B, 99
74 Brother Thomas Berry to the Reverend William West (nd, circa 1840). Letters of St Ignatius, Preston, *Letters and Notices*, IX, Jesuit Archives, London
75 Ibid.
76 *Annual Report of the Catholic Poor School Committee, 1866*, Westminster Cathedral Archives, London
77 *Protest of J.T. Hogg Against Report of Commissioners on Municipal Corporations*, PP, 1835, XL, 14
78 'History of Mormonism in Lancashire County' and Programme of Events During 113th Anniversary July, 1950,' Preston Library manuscript
79 While many new 'religious' movements were launched at the Preston Cockpit, the Mormons met there only intermittently.
80 *Census of Religious Worship, 1851*, cxi–cxii

162 Notes for pages 54–6

81 *Millenial Star*, I, 1, May 1840
82 A bound volume of Preston Anti-Mormon tracts can be found in the Lancashire Record Office.
83 Reverend Denis Duckworth, *The Story of a Church* (Preston, nd)
84 This is true generally of local records in England.
85 Though these ideas might seem transposed, in point of fact the self-help idea was important to working-class people. It was a way of achieving independence from the propertied classes – thereby being free to improve themselves even more. The middle-class idea of social improvement was also in the minds of the upper strata of workingmen to a degree. Preston Teetotalism, however, pioneered new ideas and techniques as much as being influenced by other ideas. Brian Harrison, *Drink and the Victorians* (London 1971), 126
86 This was especially true of nation-wide Teetotal leadership. See ibid., chap. V.
87 The 'seven men of Preston' were Henry Anderton, schoolmaster and Wesleyan; John Smith, tallow chandler; Edward Dickinson, doorkeeper and 'reformed drunkard'; John Gratix, Congregationalist; John King, clogger and Quaker; John Brodbelt, teacher at adult school and Nonconformist; Joseph Livesey, cheesemonger and Baptist. *Blackburn Times*, 11 Aug. 1932
88 Harrison in *Drink and the Victorians* points to the attraction of the lower middle class and working class to the sect (125), and to the problems of precise measurement of the social background of the membership as a whole (147).
89 Joseph Livesey (1794–1884), a Baptist and factory weaver turned cheesemonger, was leader of the movement in Preston and in the north generally from the 1830s. In 1835 he, with the help of others, founded the British Temperance Association in the town.
90 Joseph Livesey, 'Lecture on the Properties of Malt Liquor,' *Ipswich Temperance Tracts*, no 133, nd
91 The Radical background of many of the Preston Teetotal leaders is explored by Harrison in *Drink and the Victorians*, 117.
92 John Finch, a Socialist, preached temperance as 'the forerunner to an improved Social System' in Preston and a number of other northern English and Scottish towns. He also opposed temperance societies in which 'religious sectarianism and party politics existed.' J. Finch to R. Owen, 12 Oct. 1836. R. Owen Collection, no 831, Co-operative Union Library
93 *Reasoner*, XII, new ser. 20, 1852, 307–8
94 There were a few problems. In 1832 wardens complained about large numbers of people who refused to pay the rate, against whom legal proceedings were taken. *Preston Parish Select Vestry Book*, 14 Aug. 1832, PR 1481, LRO. In 1842 an Anti-Easter Dues Association was formed principally by Dissenters and Roman Catholics. The climax of their campaign came with the defiance of the Teetotal

Notes for pages 56–61

leader (Joseph Livesey) in refusing to pay his Easter dues. Two cheeses were taken from his shop by church-wardens in lieu of the 6½d. See *Autobiography of Joseph Livesey* (Preston nd), 52. In an address before the Church Institute on 13 November 1863 G. Howels Davies stated that in that year there was a majority of ten for the rate at the annual vestry meeting. He asserted that four years earlier there had been a majority of seventy-two for abolition. He credited the change of heart with the work of the Church Institute (founded in 1859).

95 Robert Halley, *Lancashire: its Puritanism and Nonconformity* (2nd ed., London 1972), 514
96 On 7 May 1870 the *Preston Chronicle* questioned why the corporation should support an 'elitist' school.
97 Joseph Livesey had much to do with the establishment of the institute. Elias de la Roche Rendell, a New Church minister, was very much involved in the activities of the institute in the 1850s.
98 *Preston Guardian*, 15 Jan. 1870
99 *Preston Chronicle*, 17 Dec. 1870. The statement is published in this issue.
100 John Foster, *Class Struggle and the Industrial Revolution* (London 1974), 216
101 Frederick Engels, *The Condition of the Working-Class in England* (London 1969), 141
102 October 1860, Letters of St Wilfrid's, Preston, *Letters and Notices*, IX, Jesuit Archives, London
103 The Municipal Reform Act ended the Court Leet and many of the ancient trading privileges of the town. The Preston Guild, however, could still be held every ten years, as in 1842 (though there was a debate as to its worth at that time). E.P. Thompson is incorrect in his view that the institution showed remarkable vigour in the early nineteenth century. The 1802 processions were the last of any consequence. See Thompson, *The Making of the English Working Class* (London 1963), 425.
104 *Times*, 31 Dec. 1835
105 *Preston Pilot*, 27 Oct. 1838
106 *Preston Chronicle*, 8 April 1837
107 Livesey also felt that government frequently failed to work in the interests of the people. Locally controlled government could be watched more easily on the people's behalf.
108 See W. Procter, 'Poor Law Administration in the Preston Union, 1838–48,' *Transactions of the Historic Society of Lancashire and Cheshire*, CXVII, 1966.
109 *Preston Pilot*, 28 Oct. 1837
110 *Preston Chronicle*, 31 Oct. 1846
111 *Preston Pilot*, 5 Nov. 1842
112 Livesey also involved himself in sectarian and political disputes over the burial board in 1856. *Preston Guardian*, 15 March 1856

164 Notes for pages 61–5

113 'Atticus' [A. Hewitson], *Preston Town Council* (Preston 1870), 5. For many references to the ineptitude of the reformed corporation in a number of areas see E.C. Midwinter, *Social Administration in Lancashire, 1830–1860: Poor Law, Public Health and Police* (Manchester 1969), passim.
114 *Preston Guardian*, 5 Nov. 1853
115 In February 1836 there were 4204 parliamentary voters compared with only 2369 municipal voters (PP, 1836, XLIII). The regulations that municipal voters must pay the poor rate and have two and one-half years' residence undoubtedly limited the number of people with the local franchise. For the parliamentary franchise, however, a large number of people retained their old voting privileges – as freemen, lot and scot, as so on. The Rating of Tenements Act of 1850, however, allowed working-class dwellings under £6 to be rated. Thus, the number of municipal voters in Preston increased from 1892 to 5738 in the 1850s with the adoption of the Act in the township of Preston. Unaccustomed to municipal politics, and especially the dull Preston municipal politics by that time, these new municipal voters took little action.
116 Sometimes it is referred to as potwalloper. See Charles Seymour, *Electoral Reform in England and Wales: the Development and Operation of the Parliamentary Franchise, 1832–1885* (New Haven 1915), 287. In May 1831 there was a public meeting in Preston chaired by J. Hanson and addressed by John Doherty, the great trade unionist, urging the same franchise as in Preston for other towns. See *The Voice of the People*, XXII, 1, 1831.
117 Some professional people, such as lawyers, should have been anxious for business from the Whig landed interest. It appears by 1840 that this consideration, if it still existed, did not entail voting Whig in gratitude. In the 1841 parliamentary election town attorneys voted overwhelmingly Tory. Preston pollbook for 1841
118 Charles Hardwick, *History of the Borough of Preston* (Preston 1857), 341–2. For a picture of pre-reform bribery and use of 'roughs' at elections see 330–40.
119 The courtesy title given to Edward George Stanley (1799–1869). Stanley joined Earl Grey's Whig ministry in 1830. He resigned in May 1834 over policy toward the Church of Ireland. In 1841 he joined Peel's Conservative cabinet but resigned in 1844 in opposition to Peel's decision to repeal the Corn Laws. He was Conservative prime minister in the years 1852, 1858–9, 1866–8. He became fourteenth Earl of Derby in 1851. See W.D. Jones, *Lord Derby and Victorian Conservatism* (Athens, Georgia 1956).
120 See *Preston Pilot*, 12 Nov. 1831.
121 There was a net decrease in the number of parliamentary electors of 3703 between 1832–3 and 1865–6. *Parliamentary Representation Returns*, Return A, PP, 1866, LVII

Notes for pages 65–7

122 James Heywood to George Melly, 26 April 1859. George Melly Papers, I, no 335, LRO
123 Joseph Lackwood to George Melly, 19 April 1862. Ibid., I, no 1296. Also see H.A. Taylor, 'Politics in Famine-Striken Preston,' *Transactions of the Historic Society of Lancashire and Cheshire*, CVII, 121–39.
124 This can be seen in the voting patterns of weavers and spinners as recorded in the pollbooks. Also, according to the Reform League report by C. Wade and C. Bartlett on Preston, 18 Aug. 1863, 800 of the 1000 members of the spinners' and minders' union and two-thirds of the 370 amalgamated engineers wee Liberals. *Records of the Reform League*, Bishopsgate Institute, London
125 There were a number of serious election riots in the late 1830s and 40s. See Hardwick, *History of the Borough of Preston*, 340–7.
126 A declaration issued by Wilding, Edge, and two other Liberal millowners in July 1837 stated that handloom weavers, who lost their jobs because they voted against the Conservative candidate, could find employment with them. *Preston Election Squibs, 1796–1841*, LRO
127 31 Jan. 1862, Melly Papers, I, no 1327
128 This subject is explored to some extent in James Aldridge's 'The Parliamentary Franchise at Preston and the Reform Act of 1832' (Manchester University, Honours BA thesis, 1948). Aldridge claims that only five firms were in favour of free trade in 1844. He sees this as part of the continuing allegiance of most cotton manufacturers to the Tory party since the very early nineteenth century. J.D. Marshall's observation that many manufacturers opposed the New Poor Law might be explained in the same way. J.D. Marshall, *The Old Poor Law, 1795–1834* (London 1968), 44–5
129 A vigorous attack on the *Preston Pilot* and 'its one-sided censure of the operatives' can be found in the *Preston Guardian*, 29 Oct. 1853. The pro-working-class attitude of the *Guardian* is understandable when one recalls that Joseph Livesey for a great many years was its proprietor.
130 This interpretation is found in a great many sources, including local newspapers and the Melly Papers (for example, I, nos 366 and 1371).
131 Sir Peter Hesketh-Fleetwood, a Liberal candidate, wrote to one of the local Temperance leaders promising that, as a member of the society, he would not use drink to get votes. P. Hesketh-Fleetwood to Henry Bradley, 26 Jan. 1836, Letters of P. Hesketh-Fleetwood, DDP 130/24, LRO. During the election of 1841 Joseph Livesey had to issue a special proclamation correcting a counterfeit squib urging Teetotallers to vote Tory. Both of these incidents indicate the seriousness with which people treated the Teetotal voters.
132 *Preston Guardian*, 28 March 1868

166 Notes for pages 67–70

133 The words of the Liberal *Preston Guardian*, 29 July 1868. Lord Edward Howard, son of the Catholic Duke of Norfolk, and Joseph Leese, a cotton manufacturer, were the Liberal candidates. They were matched by two Conservative candidates – a gentleman resident of the town, Sir Thomas Fermor-Hesketh, and Edward Hermon of the cotton firm of Horrockses, Miller, and Company.
134 Mentioned in Anthony Hewitson's *History of Preston* (Preston 1883), 343. No specimen of the paper appears to have survived.
135 John Foster's proposed measurement through marriage registers has not been taken up by other historians to date.
136 Henry Pelling, *A History of the British Trade Unionism* (London 1963), 39
137 Colonel Joseph Hanson, a Manchester manufacturer, was eventually imprisoned in 1808 because of his agitation over the minimum wages bill. The town Radicals called themselves the Independent party, in defiance of the alleged collusion between Whigs and Tories after 1802.
138 During the depression of 1829 workers agreed not to buy milk and butter until prices went down. Similar tactics were used in Bolton. Such action demonstrated working-class unity. Violence was used against some merchants who refused to co-operate. Bythell, *The Handloom Weavers*, 180–1
139 See G. Kitson Clark, 'Hunger and Politics in 1842,' *Journal of Modern History*, XXV, 1953, 355–74, and A.G. Rose, 'The Plug Riots of 1842 in Lancashire and Cheshire,' *Transactions of the Lancashire and Cheshire Antiquarian Society*, LXVII, 1957, 83–104.
140 Almost all of this factual material was obtained from local newspapers, riot depositions, and town histories.
141 *Quarterly Review*, CVI, July-Oct. 1859, 485
142 W. Cooke Taylor, *Notes of a Tour in the Manufacturing Districts of Lancashire*, Letter V, 'A Visit to Preston, 1842'
143 They also attracted the attention of contemporary writers. See Geoffrey Carnall, 'Dickens, Mrs. Gaskell, and the Preston Strike,' *Victorian Studies*, VIII, 1964, 31–48.
144 Henry Ashworth, *The Preston Strike, an Enquiry into its Causes and Consequences* (Manchester 1854). Ashworth had a close relationship with the Preston millowners and with others throughout Lancashire.
145 *Preston Guardian*, 8 April 1854. A bound volume entitled *Preston Strike, 1853-4* in the Lancashire Record Office contains much useful information (mostly newspaper cuttings) on the strike.
146 Charles Hardwick, *History of the Preston Strikes and Lock-Outs* (Preston nd), 3. By the time the struggle had ended in Preston, support had disappeared for the workers in most neighbouring towns and indeed in Stockport, where there had been a repudiation of the 10 per cent wage increase victory of 1853.

Notes for pages 70–4

147 See Peter N. Stearns, 'Measuring the Evolution of Strike Movements,' *International Review of Social History*, XIX, 1974 – Part I, 16–27
148 For Bolton, specific information on wage scales can be found in 'Bolton Cotton Spinning Past and Present,' Bolton Journal Cuttings 1885–6, compiled by F. Ritson and kept in the Bolton Library; for Blackburn see J.G. Shaw's article on wages in the *Blackburn Times*, 27 March 1937; for Preston see Hardwick, *History of the Preston Strikes and Lockouts*. See also the Place Collection of Newspaper Cuttings, vols. 51 and 53, BM.
149 See E.H. Hunt, *Regional Wage Variations in Britain 1850–1914* (London 1973), 37–8.
150 Henry Ashworth, *An Inquiry Into the Origin, Progress, and Results of the Strike of the Operative Cotton Spinners of Preston* (Manchester 1838), 2
151 Stearns, 'Measuring the Evolution of Strike Movements,' 24
152 Pelling, *History of British Trade Unionism*, 39–40

CHAPTER FOUR: STOCKPORT AND THE 'DARK SATANIC MILLS'

1 Although the main part of the town was located on the Cheshire side of the Mersey, Heaton Norris was on the Lancashire side. The town had closer ties at this time, however, with urban, industrial Lancashire than with the Cheshire hinterland. Like Bolton, Stockport preserved its own identity. There was no Manchester conurbation in this part of the century. See T.W. Freeman, 'The Manchester Conurbation,' in *Manchester and its Region* (Manchester 1962), 51.
2 See George Unwin, *Samuel Oldknow and the Arkwrights: the Industrial Revolution at Stockport and Marple* (Manchester 1924).
3 Stockport was also said to have been the setting for Frances Trollope's novel, *The Life and Adventures of Michael Armstrong, Factory Boy* (London 1840).
4 Duncan Bythell, *The Handloom Weavers: a Study in the English Cotton Industry during the Industrial Revolution* (Cambridge 1969), 265. In periods of labour shortage, as in 1833, there were few unemployed handloom weavers. See Arthur Redford, *Labour Migration in England, 1800–1850* (Manchester 1964), 101.
5 Census of Population, PP, 1852–3, LXXXVIII.II
6 Franklin Baker, *The Moral Tone of the Factory System Defended* (London 1850), 29
7 J.L. and B. Hammond, *The Skilled Labourer, 1760–1832* (London 1919), 276
8 See Malcolm I. Thomis, *The Luddites: Machine Breaking in Regency England* (London 1970).
9 Since 1799 Stockport weavers had involved themselves in all of the major petitioning movements in the north. See Bythell, *The Handloom Weavers*, 185.
10 PP, 1842, XXXV

168 Notes for pages 74–8

11 Hammond, *The Skilled Labourer*, 93
12 Acts of parliament prohibiting combinations of masters or workers. These laws (the first passed in 1799) covering the period up to the mid 1820s were usually used against workers' unions.
13 William Smith to the Rt. Hon. Robert Peel, secretary of state for the home department, Stockport, 5 June 1829. HO 40 / 24 / 1, PRO
14 Malcolm Thomis has described an earlier magistrate in the period of the Luddite disturbances of 1812, John Lloyd, as 'a fanatic' in his pursuit of subversion among workingmen (*The Luddites*, 140). It is possible that the Stockport magistracy, in general, was very reactionary during much of the early nineteenth century.
15 Hammond, *The Skilled Labourer*, 95
16 G. Kitson Clark, 'Hunger and Politics in 1842,' *Journal of Modern History*, XXV, 1953, 367. Also see reports in *Stockport Advertiser*, 12 and 19 Aug. 1842.
17 William Downall to Mrs H. Nicholson dated at Stockport, 25 April 1842. C17 / 2 / 13 / 9, Manchester Reference Library
18 The hatting industry also expanded rapidly in the early nineteenth century, as did combinations of makers and finishers in the labour force. See P.M. Giles, *The Felt-hatting industry, c. 1500–1850, with special reference to Lancashire and Cheshire* (Manchester 1960).
19 Dr Rayner to Lord Palmerston, home secretary, dated at the Court House, Stockport, 17 May 1854. HO 45 / 5244C, PRO
20 Pugsley to W.H. Cooper, 15 July 1815. L52/3/55, Letter Books, New College Archives, London
21 Kept at the Parish Church of St Mary's, Stockport
22 See R.B. Walker, 'Religious Changes in Cheshire, 1750–1850,' *Journal of Ecclesiastical History*, XVII, 1966, 77–94.
23 The Rev. C.K. Prescot noted in a visitation return (5 April 1825) that his church would be better attended if pews were not 'all private property.' EDV 7 / 7 / 446, CRO. At the end of the century a petition to the Lord Bishop of Chester written by laymen of the town (nd, probably about the time of the consecration of St George's, Heavily, in 1896, Stockport Central Library) indicates concern not only about having a mixed choir of Dissenters and Churchmen at a Eucharist Choral but also the arrangements in a new church (St George's) which gave too few sittings to the poor. This concern may have been as a result of earlier troubles – principally from Chartists – in Stockport churches.
24 The Reverend Charles Prescot, acting as magistrate, vigorously put down rioters in 1818. His son, also a clergyman, was a specific figure of hate for Stockport Chartists twenty years later.

Notes for pages 78-80

25 W.R. Ward, *Religion and Society in England, 1790-1850* (London 1972), 201
26 *Times*, 29 July 1839. The sources of information came almost exclusively from the *Times*, the *Northern Star*, and provincial newspapers. Neither Home Office correspondence nor the papers of Chartist leaders have much to say about the subject. Chartist Sunday deserves much more attention from historians. See H.U. Faulkner, *Chartism and the Churches* (New York 1916), 35; see also N.J. McLellan, 'Chartism and the Churches with reference to Lancashire' (PHD thesis, University of Edinburgh, 1947).
27 Pugsley to W.H. Cooper, 15 July 1815. L 52 / 3 / 55, Letter Books, New College Archives, London
28 See Tiviot Dale Pew Rents and Account Book C, 1826-53, B / W / 3 / 11, Records of Tiviot Dale Wesleyan Chapel, Stockport Central Library
29 Ibid., A Register for the People called Methodists, B / W / 2 / 13. The Marriage Register contains the occupations of 61 husbands from early 1852 to late 1862 including almost every type of factory hand and tradesman, B / W / 3 / 2.
30 The occupations of 146 fathers between 1 July 1831 and 17 November 1834 includes: 32 tradesmen, 35 weavers, 17 operative spinners, 16 skilled labourers, 24 unskilled manual labourers, 1 shopkeeper, 1 professional man, 2 cotton manufacturers, and 18 assorted, unclassified, or unknown occupations. RG 4 / 550, PRO
31 Registers of Mount Tabor Chapel, Stockport 1793-1832 (3 notebooks), English Manuscripts no 710, John Rylands Library, Manchester
32 W.H. Lockley, *The Story of Stockport Circuit of the United Methodist Church: a Series of Lectures* (Stockport 1909), 148
33 Visitation return, 11 March 1811, EDV 7 / 4 / 221, CRO
34 MS history of the Hanover Chapel by N.K. Pugsley, dated February 1859, found in the records of Hanover Chapel, Stockport Central Library
35 RG 4/420, PRO
36 The first trustees listed in the 1838 deed included three Manchester manufacturers.
37 The Stockport Ministerial Association was formed by Baptist and Independent ministers of the district in 1856.
38 L.M. Wheeler, 'Forty Years of a Minister's Fraternal,' *Congregational Quarterly*, XVIII, 1940, 304
39 There were sixty-nine members in 1857, Records of Stockport Preparative Meeting, EFC 12 / 1, CRO
40 Stockport Unitarian Chapel minutes, 19 Sept. 1829, in care of chapel secretary
41 Henry Coppock (1806-1870), a wealthy Stockport lawyer, was the patriarch of the town's Liberal party in the mid-Victorian years.

170 Notes for pages 81–5

42 Chapel minutes, 13 May 1863. The exact nature of the 'Ministers' Stipend Augmentation Fund, Liverpool' is not stated. The congregation approved Coppock's position.
43 James Coppock (1798–1857), born in Stockport, was a Unitarian and lawyer. He helped to establish the London Reform Club and was perhaps the best known Liberal electioneering agent in early Victorian England. It is not clear that he was a relative of Henry Coppock. In his youth he was a member of the Unitarian chapel and probably did work for the town's Liberals. His death was commemorated by the chapel. Chapel minutes, Dec. 1857
44 Unless one sees the heavy contribution to the Mechanics' Institute (Chapel minutes, autumn 1834) or the school board (Chapel minutes, 1870). Both of these actions might also be regarded as basically political moves by the chapel elite.
45 See Herbert E. Perry, 'Historical Notes on the Stockport Unitarian Chapel,' *Transactions of the Unitarian Historical Society*, III, 1923–6, 148–52.
46 The Municipal Corporations Commissioners noted in 1833 that there was a Catholic church in town accommodating 700 persons. It was said to be 'much frequented by the Irish.'
47 Annual Report of the Catholic Poor School Committee for 1852
48 The Rev. Charles Prescot felt in 1811 that most Catholics in Stockport were 'chiefly of the rank of Irish weavers,' Visitation Return, 11 March 1811, EDV 7/4/221, CRO
49 In the Stockport section of the Appendix to the Report of the State of the Irish Poor in Great Britain, PP, 1836, XXXIV. For a similar picture of the Manchester Irish 'ghetto' see John M. Werly, 'The Irish in Manchester, 1832–49,' *Irish Historical Studies*, XVIII, 1973, 345–58.
50 Ibid.
51 *Stockport Advertiser*, 8 July 1852, and William Astle, *'Stockport Advertiser' Centenary History of Stockport* (Stockport 1922), chap. XII. Many handloom weavers may also have been Irish.
52 *The Reasoner*, XII, II, 1852, 29
53 Ibid., XVI, 23, 1854, 374
54 The rules of the society prohibited discussions of religious and political issues, though a liaison was attempted by some co-operators with the Chartists in 1848. See T.W. Gough, *Stockport Great Moor Cooperative Society, Ltd. 1831–1931: a Centenary History* (Stockport 1931).
55 PP, 1835, XXVI
56 The attempt to rebuild the parish church by levying rates between 1812 and 1834 under a local Act of parliament was never quite forgotten by some Nonconformists. It was even brought up during the heated discussion over the appointment of a burial board in 1856. *Stockport Advertiser*, 28 March 1856

Notes for pages 86–92

57 The Institute was very much connected to the Church. As the First Report of the *Stockport District Society for the Promotion of Christian Knowledge* stated, 'the Christianity of the Church of England is the Christianity of the truly enlightened and noble of the human species.'
58 *Stockport Advertiser*, 2 Dec. 1870. The original compromise list contained two Roman Catholics, one Unitarian, and, of course, one less representative for both the Churchmen and the Independents. *Stockport Advertiser*, 11, 18, 25 Nov. 1870
59 J.M. Morgan, *A Brief Account of the Stockport Sunday School* (London 1838). Morgan points out that in 1832 the school had an Anglican priest as treasurer, a Unitarian minister as secretary, and a Wesleyan layman as librarian.
60 Joseph Butterworth to J. Mayer, 23 Dec. 1819. Butterworth urged Mayer to disclose any information he could to help ease the situation – asserting that serious consideration had been given to placing the school under the magistrates. Butterworth had heard that the rules of the school had been written up by Major Cartwright. Letters B/S/5/3, Records of the Stockport Sunday School, Stockport Central Library
61 J. Mayer to J. Turner, T. Swan, and J. Lomax, 29 July 1846, B/S/5/7, Records of Stockport Sunday School
62 J.W. Clarke, DD, to William Smith, 2 Sept. 1872, Records of Stockport Sunday School
63 For an attack in print of the Stockport Sunday School see C.J. Haslam, *Letters to the Clergy of all Denominations* (Manchester nd [circa 1838–41]), letter XIII
64 Andrew Ure, *The Philosophy of Manufactures* (London 1835), Book the Third, 410
65 T.W. Laqueur, *Religion and Respectability* (New Haven 1976), 45–6
66 Ure, *Philosophy of Manufactures*, 412
67 Walker, 'Religious Changes in Cheshire, 1750–1850,' 92–3
68 See Benjamin Varley, *The History of the Stockport Grammar School* (Manchester 1946); *Stockport Advertiser*, 6 Jan. 1860
69 PP, 1836, XXXIV
70 See Henry Heginbotham, *Stockport: Ancient and Modern*, II (London 1892), chap. XII. For sketches of the riots and damaged buildings see the *Illustrated London News*, 10 July 1852.
71 Municipal Commissioners' Report on the Borough of Stockport, 129, PP, 1837–8, XXXV
72 The police commissioners were set up by a local Act of parliament, 7 Geo. IV. The essential powers of the commissioners were clearly defined but later became complicated by subsequent 'gas and water' acts.
73 Municipal Commissioners' Report, 134, PP, 1837–8, XXXV
74 Unwin, *Samuel Oldknow and the Arkwrights*, 39

75 *Stockport Advertiser*, 6 Nov. 1845
76 See P.M. Giles, 'The Economic and Social Development of Stockport, 1815–1836' (MA thesis, University of Manchester, 1950), 542–4.
77 'History of the Municipality of Stockport: Paper V,' *Stockport Advertiser*, 18 April 1873
78 *Stockport Advertiser*, 8 Jan. 1836
79 *North Cheshire Reformer*, 10 Feb. 1837
80 Tory manufacturers may have initially resisted the New Poor Law, an attitude not uncommon among manufacturers in the north. See J.D. Marshall, *The Old Poor Law, 1795–1834: Studies in Economic History* (London 1968), 44.
81 This phrase was used by the *Stockport Advertiser*.
82 The different estimates were given at a public meeting at the Lyceum sponsored by the Conservative Workingmen's Ratepayers' Association in 1848. *Stockport Advertiser*, 26 Oct. 1848
83 An examination of assessment books now deposited in the Stockport Central Library, such as the Rate Collection Ledger for 1841-2 (B / L / 3 / 3), gives an idea of the structure of property ownership in the town. Henry Coppock and other men of moderate wealth (Coppock's estate at death was valued at under £25,000) owned a considerable number of houses, undoubtedly adding to their influence and prestige. Their wealth, of course, could not compare with that of a great millowner such as James Heald, worth about £350,000 at death.
84 *Stockport Advertiser*, 19 May 1837
85 H.J. Hanham, *Elections and Party Management* (London 1959), Appendix I, 'A Note on Municipal Elections'
86 From the Lyceum meeting. *Stockport Advertiser*, 26 Oct. 1848
87 Some of these views would be at variance with those of E.P. Hennock for Leeds and Birmingham. See E.P. Hennock, *Fit and Proper Persons: Ideal and Reality in Nineteenth-century Urban Government* (London 1973). This may be explained to some extent by the different locales under examination.
88 Hanham, *Elections and Party Management*, Appendix I: 'A Note on Municipal Elections'
89 The *Stockport Advertiser*, 6 Nov. 1845, cited at least three factions – the Coppock men, the 'moderates,' and the 'loco-focos' or extreme Radicals.
90 *Stockport Advertiser*, 12 Oct. 1843
91 Ibid., 21 Jan. 1848
92 *Stockport Mercury*, 2 Nov. 1848
93 At a Conservative Lyceum meeting before the election, Mr Hill of the Tory Ratepayers' Association pointed out that the money allocated for Coppock's visit to London (£289.10.4) to lobby for the passage of the 1847 Improvement bill could have supplied '500 families with 4½ pounds of bread per day for twelve

Notes for pages 99-105

months successively.' Hill concluded by saying, 'these rulers may talk about improvement as they like, but what the people most require is physical improvement in the shape of bread and beef.' Thomas Williams, identified as an Irishman, also urged his fellow countrymen with the municipal franchise to vote against the 'Whig regime' for its financial mismanagement.

94 *Stockport Mercury*, 23 Nov. 1848
95 Reference to James Heald, the prominent Stockport Conservative
96 *Stockport Mercury*, 8 Nov. 1850
97 *Stockport Advertiser*, 20 Dec. 1850
98 The Rev. J. Merdith, curate of St Peter's Church, tried to suggest in a letter to the Liberal candidate, J.B. Smith, that he should oppose Popery. J. Merdith to J.B. Smith, 25 March 1852, Stockport Letters MS 923.9.S341, J.B. Smith Papers, Manchester Reference Library
99 *Stockport Advertiser*, 17 Jan. 1851
100 E.D. Steele, 'Leeds and Victorian Politics,' *University of Leeds Review*, XVII, 1975, 277
101 Ibid., 8 Nov. 1850
102 *Stockport Advertiser*, 15 Feb. 1856
103 According to the Parliamentary Return of electors (PP, 1836, XLIII) there were 895 parliamentary electors compared with 2295 municipal electors in town in February 1836. There were, therefore, 1400 municipal electors without the right to vote in parliamentary elections. In 1866 the number of parliamentary electors had only risen to 1348, of which only 9.2 per cent were 'working class.' PP, 1866, LVII
104 These events were dramatized in a play by Charles Smith entitled *We are all Reformers* (Stockport 1938). The play was decidedly anti-Coppock.
105 Richard Cobden to Henry Coppock, 17 July 1846. Cobden Papers, MS 41 / E 42, West Sussex RO
106 See J.B. Smith to W. Gosling, 12 March 1857, and W. Gosling to J.B. Smith, 13 March 1857, J.B. Smith Papers. It appears that the local Liberal Association was prepared to fight Coppock if he chose another candidate.
107 Langley was an important newspaperman who edited a number of northern newspapers, including the *Preston Guardian*. He was an enthusiastic advocate of Liberal causes. See H.W. Nicholas, 'John Baxter Langley,' *The Commonwealth*, 13 Oct. 1866
108 *Stockport Advertiser*, 30 Aug. 1839
109 Ibid., 18 June 1835
110 According to the stamps issued (PP, 1851, XVII), the *Advertiser* through the years had a high and consistent following when compared with other papers.
111 *Stockport Advertiser*, 22 April 1852
112 A pollbook complete with occupations survives for the 1847 election.

CHAPTER FIVE: BLACKBURN: AN ARCHETYPAL COTTON TOWN

1 Birley and Hornby Company employed about 550 handloom weavers in the first decade of the nineteenth century. Duncan Bythell, *The Handloom Weavers* (Cambridge 1969), 29
2 Anon. (possibly R. Dobson), *Remarks on Weaving with Reflections on Recent Events in Lancashire* (Blackburn 1834),4
3 Much of this biographical information on families can be found in William Alexander Abram, *The History of Blackburn, Town and Parish* (Blackburn 1877).
4 In 1831 there were 170,000 spindles and about 15,000 spinners. P.A. Whittle, *Blackburn As It Is* (Blackburn 1851), 240
5 Reports of the Inspectors of Factories, PP, 1842, XXII
6 Franklin Baker, *The Moral Tone of the Factory System Defended* (London 1850), 27
7 PP, 1852-3, LXXXVIII.I
8 Messrs. W. Eccles and Co, W.H. Hornby and Co, R. Hopwood and Son, Pilkington Brothers and Co each employed over one thousand operatives at mid century. See Whittle, *Blackburn As It Is*, 243. The average per mill in 1841 was about 281. D.S. Gadian, 'Class Consciousness in Oldham and Other North-West Industrial Towns 1830-1850,' *Historical Journal*, XXI, 1978, 168, Table 2
9 See J.D. Marshall, 'Colonisation as a Factor in the Planting of Towns in North-West England,' *Studies in Urban History* (London 1968), ed. H.J. Dyos, especially 226-8.
10 See Patrick Joyce, 'The Factory Politics of Lancashire.'
11 *Historical Journal*, XVIII, 1975, 525-53. Whittle, *Blackburn As It Is*, 244
12 George Dewhurst (1790-1857), Unitarian, reedmaker, and Blackburn's most popular Radical leader. Dewhurst was arrested and sentenced to two years at Lancaster Castle for his 1819 speech given to handloom weavers in nearby Burnley.
13 Thomas Greenwood to J.W. Whittaker, 5 May 1826, Correspondence of the Rev. John W. Whittaker, Blackburn Library
14 *Blackburn Mail*, 12 April 1826
15 Ibid., 7 June 1826
16 According to Bythell, *The Handloom Weavers*, there were only 1000 docile handloom weavers in Blackburn by 1841. See especially 176 and 266.
17 *Blackburn Gazette*, 5 Oct. 1836. The incident supposedly took place two weeks before.
18 Ibid., 20 Aug. 1842. The Highlanders were eventually reinforced by the 11th Hussars.

175 Notes for pages 111–14

19 For a discussion of the price problem for cuts (or lengths) paid to weavers see the *Blackburn Standard*, 9 June 1847.
20 See article on wages by John G. Shaw in the *Blackburn Times*, 27 March 1937.
21 See Mary Ellison, *Support for Secession: Lancashire and the American Civil War* (Chicago and London 1972).
22 According to William Gourlay, 89 per cent of Blackburn's population suffered directly from the effects of the Famine, more than in any other Lancashire town. See William Gourlay, *The History of the Distress in Blackburn, 1861–5, and the Means Adopted for its Relief* (Blackburn 1865).
23 Mrs Whittaker to the Rev. J.W. Whittaker, 1 June 1826, Correspondence of the Rev. John W. Whittaker
24 Walter Chamberlain, *Parochial Centralization* (Bolton 1850). In January 1848 a meeting was in fact called at Accrington by five Blackburn curates to try to overthrow the authority of the vicar. See W.R. Ward, *Religion and Society in England 1790–1850* (London 1972), 226
25 See Books 5 and 6 of the Rev. John Ruston's 'M.S. Notes on Churches in Lancashire and Cheshire,' English Manuscripts no 706, John Rylands Library, Manchester
26 There were only seven gentlemen of independent means in Blackburn in 1851, Census of Population, PP, 1852–3, LXXXVIII.II. Chamberlain had claimed in his pamphlet that millowners and senior clergy were drawing too close together to serve the church properly.
27 George C. Miller, *Blackburn: the Evolution of a Cotton Town* (Blackburn 1951), 170
28 Wills at Somerset House
29 The Rev. George Cole to the National Society, 25 Oct. 1889, Blackburn file, National Society, London
30 The Rev. H. Wescoe to the National Society, Oct. 1867
31 National Society Correspondence
32 How well the Church was doing in comparison with other denominations as a place for such functions can be ascertained from the following table:

Statistics for Blackburn, 1841

	At Church	At Roman Catholic chapel	Other places
Marriages	520	17	19
Burials	1333	94	91
Christenings	1921	182	161

Blackburn Standard, 8 Jan. 1842

176 Notes for pages 114–17

33 T.D. Whitaker, *A Sermon Preached ... in Aid of a Subscription for the Relief of the Poor in the Town of Blackburn* (Blackburn 1820). The Rev. T.D. Whitaker, vicar of both Blackburn and Whalley (1818–21), should not be confused with his successor at Blackburn, J.W. Whittaker (1822–54). T.D. Whitaker had a greater preference for the gentry than the manufacturers. Gentry influence on the town, however, was declining even in his day.
34 Rev. J.W. Whittaker, *A Sermon Preached at the Parish Church, August 4, 1839* (London 1840)
35 Northeastern Lancashire was historically a Nonconformist breeding ground. This is an example of sub-regional characteristics within a county.
36 D.T. Carnson to the Blackburn Academy, 26 Sept. 1827. This letter is reproduced in *An Appendix of Blackburn Academy Correspondence* held at Dr Williams's Library, London. For a general idea of the importance of Dissenting academies in Warrington, Manchester, and other Lancashire towns see Herbert McLachlan, *English Education under the Test Acts: being the History of the Non-Conformist Academies, 1662–1820* (Manchester 1931).
37 This trust deed is reproduced in W.A. Abram, *A Century of Independency in Blackburn* (Blackburn 1878), 15–16.
38 Joyce, 'The Factory Politics Of Lancashire,' 537
39 Letter of A.W. Selbie of Chesterfield to W.H. Ainsworth, 6 May 1865. It is found in the Chapel Street Chapel deaconal minute book, Chapel St Chapel, Blackburn
40 See Abram, *A Century of Independency in Blackburn*.
41 This information is contained in a pamphlet entitled *St. George's Presbyterian Church, Blackburn*, found in the records of Mount Street Chapel, Presbyterian Archives, London.
42 This vestry meeting was held on 6 Sept. 1832. A report of the meeting is found in W.A. Abram, *Blackburn Characters of a Past Generation* (Blackburn 1894), 30.
43 Deed dated 4 June 1842, C 53 / 1842, 139.9, PRO
44 J. Lea, 'Baptists and the Working Classes in Mid-Victorian Lancashire,' in *Victorian Lancashire* (Newton Abbot 1974), ed. S.P. Bell, 60
45 Blackburn Primitive Methodist Circuit, RG 4 / 2003, PRO. For an interesting account of the early sufferings of Methodist preachers in Blackburn see James Sigston, *A Memoir of the Life and Ministry of Mr. W. Bramwell, Lately an Itinerant Methodist Preacher* (London 1821).
46 For the 51 baptisms in 1863, for example, the occupations of fathers were as follows: 1 gentleman, 1 stationer, 1 printer, 1 stone mason, 1 blacksmith, 1 chair-maker, 1 milliner, 14 weavers, 7 spinners, 1 self-minder, 1 piecer, 1 taper, 1 winder, 2 woolstaplers, 1 mixer of cotton, 2 clothlookers, 1 forger, 1 moulder,

Notes for pages 117–20

1 grinder, 1 shipper, 1 machinist, 1 engine cleaner, 3 labourers, 1 woodman, 1 carter, and 1 commercial traveller. Primitive Methodist Connexion, Register of Baptisms in the Blackburn Circuit, kept at the Methodist Church, Wilpshire, Blackburn
47 Catholic Poor School Committee, 2nd annual report, 1849, 35. Two letters can be found in the Leeds Diocesan Archives for the 1820s which touch upon the financial state of Blackburn Catholicism.
48 *Millenial Star*, I, 1, May 1840
49 See E. Stones, 'The Rev. Dr. Jonathan Bayley of Accrington: a Nineteenth-Century Educationalist,' *Transactions of the Lancashire and Cheshire Antiquarian Society*, LXX, 1960; Rev. Dr Bayley, *New Church Worthies* (London 1884).
50 Deed dated 7 Sept. 1860, C 53 / 1860.104.16, PRO
51 *The Reasoner*, XX, 7, 1856, 54
52 Stephenson was the future editor of the short-lived *Preston Observer* in 1869.
53 The Hammonds in *The Age of the Chartists, 1832–54* (London 1930) use this incident as an example of the strength of the friendly societies in Lancashire.
54 According to the report of the parliamentary committee investigating the Orange institutions of Great Britain and the colonies (PP, 1835, XVII.1, Appendix, 145) there were five warrants issued for lodges in the parish containing an official membership of ninety-five.
55 The church question in Rochdale revolved around a Dissent-led, Quaker-inspired popular opposition to the church rate, which brought the Reformist forces into a violent clash with Tory Anglicans led by their High Church vicar, Dr J.E.N. Molesworth. The high point of the clash was between 1834 and 1840. See J.E.N. Molesworth, *Remarks on Church Rates and the Rochdale Contest* (Rochdale 1841), and William Robertson, *The Social and Political History of Rochdale* (Rochdale 1889), 31.
56 The meeting was held on Monday, 10 Sept. 1827. For a report see the *Blackburn Mail*, 12 Sept. 1827.
57 Ibid.
58 Among the leypayers were 3 gentlemen, 23 cotton manufacturers, 2 other manufacturers, 19 shopkeepers and tradesmen, 11 victuallers, spirit dealers, and brewers, 28 in other assorted occupations, and 16 with unknown occupations. Compiled from the *Blackburn Mail*, 19 Sept. 1827, and the Greater Manchester Directory for 1824
59 A collection of the squibs surviving from the 1834 contest can be found in the Lancashire Record Office.
60 There was, of course, a running debate over the question of Disestablishment in all four northern towns in the 1830s. In 1836 there was a rather nasty pamphlet war between the vicar of Blackburn and Francis Skinner, the outspoken Presbyterian minister, on the subject.

178 Notes for pages 120–6

61 Gourlay, *History of the Distress in Blackburn*, 33
62 For example, the Congregationalists' Lancashire Union decided to relieve only Congregationalist operatives who were distressed. For the controversey that ensued over this amongst Dissenters see the letters to the editor entitled 'Sectarian Modes of Doing Good' in the *Nonconformist*, 17 and 24 Sept. 1862.
63 *Blackburn Times*, 17 Dec. 1870
64 Alderman Baynes, *The Cotton Trade* (Blackburn 1857), 68. It appears that there was a 'Lit and Phil' society in the town by 1861. Previous to this, the only lit and phil society was in Preston, though Blackburn did have the Bank Foundry and Highfield Mill Athenaeum. Literary and Scientific Societies, PP, 1852-3, XC
65 A series of public letters addressed to the priests of Stonyhurst College in 1829 can be found in Vicar Whittaker's correspondence kept at the Blackburn Library.
66 43 Geo. III, c CXXV
67 *First Report of the Committee of the Blackburn National and Sunday Schools, 1828* (National Society, London)
68 Thomas Ainsworth to the Poor Law Commission, 10 Oct. 1838, MH 12/5529, PRO
69 *Blackburn Gazette*, 4 April 1838
70 Cobbett attacked the New Poor Law because it gave greater voting power to the rich. See Bryan Keith-Lucas, *The English Local Government Franchise* (Oxford 1952), chap. II.
71 *Blackburn Gazette*, 4 April 1838. Peter Ellingthorpe (1809–1874), a wealthy Anglican solicitor and Tory, was clerk to the Board of Guardians between 1837 and 1874.
72 A. Power to the Poor Law Commission, 31 Jan. 1837, MH 32/63, PRO. Alfred Power was Edwin Chadwick's hand-picked subordinate, who travelled about Lancashire in 1837–8 making reports on the state of local unions.
73 Ibid., 13 Feb. 1840
74 Every male, twenty-one years old and over, resident within three miles of township, being assessed for the poor rate at £30 or over. 4–5 Vic. c cxii
75 Alderman Baynes, *The Cotton Trade* (Blackburn 1857), 68
76 *Blackburn Directory for 1852*. By comparing the lists of gentlemen in the front of directories with the various lists of manufacturers (further on in the directories), one can see that most 'gentlemen' were in fact commercial men rather than gentlemen of independent means. This was common in Lancashire directories. For the various motives for producing directories see Jane E. Norton, *Guide to the National and Provincial Directories of England and Wales, Excluding London, Published before 1856*, Royal Historical Society Guides and Handbooks, No. 5 (London 1950).

Notes for pages 126–33

77 Lists of appointments to the borough bench, 19 July 1852 and 25 April 1860, Blackburn File, Duchy of Lancaster Records, London
78 W.H. Hornby was one of the largest Tory-Anglican cotton manufacturers in Blackburn.
79 *Blackburn Standard*, 2 Nov. 1853
80 See George C. Miller, *Blackburn: the Evolution of a Cotton Town* (Blackburn 1951), local government sections. William Hoole as its chairman no doubt caused such concern, though its secretary, J. Hargreaves, was a Tory Churchman.
81 For example, John Vincent, *The Formation of the Liberal Party, 1857–1868* (London 1966), 67, though Patrick Joyce would err even more in this respect.
82 *Blackburn Standard*, 16 Nov. 1853. James Boyle (1804–1873) was a confectioner by trade and an Independent in religion. A staunch supporter of the Anti-Corn Law League and other Liberal causes, he was elected to the town council in 1851. He later became an alderman.
83 Abram, *Blackburn Characters of a Past Generation*, 349–50
84 Borough of Blackburn, *Watch Committee Minutes*, 6 Dec. 1852, Town Hall, Blackburn
85 See J.J. Tobias, *Crime and Industrial Society in the Nineteenth Century* (London 1967).
86 The Liberal regime managed to involve itself in a few projects: water fountains were erected in 1858, lands were also purchased for a public park in 1855. *Corporation Promiscuous Minute Book, 1851–72* passim, Town Hall, Blackburn
87 See C. Aspin, *Lancashire: the First Industrial Society* (Preston 1969), 136.
88 J.C. Lowe, 'The Tory Triumph of 1868 in Blackburn and Lancashire,' *Historical Journal*, XVI, 1973, 739
89 See Abram, *Blackburn Characters of a Past Generation*, 160. It can, of course, be noted that butchers in some places tended toward Toryism often to please farmer-creditors. But Mullineaux was an outspoken member of council at times opposing the Conservative leadership in the mid 1860s. Abram, *Blackburn Characters of a Past Generation*, 160
90 See J.R. Vincent, 'The Electoral Sociology of Rochdale,' *Economic History Review*, 2nd ser., XVI, 1963, 76–90.
91 *Blackburn Times*, 2 Nov. 1861
92 J. Pilkington of Blackburn to the Rt Hon. Sir George Grey, home secretary, 11 Dec. 1861, Duchy of Lancaster Records, Blackburn file
93 Salter's workshop at the bottom of Church Street. People met there to read Radical journals and the like.
94 *Blackburn Standard*, 10 March 1852

180 Notes for pages 134–40

95 Borough of Blackburn, *Watch Committee Minutes*, 17 Nov. 1862 and 28 Oct. 1868. See also 'M.S. Notebook of Police Sergeant Whitehead,' Blackburn Library, for 1868.
96 Ellen Barlee, *A Visit to Lancashire in December, 1862* (London 1863), 141
97 The vicar, Dr Rushton, refused to have church bells rung at the time of Cobden's death in the spring of 1865, and was violently attacked by the Liberal press. See *Blackburn Times*, 8 and 22 April 1865.
98 See Abram, *Blackburn Characters of a Past Generation*, chap. XII.
99 *Blackburn Times*, 28 July 1866
100 *Blackburn Patriot*, 7 Nov. 1868
101 See Abram, *Blackburn Characters*, chap. II.
102 According to J.D. Marshall, forty to forty-five of the seventy mills in Blackburn were under the control of Tories. J.D. Marshall, 'Colonisation as a Factor in the Planting of Towns in North-West England,' *Study of Urban History*, 227
103 *Blackburn Gazette*, 18 March 1835
104 Ibid., 22 May 1833
105 The *Blackburn Standard* ran until 1893.
106 See John and George Toulmin, *Bits of Old Blackburn* (Blackburn 1888), Part I.
107 Gilbert Wardlow to George Hadfield of Manchester, 14 Jan. 1835, *Appendix of Blackburn Academy Correspondence*, Dr Williams's Library, London
108 *Blackburn Times*, 19 July 1865
109 Rule number 2 of the Rules and Regulations of the Blackburn Operative Conservative Association (originally founded 4 Jan. 1836) was 'to uphold the necessary connexion between the Established Church and State.'
110 The well-known clergyman attended a Darwen meeting supporting striking colliers at Church and Oswaldtwistle in 1860. *Blackburn Standard*, 28 May 1860
111 Murrough was a close friend of the famous atheist, Charles Bradlaugh. He was also on good terms with local Secularists such as W. Johnson.
112 *Blackburn Patriot*, 21 Nov. 1868. Intimidation, of course, was always an accusation hurled at millowners. According to the *Blackburn Gazette*, 30 June 1841, Liberal millowners had hired bludgeon men during the election to support the free trade cause.
113 See J.C. Lowe, 'The Tory Triumph of 1868 in Blackburn and in Lancashire,' and J.R. Vincent's, 'The Effect of the Second Reform Act in Lancashire,' *Historical Journal*, XI, 1968, 84–94.
114 *Blackburn Times*, 24 Dec. 1869

CHAPTER SIX: WIDER PERSPECTIVES

1 Geoffrey Best, *Mid-Victorian Britain, 1851–75* (London 1971), 171, and R.J.

Notes for pages 140-2

Helmstadter, 'The Victorian Churches,' in *Victorian Prose: a Guide to Research* (New York 1973), ed. D.J. DeLaura, 421-3
2 Stephan Thernstrom, *Poverty and Progress: Social Mobility in a Nineteenth Century City* (Cambridge, Mass. 1964), 204
3 See B.D. White, *A History of the Corporation of Liverpool, 1835-1914* (Liverpool 1951), and R.B. Walker, 'Religious Changes in Liverpool in the Nineteenth Century,' *Journal of Ecclesiastical History*, XIX, 1968, 195-211.
4 Ian Sellers, 'Nonconformist Attitudes in Later Nineteenth-Century Liverpool,' *Trans. Hist. Soc. of Lancashire and Cheshire*, CXIV, 1962, 217
5 See A. Redford, *The History of Local Government in Manchester, II: Borough and City* (London 1940); L.S. Marshall, *The Development of Public Opinion in Manchester* (Syracuse 1946); W.E.A. Axon, ed., *The Annals of Manchester* (London 1886); Richard Wade, *The Rise of Nonconformity in Manchester* (Manchester 1880); John M. Werly, 'The Irish in Manchester, 1832-49,' *Irish Historical Studies*, XVIII, 1973, 345-58. For an idea of the strife in the pre-Reform period see Frida Knight, *The Strange Case of Thomas Walker: Ten Years in the Life of a Manchester Radical* (London 1957), chap. IV.
6 Conrad Gill, *History of Birmingham*, I: *Manor and Borough to 1865* (London 1952); Asa Briggs, *History of Birmingham*, II: *Borough and City, 1865-1938* (London 1952) and *Victorian Cities* (London 1963) chap. V; E.P. Hennock, *Fit and Proper Persons: Ideal and Reality in Nineteenth-Century Urban Government* (London 1973), Book I. See also David E.H. Mole, 'Challenge to the Church, Birmingham 1815-1865,' *The Victorian City: Images and Realities*, II, ed. H.J. Dyos and M. Wolff (London and Boston 1973), 815-36. Trygve Tholfsen, 'The Chartist Crisis in Birmingham,' *International Review of Social History*, III, 1958, 461-80, discusses a very brief period in which class cohesion was less evident.
7 p. 279
8 See Hennock, *Fit and Proper Persons*, Book II.
9 See William Cudworth, *Historical Notes on the Bradford Corporation* (Bradford 1881).
10 See John Prest, *The Industrial Revolution in Coventry* (London 1960), 138-9.
11 See John Latimer, *The Annals of Bristol in the Nineteenth Century* (Bristol 1887); A.B. Beavan, *Bristol Lists: Municipal and Miscellaneous* (Briston 1899); J.F. Nicholls and J. Taylor, *Bristol Past and Present*, I (Bristol 1881), and William Hunt, *Bristol* (London 1887), in Freeman and Hunt series on Historic Towns, chaps. VIII, IX, and X.
12 See my 'The Religious Side of Victorian Bath, 1830-70,' *Histoire sociale / Social History*, VI, 1973, 224-40.
13 See Robert Newton, *Victorian Exeter* (Leicester 1968), and Allan Brockett, *Nonconformity in Exeter, 1650-1875* (Manchester 1962).

182 Notes for pages 142–3

14 See my article, 'Religion and Society in the Cloth Region of Wiltshire, c. 1830–1870,' *Journal of Religious History*, XI, 1, 1980, 95–110.
15 H.J. Hanham, *Elections and Party Management*, Appendix I, 'A Note on Municipal Elections,' 393
16 Gill, *History of Birmingham*, I, 217
17 For example, see James Cornford, 'The Transformation of Conservatism in the Late Nineteenth Century,' *Victorian Studies*, VII, 1963, 35–66, and E.J. Feutchwanger, *Disraeli, Democracy and the Tory Party* (Oxford 1968).
18 Donald Read, *The English Provinces* (London 1969), 224–5
19 See Ken Young, *Local Politics and the Rise of Party* (Leicester 1975).
20 Term used today to explain those values in individuals predisposing them to vote at every election for the same party. David Butler and Donald Stokes, *Political Change in Britain* (Harmsworth, Middlesex 1971), 56–64
21 See Hanham, *Elections and Party Management*, Appendix I, 388.
22 Pp. 67 and 110

Note on Sources

Most of the materials used for the writing of complete local histories were consulted until a pattern began to emerge from the evidence. With a more clear-cut framework of investigation came more selectivity, though a topic of this nature always requires an eclectic approach.

Some of the sources were those employed by ecclesiastical historians. Lacking direct documentation for sectarianism, I found such pieces of evidence as religious censuses a convenient starting-point. As the text, notes, and appendix should reveal, more data were available than those found in the *Census of Religious Worship, 1851*. For a more complete discussion of data sources see R. Currie, A. Gilbert, and L. Horsley, *Churches and Churchgoers: Patterns of Growth in the British Isles Since 1700* (Oxford 1977). However, there were limits to the usefulness of such material for a study of this nature. More detailed evidence on the social composition of congregations came from the Non-Parochial registers kept at the PRO and denominational records – usually at the local level.

The Non-Parochial registers (which normally cover periods from the late eighteenth century to the end of the 1830s) are a neglected historical source. See R.W. Ambler, 'Non-Parochial Registers and the Local Historian,' *The Local Historian*, X, 1972, 59-64. Such registers, of course, must be handled with statistical caution. For further information see Edwin Welch, 'Nonconformist Registers,' *Journal of the Society of Archivists*, II, 1964, 411-17, and Janet Smith, 'The Local Records of Nonconformity,' *The Local Historian*, VIII, 1968, 131-43. Marriage registers can also be found in regional registry offices and used when permission can be obtained. There is also the question of how far any set of chapel registers reflects the allegiance of the participants to the chapel. The current orthodoxy amongst most historians, one I agree with, is that a very high proportion of those using Nonconformist chapels for weddings and christenings were Nonconformists, the 'convenience argument' usually pertaining more to the parish church. Complete membership lists, where available, would of course be even more reliable but also would reveal only a portion of the true number of attenders and others affiliated with the chapel.

In general, for the four cotton towns the local records of Unitarians, Baptists, and Congregationalists were among the best, with less luck for the Wesleyan Methodists. Few chapel sources could pin-point with great accuracy the complete social composition (in quantitative terms) of congregations for this period. These observations, of course, may not pertain to other regions of the country and are also subject to the discovery of new sources in these towns and new techniques of investigation at any time. R.J. Helmstadter of the University of Toronto, for example, is doing some interesting work correlating census enumerators' lists with the more complete chapel membership lists for late nineteenth-century Leeds. The local records of Roman Catholics and new sects tended to be almost non-existent.

Records for the Church of England were mostly of an official nature – parish registers of baptisms, marriages, and burials. Some of these documents give occupations of registrants. However, there is a question as to how many enumerated here were committed and practising Anglicans. A great many people simply viewed (and still do) the Church as a sort of public registration agency for important events in life. It was necessary to explore more committed and personalized sources of evidence, such as National Society reports and visitation papers, for a better picture of the social background of Anglicanism in each locale.

For all groups – Churchmen, Nonconformists, Roman Catholics, and the new sects – it was necessary to seek much information from indirect sources, particularly local newspapers. Weekly newspapers, of course, are an indispensable source for the local and urban historian. They not only provided reasonably accurate reporting of major developments in the locale but usually, through editorials, reflected the views of the major political-sectarian groups. All four cotton towns possessed newspapers throughout the period representing Tory and Liberal opinion.

Select Bibliography

I Primary Sources
A   Manuscript Material   (1) Private Papers
                               (2) Government Records
                               (3) Records of Church and Chapel
                               (4) Other Manuscript Sources
B   Printed Sources   (1) Newspapers
                               (2) Periodicals
                               (3) Parliamentary Sessional Papers
                               (4) Directories and Pollbooks
                               (5) Memoirs and Observations
                               (6) Sermons and Pamphlets
                               (7) Other Primary Materials
II Secondary Sources

I PRIMARY SOURCES

A *Manuscript material*

(1) Private papers

Franklin Baker Collection (Unitarian College, Manchester)
Richard Cobden Papers (BM and West Sussex RO)
Letters of P. Hesketh Fleetwood (LRO)
Reminiscences of Robert Greenhalgh (Bolton Library)
G.J. Holyoake Papers (Co-operative Union Library, Manchester)
George Melly Correspondence (Liverpool RO)
Robert Owen Papers (Co-operative Union Library, Manchester)

186 Select Bibliography

John Rushton Papers (John Rylands Library, Manchester)
J.B. Smith Papers (Manchester Central Reference Library)
Letters of R. Townley Parker (LRO)
David Urquhart Papers (Balliol College, Oxford)
Correspondence of the Rev. J.W. Whittaker (Blackburn Library)

(2) Government records

(a) National
Chapel Trust Deeds (PRO)
Duchy of Lancaster Papers (Duchy Office, London)
Home Office Papers (PRO), especially on Disturbances and the Religious Census of 1851
Non-Parochial Registers (PRO)
Poor Law Commission Correspondence (PRO)

(b) Regional
Register of Dissenting Meeting Houses (Quarter Session Records, Cheshire RO)
Riot Depositions (LRO)

(c) Local
BOLTON: Great Bolton Overseers of the Poor Minute Book, 1848–52 (Bolton Library); Rate Collection Ledgers (Bolton Library); Proceedings of the Court Leet and Court Baron of Little Bolton, 1797–1841 (Bolton Library)
PRESTON: Preston Parish Select Vestry Books 1829–51 (LRO); Preston Prison Chaplain Reports – some manuscript and some printed (LRO)
STOCKPORT: Rate Collection Ledgers (Stockport Library)
BLACKBURN: Borough of Blackburn, Promiscuous Minute Book, 1851–72 (Blackburn Town Hall); Borough of Blackburn, Watch Committee Minute Books, 1852–70 (Blackburn Town Hall); Blackburn Union, Minute Books of Guardians, 1837–70 (LRO); Notebook of Police Sergeant Whitehead (Blackburn Library)

(3) Records of church and chapel

(a) National
CHURCH OF ENGLAND: Correspondence of the National Society (National Society Archives, London)
NONCONFORMIST: Records of the Liberation Society (London County RO); Correspondence of Methodist Ministers (Methodist Church Archives, London); Records of

187 Select Bibliography

New College, London; Quaker Digest of Marriages (Friends' House, London)
ROMAN CATHOLIC: Jesuit Letters and Notes, vol. IX, The Preston Mission (Jesuit Archives, Farm St Church, London)

(b) Regional
CHURCH OF ENGLAND: Articles of Enquiry for Episcopal Visitations (Cheshire RO)
ROMAN CATHOLIC: Archdiocese of Liverpool, Correspondence 1839–70 (LRO); Diocese of Leeds – Correspondence relating to Lancashire; Correspondence of Ushaw College (Ushaw College Library, Durham)

(c) Local
BOLTON: Records of Bank St Chapel (Bank St Chapel and the Unitarian College, Manchester); Moor Lane Unitarian Chapel Minutes 1821–37 (kept at Bank St Chapel, Bolton); Society of Friends, Edgworth, and Bolton Preparative Meeting Records (LRO)
PRESTON: Archdeacon's Visitation Book, 1839 (LRO); Records of Canon St Chapel; Records of Fishergate Chapel (Held at Canon St Chapel); Records of Grimshaw St Chapel; Records of Lune St and Orchard Methodist Circuit; Roman Catholic Episcopal Visitation Return for 1858 (LRO); Records of Preston Pleasant Retreat Lodge and Duke of York Lodge of Oddfellows (LRO); Society of Friends, Preston Preparative Meeting Records (LRO); Records of the Unitarian Chapel, Preston
STOCKPORT: Records of Greek St Baptist Chapel; Records of Hanover St Congregational Chapel (Stockport Library); Records of Mt Tabor Chapel (John Rylands Library, Manchester); Society of Friends, Stockport Preparative Meeting Records (Cheshire RO); Records of Stockport Sunday School (Stockport Library); Records of Stockport Unitarian Chapel (some in hands of chapel secretary, some now transferred to Stockport Library); Tiviot Dale Wesleyan Methodist Records (Stockport Library); Records of Woodford Methodist Chapel (Stockport Library)
BLACKBURN: An Appendix to Blackburn Academy Correspondence (Dr Williams's Library, London); Parish of Blackburn, Coucher Books (LRO); Parish of Blackburn, Marriage Registers, 1838, 1853, 1871 (on loan to Blackburn Library); Records of Blackburn Baptist Chapel; Records of Chapel St Chapel; Records of Mount St Presbyterian Chapel (Presbyterian Archives, London)

(4) Other manuscript sources

Records of Blackburn Grammar School (LRO); Records of National Reform League (Howell Collection, Bishopsgate Institute, London); Proceedings of Conferences of the National Union (Conservative Political Centre, London)

188 Select Bibliography

B *Printed sources*

(1) Newspapers

Bolton Chronicle
Bolton Evening News
Bolton Free Press
Bolton Guardian
Blackburn Alfred
Blackburn Mail
Blackburn Mercury
Blackburn Standard
Manchester Guardian
Nonconformist
North Cheshire Reformer (Stockport)
Northern Star
Preston Chronicle
Preston Guardian
Preston Pilot
Stockport Advertiser
Stockport Free Press
Stockport Mercury
Times

(2) Periodicals

Bolton Protestant Association Monthly Paper
British Temperance Advocate (Bolton)
Catholic Standard
Chartist Circular and Temperance Record
Conservative Bulwark (Bolton)
Dissenters' Magazine for Yorkshire and Lancashire
Millennial Star
Moral Reformer (Preston)
Preston Almanacs, 1835, 1836, 1844, 1847, 1854
Preston Temperance Advocate
Protestant Magazine
Reasoner and Theological Examiner
Revivalist

189 Select Bibliography

Staunch Teetotaller (Preston)
Struggle (Preston)
Voice of the People

(3) Parliamentary Sessional Papers

House of Commons
Census returns 1801–71
Factory Inquiry Commission Report 1834, XIX
Reports of Factory Inspectors 1842, XXII
Reports from the Commissioners on Handloom Weavers 1840, XXIII and XXIV
Report on the State of the Irish Poor in Great Britain 1836, XXXIV
Return of the Number of Parish Churches and Chapels; and Chapels of Ease of the Church of England, and of the Number of Places Not of the Church of England for the County of Lancaster 1830, XIX
Reports of Commissioners appointed to inquire into the Municipal Corporations of England and Wales especially 1835, XXIV, XXV, and 1837–8, XXXV
Report of Select Committee on Newspaper Stamps 1851, XVII
Report of Select Committee on Orange Institutions 1835, XVIII
Report on the Poor 1842, XXXV
Report on Religious Worship 1852–3, LXXXIX
Reports on Number of Voters 1836, XLIII, 1866, LVII, and 1867, LVI
House of Lords
Report from the Select Committee inquiring into Deficency of Means of Spiritual Instruction 1857–8, IX
Report from the Select Committee to inquire into the Operation of 13 and 14 Vic. c 99, for the better assessing and collecting the Poor Rates and Highway Rates in respect to Small Tenements and of the Act of the Last Session, cap. 43, to amend the Municipal Franchise in certain cases 1859, XIIX

(4) Directories and pollbooks

Bolton pollbooks for 1832, 1835, 1837, and 1841
Brown, J.W. *Commercial Directory of Preston, Fleetwood etc.* Preston 1860
Dod's Parliamentary Companion. London 1833–70
P. Mannex and Co. *History, Topography and Directory of the Borough of Preston.* Beverley 1851
– *History, Topography and Directory of Mid-Lancashire.* Preston 1854
Mitchell, C. & Co. *The Newspaper Press Directories.* London 1847–71

Preston pollbooks for 1831, 1835, 1837, and 1841
Stockport pollbook for 1847
Whittle, P.A. *Blackburn As It Is.* Preston 1852

(5) Memoirs and observations

Abram, W.A. 'Social Condition and Political Prospects of the Lancashire Workman,' *Fortnightly Review*, new series, IV, 1868, 426–41
Barlee, Ellen. *A Visit to Lancashire in December, 1862.* London 1863
Autobiographical Reminiscences of Sir John Bowring. London 1877
Citizen of the World (pseudo.). *Manchester and the Manchester People; with a Sketch of Bolton, Stockport, Ashton, Rochdale, and Oldham and Their Inhabitants.* Manchester 1843
Engels, Frederick. *The Condition of the Working Class in England in 1844.* London, reprint, 1969
Fletcher, Rev. Joseph, Jr, ed. *The Selected Works and Memoirs of the Late Reverend Joseph Fletcher.* London 1846
Grimshaw, Timothy. *The Cognitions and Opinions of Timothy Grimshaw, Esq., formerly of Dean.* Bolton 1838
Hewitson, A. *Our Churches and Chapels.* Preston 1869
Autobiography of Joseph Livesey. Preston nd
Livesey, Joseph. *Reminiscences of Early Teetotallism.* Preston nd
Morgan, J.M. *A Brief Account of the Stockport Sunday School.* London 1838
Richardson, H.M. *Reminiscences of Forty Years in Bolton.* Bolton 1835
Taylor, John. *Autobiography of a Lancashire Lawyer: Being the Life and Reminiscences of John Taylor, Attorney-at-Law and First Coroner of the Borough of Bolton.* Ed. James Clegg. Bolton 1883
Taylor, W. Cooke. *Notes of a Tour in the Manufacturing Districts of Lancashire.* London 1842
Ure, Andrew. *The Philosophy of Manufactures.* London 1835
Watts, John. *The Facts of the Cotton Famine.* London 1866

(6) Sermons and pamphlets

Ashworth, Henry. *An Inquiry into the Origin, Progress and Results of the Strike of the Operative Cotton Spinners of Preston.* Manchester 1838
– *Statistical Illustrations of the past and Present State of Lancashire.* Manchester 1842
– *The Preston Strike.* Manchester 1858
Axon, W.E.A. *The Special Results of Temperance in Blackburn.* Manchester and London 1886

191 Select Bibliography

Baker, Franklin. *A Lecture on the Evils of Church Establishments.* Bolton 1832
- *A Letter to the Rev. John Lyons, M.A. occasioned by a Sermon Preached in St. George's Church, Little Bolton, on Sunday, June 27, 1841.* London 1841
- *A Voice for Ireland.* London 1847
- *The Moral Tone of the Factory System Defended in a Letter to the Lord Bishop of Manchester.* London 1854
- *The Rise and Progress of Nonconformity in Bolton.* London 1854

Bingham, John. *Waiting For the Verdict on the Defence of the Church of Ireland.* Preston 1868

Chamberlain, Walter. *Parochial Centralization: or Remarks on the Present State of the Church of England in Provincial Towns.* Bolton 1850

Church Defence Institution. *List of Associations in Union Throughout the Country.* Westminster 1872

Cooper, Samuel. *A Treatise on Odd-Fellowship or an Address to Secret Orders in General.* Stockport 1833

Davies, G.H. *Address delivered before the Members of the Church Institution.* Preston 1863

Fallon, Rev. W.M. *Which is the Rock, Christ or St. Peter?* Preston 1852

Hamilton, J. *A Socialist Doctrine Scrutinized.* Preston 1844

Haslam, C.J. *A Defence of the Social Principles.* Manchester 1837
- *Who are the Infidels? Socialists or Christians.* Manchester 1840
- *Letters to the Clergy of all Denominations.* Manchester 1841
- *How to Make the People Virtuous.* Manchester 1858

Holyoake, G.J. *Secularism: A Religion.* London 1881

Hume, A. *The Church of England: the Home Missionary to the Poor.* London 1862

Address of Ernest Jones, Esq. in reply to Rev. W. Chamberlain's 'Remonstrance' to John Bright, Esq., M.P. Bolton 1867

Livesey, Joseph. *A Temperance Lecture based on the Teetotalism Principle.* Preston 1836
- *An Address to the Working Classes.* Preston 1836
- *A Letter to J. Wilson Patten, M.P.* Preston 1855
- *True Temperance Teachings.* Preston 1873
- *Lectures on the Properties of Malt Liquor.* Ipswich Temperance Tracts, no 133, nd

Newman, J.H. *Lectures on the Present Position of Catholics in England.* London 1851

Parr, Rev. J. Owen. *The Christian Rule in the Election of Members to serve in Parliament.* Preston 1852
- *A Lecture on Capital and Labour.* Preston 1860
- *The Recent Attacks on the Church of England.* Preston 1866

Preston Liberation Society. *The Liberation Society Vindicated.* Preston 1861

Preston Protestant Association. *Pamphlet No. 3. Report of Addresses by the Rev. Hugh*

192 Select Bibliography

McNeile and other gentlemen to petition Parliament for the Repeal of the Maynooth Endowment Act. Preston 1852
Stephens, J.R. *The Political Preacher.* London 1839
- *The Unemployed Operatives of Lancashire and Cheshire.* Oldham 1863
- *Co-operation.* Stalybridge 1866
- *The Altar, the Throne, and the Cottage.* Stalybridge 1868
List of Subscriptions to the Stockport Temperance Society. Stockport 1833
Sutcliffe, Rev. William. *A Correspondence between the Rev. William Sutcliffe, Curate of Farnsworth, near Bolton, and the Rev. John Bedford, Wesleyan Minister.* Bolton 1842
Taylor, Edward, *An Account of Orangeism: Key to the Late Religious Riots*, London 1868
Thelwall, Rev. A.S., ed. *Proceedings of the Anti-Maynooth Conference of 1845.* London 1845
Vicar of Preston. *Which are the Heretics?* Preston 1852
Verity, E.A. *Church Reform.* London 1854
Whitaker, Rev. T.D. *Church Property.* 2 vols. Blackburn 1837
Whitehead, Rev. E. *The Duty of Bearing One Another's Burdens.* Manchester 1774
Whittaker, Rev. J.W. *A Sermon preached at the Parish Church, August 4, 1839.* London 1840
- *The Romish Controversy, 1822-1854.* Blackburn nd

(7) Other printed primary materials

Bolton Biographical Cuttings (Bolton Library)
Annual Reports of the British and Foreign Bible Society
Annual Reports of the British and Foreign School Society
Catholic Poor School Committee Annual Reports, 1848-1870 (Westminster Cathedral Archives)
Early Mormon Tract Collection (LRO)
Election squibs - collections for Blackburn (Blackburn Library), Preston (LRO), and Stockport (Stockport Library)
Annual Reports of the Evangelical Alliance (Alliance Headquarters, London)
Place Collection of Newspaper Cuttings (BM)
Preston Town Council, Proceedings 1836-70 (Preston Library)
Consolidated Minutes of the Primitive Methodist Connexion (Methodist Church Archives, London)
Religious Statistics of Eight Towns in South Lancashire (Bruce Collection of Pamphlets, Congregational Union Library, London)
Annual Reports of the SPCK

193 Select Bibliography

Borough of Stockport Minutes of Council Meetings 1836-70 (Stockport Library)
Annual Reports of the Unitarian Home Missionary Board

II SECONDARY SOURCES

Abbatt, P. *Quaker Annals of Preston and the Flyde, 1653-1900*. Preston 1931
Abram, W.A. *A History of Blackburn, Town and Parish*. Blackburn 1877
- *A Century of Independency in Blackburn, 1778-1878*. Blackburn 1878
- *Blackburn Characters of a Past Generation*. Blackburn 1894
Ainsworth, A.J. 'Religion in the Working Class Community and the Evolution of Socialism in Late Nineteenth Century Lancashire: A Case of Working Class Consciousness,' *Histoire sociale / Social History*, X, 1977, 354-80
Aldridge, J. 'The Parliamentary Franchise at Preston and the Reform Act of 1832.' Honours BA thesis, Manchester University, 1948
Ambler, R.W. 'Non-Parochial Registers and the Local Historian,' *Local Historian*, X, 1972, 59-64
Anderson, Michael. *Household Structure and the Industrial Revolution: Mid-nineteenth Century Preston in Comparative Perspective*. Edinburgh 1969
- *Family Structure in Nineteenth Century Lancashire*. Cambridge 1971
Antliff, Rev. Samuel. *Historical Sketches of the Canon Street Independent Church*. Preston 1880
Arnold, R.A. *The History of the Cotton Famine*. London 1864
Aspin, C. *Lancashire: the First Industrial Society*. Preston 1969
Astle, William, ed. *History of Stockport*. Reprint, Wakefield 1972
Atkinson, Rev. J.A. *Memoir of the Reverend Canon Slade, Vicar of Bolton*. Bolton 1892
Axon, W.E.A. *Annals of Manchester*. London 1886
Ayerst, D.G. *The Manchester Guardian: Biography of a Newspaper*. Ithaca 1971
Baines, Edward. *History of the Cotton Manufacture in Great Britain*. London 1835
- *History of the County Palatine and Duchy of Lancaster*. London 1836
Baines, Thomas. *Lancashire and Cheshire, Past and Present*. 2 vols. London nd
Bank St Chapel, Bolton. *Bi-Centenary Commemorative, 1696-1896*. Manchester 1896
Banks, Thomas. *A Short Sketch of the Cotton Trade of Preston in the Last Sixty-Seven Years*. Preston nd
Barber, E. and P.H. Ditchfield. *Memorials of Old Cheshire*. London 1910
Barton, B.T. *Historical Gleanings of Bolton and District*. 3 vols. Bolton 1881
Bayley, Rev. Dr Jonathan. *New Church Worthies*. London 1884
Beck, G.A. *The English Catholics, 1850-1950*. London 1950
Bell, S.P., ed. *Victorian Lancashire*. Newton Abbot 1974

194 Select Bibliography

Binfield, Clyde. *So Down to Prayers: Studies in English Nonconformity 1780–1920*. London 1977

Birch, A.H., ed. *Small Town Politics: a Study of Political Life in Glossop*. Oxford 1959

Bottomore, T.B. *Elites and Society*. London 1964

Boyson, Rhodes. *The Ashworth Cotton Enterprise: the Rise and Fall of a Family Firm, 1818–1880*. London 1970

Briggs, Asa. 'The Background of the Parliamentary Reform Movement in Three English Towns,' *Cambridge Historical Journal*, x, 1952, 293–317

– ed. *Chartist Studies*. London 1965

Brimelow, W. *Political and Parliamentary History of Bolton*. Bolton 1882

Burke, T. *Catholic History of Liverpool*. Liverpool 1910

Bythell, Duncan. *The Handloom Weavers: a Study in the English Cotton Industry during the Industrial Revolution*. Cambridge 1969

Cahill, G.A. 'Irish Catholicism and English Toryism,' *Review of Politics*, xix, 1957, 62–76

Carnall, Geoffrey. 'Dickens, Mrs. Gaskell, and the Preston Strike,' *Victorian Studies*, viii, 1964, 31–48

Carter, G.D. 'Affairs Overseas and the Cotton Operatives of Bolton.' Honours BA thesis, Leeds University, 1963

Cartwell, Henry. *The Preston Churches and Sunday Schools*. Preston 1892

Chadwick, Owen. *The Victorian Church*. Parts i and ii. London 1966 and 1970

Challinor, Raymond. *The Lancashire and Cheshire Miners*. Newcastle upon Tyne 1972

Chaloner, W.H. *The Skilled Artisans during the Industrial Revolution*. London 1969

Clark, G. Kitson. 'Hunger and Politics in 1842,' *Journal of Modern History*, xxv, 1953, 355–74

– *The Making of Victorian England*. London 1962

– *Churchmen and the Condition of England, 1832–1885*. London 1973

– 'The Leeds Elite,' *University of Leeds Review*, xvii, 1975, 232–58

Clarke, P.F. *Lancashire and the New Liberalism*. Cambridge 1971

Clay, Rev. Walter L. *The Prison Chaplain: a Memoir of the Rev. John Clay, B.D., Late Chaplain of the Preston Gaol*. Cambridge 1861

Clegg, James. *Annals of Bolton: History, Chronology and Politics, Parliamentary and Municipal Poll*. Bolton 1888

Clemesha, H.W. *A Bibliography of the History of Preston in Amounderness*. Preston 1923

Cottrell, Hannah. *Gate Pike: the Story of Eighty Years' Methodism, 1843–1923*. Bolton 1924

Crossick, Geoffrey. *An Artisan Elite in Victorian Society: Kentish London 1840–1880*. London and Totowa, NJ 1978

195 Select Bibliography

Currie, R., A. Gilbert, and Lee Horsley, eds. *Churches and Churchgoers: Patterns of Church Growth in the British Isles since 1700.* Oxford 1977
Dahrendorf, Ralf. *Class and Class Conflict in Industrial Society.* Stanford 1957
Daleyne, James. *History of the Bolton New Church Society from 1781 to 1888.* London 1888
Davies, E.T. *Religion in the Industrial Revolution in South Wales.* Cardiff 1965
Dearden, J. *A Brief History of the Commencement and Success of Tee-Totalism.* Preston nd
Denvir, J. *The Irish in Britain.* London 1892
Dobson, William. *Preston Municipal Elections, from 1835-1862.* Preston 1862
- *History of the Parliamentary Representation of Preston.* Preston 1868
Durham, W. *Chronological Notes of Prominent Events in the Town and Parish of Blackburn.* Blackburn 1861
Dyos, H.J., ed. *The Study of Urban History.* London 1968
- and M. Wolff, eds. *The Victorian City: Images and Realities.* 2 vols. London and Boston 1973
Ellison, James. *Dawn of Tee-Totalism.* Preston 1932
Ellison, Mary. *Support for Secession: Lancashire and the American Civil War.* Chicago 1973
Faulkner, H. *Chartism and the Churches.* New York 1916
Fishergate Baptist Church. *Centenary Celebrations.* Preston 1958
Fishwick, Henry. *The History of the Parish of Preston in Amounderness.* Rochdale 1900
Foster, J.O. *Class Struggle and the Industrial Revolution.* London 1974
Fraser, Derek. *Urban Politics in Victorian England: the Structure of Politics in Victorian Cities.* Leicester 1976
Gadian, D.S. 'Class Consciousness in Oldham and other North-West Industrial Towns, 1830-1850,' *Historical Journal,* XXI, 1978, 161-72
Garnett, R.G. *Cooperation and the Owenite Socialist Communities in Britain, 1825-1845.* Manchester 1972
Gash, Norman. *Reaction and Reconstruction in English Politics, 1832-1852.* Oxford 1965
Gay, J.D. *The Geography of Religion in England.* London 1971
Gilbert, A.D. *Religion and Society in Industrial England: Church, Chapel and Social Change, 1740-1914.* London and New York 1976
Giles, Phyllis M. 'The Economic and Social Development of Stockport 1815-1836.' MA thesis, Manchester University, 1950
- *The Felt-hatting Industry, c. 1500-1850, with Particular Reference to Lancashire and Cheshire.* Reprint, Manchester 1950
Gosden, P.H.J.H. *The Friendly Societies in England, 1815-1875.* Manchester 1961

Select Bibliography

Gough, T.W. *Stockport Great Moor Co-operative Society Ltd., 1831-1931.* Stockport 1931

Gowland, D.A. *Methodist Secessions: the Origins of Free Methodism in Three Lancashire Towns.* Chetham Society Remains, XXVI. Manchester 1979

Greek St Baptist Church. *A Centenary of Christian Service, 1838-1938: a Short History of the Baptist Cause in Stockport.* Stockport 1938

Halley, Robert. *Lancashire: its Puritanism and Nonconformity.* Manchester 1872

Hamer, Harold. *Bolton, 1838-1938.* Bolton 1938

Hammond, J.L. and B. *The Age of the Chartists, 1832-1854.* London 1930

Hanham, H.J. *Elections and Party Management: Politics in the Time of Disraeli and Gladstone.* London 1959

Hardwick, Charles. *History of the Borough of Preston.* Preston 1857

– *History of the Preston Strikes and Lockouts.* London nd

Harrison, B. *Drink and the Victorians: the Temperance Question in England, 1815-1872.* London 1971

Harrison, J.F.C. *Robert Owen and the Owenites in Britain and America.* London 1969

Heginbotham, Henry. *Stockport: Ancient and Modern.* 2 vols. London 1892

Henderson, W.O. *The Lancashire Cotton Famine, 1861-1865.* Manchester 1934

Hennock, E.P. *Fit and Proper Persons: Ideal and Reality in Nineteenth-Century Urban Government.* London 1973

Henriques, Ursala. *Religious Toleration in England 1787-1833.* London and Toronto 1961

Herford, R.T. and E.D.P. Evans, eds. *Historical Sketch of the North and East Lancashire Unitarian Mission, and its Affiliated Churches, 1859-1909.* Bury 1909

Hewitson, Anthony. *Preston Town Council, 1835-70.* Preston 1870

– *History of Preston in the County of Lancaster, A.D. 705-1883.* Preston 1883

– *Preston Court Leet Records: Extracts and Notes.* Preston 1905

Hickey, J. *Urban Catholics: Urban Catholicism in England and Wales from 1829 to the Present Day.* London 1967

Hill, R.L. *Toryism and the People, 1832-1846.* London 1929

Hilton, J.D. *A Brief History of James Hayes Roper, Temperance Reformer, 1820-1897.* London 1898

Hindmarsh, Robert. *Rise and Progress of the New Jerusalem Church in England, America and Other Parts.* London 1861

Hobsbawm, E.J. *Labouring Men: Studies in the History of Labour.* London 1964

Hollis, Patricia, ed. *Pressure from without in Early Victorian England.* New York 1974

Holt, Raymond V. *The Unitarian Contribution to Social Progress in England.* London 1938

Hunt, E.A. *Regional Wage Variations in Britain 1850-1914.* London 1973

Select Bibliography

Hunt, Stella. 'The Radical Party in Preston, 1815-1832.' Honours BA thesis, Birmingham University, 1950
Hunter, Rev. Frederick. *Methodism in Stockport and District.* Stockport 1951
Isichei, E. *Victorian Quakers.* London 1970
Johnston, James. *Mawdsley Street Congregational Chapel, Bolton-Le-Moors, 1808-1908: a Notable Record.* London 1908
Johnstone, Rev. T.B. *The Religious History of Bolton.* Bolton 1887
Jones, Rev. J.I. *A Brief History of the Unitarian Church in Accrington from 1859 to 1909.* Accrington 1909
Joyce, Patrick. 'The Factory Politics of Lancashire in the Later Nineteenth Century,' *Historical Journal*, XVIII, 1975, 525-53
- *Work, Society, and Politics: the Culture of the Factory in Later Victorian England.* Brighton and New Brunswick 1980
Katz, M.B. 'Occupational Classification in History,' *Journal of Interdisciplinary History*, III, 1972, 63-88
Keith-Lucas, Bryan. *The English Local Government Franchise.* Oxford 1952
Kent, John. 'The Role of Religion in the Cultural Structure of the Later Victorian City,' *Transactions of the Royal Historical Society,* 5th series, XXIII, 1973, 153-73
Kenyon, Keith. *St. Thomas's Church: Blackburn Centenary, 1865 to 1965.* Blackburn 1965
Laqueur, Thomas W. *Religion and Respectability: Sunday Schools and Working Class Culture, 1780-1850.* New Haven 1976
Little, C.D. *The History and Romance of our Mother Sunday School: 150 Years of Bolton Methodism.* Bolton 1935
Lockley, W.H. *The Story of the United Methodist Church: a Series of Lectures.* Stockport 1909
Lowe, J.C. 'The Tory Triumph of 1868 in Blackburn and in Lancashire,' *Historical Journal*, XVI, 1973, 733-48
Machin, G.I.T. *Politics and the Churches in Great Britain, 1832-1868.* Oxford 1977
MacLaren, A.A. *Religion and Social Class: the Disruptive Years in Aberdeen.* London and Boston 1974
Marshall, J.D. *The Old Poor Law, 1795-1834.* London 1968
Martin, David. *A Sociology of English Religion.* London 1967
Mathias, Peter. 'The Brewing Industry, Temperance and Politics,' *Historical Journal*, I, 1958, 97-113
McCord, Norman. *The Anti-Corn Law League, 1838-1846.* London 1958
McLellan, N.J. 'Chartism and the Churches with Special Reference to Lancashire.' PHD thesis, Edinburgh University, 1947
McLeod, Hugh. *Class and Religion in the Late Victorian City.* London and Hamden, CT 1974

Meacham, Standish. 'The Church in the Victorian City,' *Victorian Studies*, II, 1968, 359-78
Middleton, Thomas. *The History of Hyde and its Neighbourhood.* Hyde 1932
Midwinter, Eric C. *Social Administration in Lancashire, 1830-1860: Poor Law, Public Health and Police.* Manchester 1969
Miller, G.C. *Bygone Blackburn.* Blackburn 1950
- *Blackburn: the Evolution of a Cotton Town.* Blackburn 1951
- *Blackburn Worthies of Yesterday.* Blackburn 1959
Moore, D.C. *The Politics of Deference: a Study of the Mid-Nineteenth Century English Political System.* Hassocks and New York 1976
Murphy, James. *The Religious Problem in English Education: The Crucial Experiment.* Liverpool 1959
Musson, A.E. 'The First Daily Newspapers in Lancashire,' *Transactions of the Lancashire and Cheshire Antiquarian Society*, LXV, 1956, 104-31
- and John Foster. 'Discussion: Class Struggle and the Labour Aristocracy, 1830-60,' *Social History*, III, 1976, 355-66
Orr, J.E. *The Second Evangelical Awakening.* London 1949
Neale, R.S. *Class and Ideology in the Nineteenth Century.* London 1972
Neibuhr, Richard. *The Social Sources of Denominationalism.* New York 1929
Nelson, G.K. *Spiritualism and Society.* London 1969
Newton, R. *Victorian Exeter.* Leicester 1968
Nightingale, Rev. B. *Lancashire Nonconformity.* Preston 1890
- *Early Stages of the Quaker Movement in Lancashire.* London 1921
Norman. E.R. *Anti-Catholicism in Victorian England.* London 1968
- *Church and Society in England 1770-1970: an Historical Study.* London 1976
Norris, G.M. 'The Nonconformist Chapel and the Local Community,' *Local Historian*, X, 1973, 253-8
Patterson, A. Temple. *Radical Leicester: a History of Leicester, 1780-1850.* Leicester 1954
Paul, William. *A History of the Origin and Progress of Operative Conservative Societies.* Leeds 1838
Peaples, F.W. *History of the Great and Little Bolton Co-operative Society Ltd.* Bolton 1909
- *History of St. George's Road Congregational Church (Bolton) and its Connections.* Bolton 1913
- *History of the Educational Department of the Bolton Co-operative Society Ltd., 1861-1914.* Manchester 1914
Pearce, John. *The Life and Teachings of Joseph Livesey.* Preston 1887
Pelling, Henry. *A History of British Trade Unionism.* London 1963

Select Bibliography

- *Social Geography of British Elections, 1885-1910.* London 1967
- *Popular Politics and Society in Late Victorian Britain.* London 1968

Perkin, Harold. *The Origins of Modern English Society, 1780-1880.* London and Toronto 1969

Perry, Herbert E. 'Historical Notes on the Stockport Unitarian Chapel,' *Transactions of the Unitarian Historical Society*, III, 1923-6, 148-52

Phillips, Paul T. 'The Religious Side of Victorian Bath, 1830-1870,' *Histoire sociale / Social History*, VI, 1973, 224-40

- 'James Fraser, Bishop of All the Denominations,' in P.T. Phillips, ed., *The View from the Pulpit.* Toronto 1978
- 'Religion and Society in the Cloth Region of Wiltshire, c. 1830-1870,' *Journal of Religious History*, XI, 1980, 95-110

Pickering, W.S.F. 'The 1851 Religious Census - a Useless Experiment?' *British Journal of Sociology*, XVIII, 1967, 382-407

Pilkington, W. *The Makers of Wesleyan Methodism in Preston and the Relation to the Temperance and Teetotal Movements.* Preston 1890

Piva, Michael. 'The Aristocracy of the English Working Class: Help for an Historical Debate in Difficulties,' *Histoire sociale / Social History*, VII, 1974, 270-92

Pollard, Sidney. *A History of Labour in Sheffield.* Liverpool 1959

- *The Genesis of Modern Management: a Study of the Industrial Revolution in Great Britain.* London 1965

Powell, W.R. 'Sources for the History of Protestant Non-conformist Churches in England,' *Bulletin of the Institute of Historical Research*, XXV, 1952, 213-27

Powicke, F.J. *A History of the Cheshire County Union of Congregational Churches, 1808-1906.* Manchester 1907

Procter, W. 'Poor Law Administration in the Preston Union, 1838-48,' *Transactions of the Historic Society of Lancashire and Cheshire*, CXVII, 1966, 145-66

Prest, John. *The Industrial Revolution in Coventry.* Oxford 1960

Read, Donald. *The English Provinces, 1760-1960: a Study in Influence.* London 1964

Rimmer, W.G. *Marshalls of Leeds: Flax-spinners, 1788-1886.* Cambridge 1960

Robicon, F.J. *A History of the Lancashire Congregational Union, 1808-1956.* Manchester 1956

Rodgers, H.B. 'The Lancashire Cotton Industry in 1840,' *Institute of British Geographers, Transactions and Papers*, XXVIII, 1960, 135-53

Rose, A.G. 'The Plug Riots of 1842 in Lancashire and Cheshire,' *Transactions of the Lancashire and Cheshire Antiquarian Society*, LXVIII, 1957, 83-104

Royle, E. *British Infidels: The Origins of the British Secularist Movement, 1791-1866.* Manchester 1974

Salter, F.R. 'Political Nonconformity in the Eighteen-Thirties,' *Transactions of the Royal Historical Society*, 5th series, III, 1953, 125-43

- *Dissenters and Public Affairs in Mid-Victorian England*. Friends of Dr Williams's Library Occasional Papers, no 21. London 1967
Sanderson, Michael. 'Education and the Factory in Industrial Lancashire, 1780–1840,' *Economic History Review*, 2nd series, XX, 1967, 266–79
Saxelby, C.H., ed. *Bolton Survey*. Bolton 1953
Scholes, J.C. *Memoir of the Reverend Edward Whitehead, M.A., Vicar of Bolton from 1737 to 1789*. Bolton 1889.
- *History of Bolton*. Bolton 1892
Sellers, I. 'Nonconformist Attitudes in later 19th century Liverpool,' *Transactions of the Historic Society of Lancashire and Cheshire*, XCIV, 1962, 215–39
Senior, H. *Orangeism in Ireland and Britain 1795–1836*. London and Toronto 1966
Slater, George. *Chronicles of Lives and Religion in Cheshire and Elsewhere*. London 1891
Smelser, Neil J. *Social Change in the Industrial Revolution: an Application of Theory to the Lancashire Cotton Industry, 1770–1840*. London 1959
Smith, F.B. 'The Atheist Mission, 1840–1900,' in R. Robson, ed., *Ideas and Institutions of Victorian England*. London 1967
Smith, Janet. 'The Local Records of Nonconformity,' *Local Historian*, VIII, 1968, 131–43
Smith, Rev. Robert. *History of Catholicity in Blackburn and the Neighbourhood*. Blackburn nd
Stearns, Peter N. 'Measuring the Evolution of Strike Movements,' *International Review of Social History*, XIX, 1974, 16–27
Steele, E.D. 'Leeds and Victorian Politics,' *University of Leeds Review*, XVII, 1975, 259–85
Sykes, R.A. 'Some Aspects of Working Class Consciousness in Oldham, 1830–1842,' *Historical Journal*, XXIII, 1980, 167–79
Symonds, W. *Forty Rectors of Stockport: an Obituary*. Stockport 1902
Taylor, A.J. 'Concentration and Specialization in the Lancashire Cotton Industry, 1825–1850,' *Economic History Review*, 2nd series, I, 1949, 114–22
Taylor, H.A. 'Politics in Famine-Stricken Preston,' *Transactions of the Historic Society of Lancashire and Cheshire*, CVII, 1956, 121–39
Tholfsen, Trygve R. *Working Class Radicalism in Mid-Victorian England*. New York 1977
Thomis, Malcolm. *The Luddites: Machine-Breaking in Regency England*. London 1970
Thompson, E.P. *The Making of the English Working Class*. London 1963
Troeltsch, Ernst. *The Social Teachings of the Christian Churches*. London 1931
Tylecote, M. *The Mechanics' Institute of Lancashire and Cheshire before 1851*. Manchester 1957

Select Bibliography

Tyrrell, A. 'Class Consciousness in Early Victorian Britain: Samuel Smiles, Leeds Politics and the Self-Help Creed,' *Journal of British Studies*, IX, 1970, 102–25

Unwin, Benjamin. *Samuel Oldknow and the Arkwrights: the Industrial Revolution at Stockport and Marple.* Manchester 1924

Varley, Benjamin. *The History of Stockport Grammar School.* Manchester 1946

Victoria County Histories of Lancashire. 8 vols. London 1906–14

Vincent, J.R. 'The Electoral Sociology of Rochdale,' *Economic History Review*, 2nd series, XVI, 1963, 76–90

– *The Formation of the Liberal Party, 1857–1868.* London 1966

– *Pollbooks: How Victorians Voted.* Cambridge 1967

– 'The Second Reform Act in Lancashire,' *Historical Journal*, XI, 1968, 84–94

Wade, R. *The Rise of Nonconformity in Manchester.* Manchester 1880

Walker, R.B. 'Religious Changes in Cheshire, 1750–1850,' *Journal of Ecclesiastical History*, XVII, 1966, 77–94

– 'Religious Changes in Liverpool in the Nineteenth Century,' *Journal of Ecclesiastical History*, XIX, 1968, 195–211

– 'The Growth of Wesleyan Methodism in Victorian England and Wales,' *Journal of Ecclesiastical History*, XXIV, 1973, 267–84

Ward, Rev. John, *The Rise and Progress of Wesleyan methodism in Blackburn.* Blackburn 1871

Ward, W.R. 'The Cost of Establishment: Some Reflections on Church Building in Manchester,' in C.J. Cuming, ed., *Studies in Church History*, III. London 1966

– *Religion and Society in England, 1790–1850.* London 1972

Wearmouth, R.F. *Methodism and the Working Class Movements of England, 1800–1850.* London 1937

Welsh, Edwin. 'Nonconformist Registers,' *Journal of the Society of Archivists*, II, 1964, 411–17

Werly, J.M. 'The Irish in Manchester, 1832–49,' *Irish Historical Studies*, XVIII, 1973, 345–58

Wheeler, L.M. 'Forty Years of a Ministers' Fraternal,' *Congregational Quarterly*, XVIII, 1940, 300–6

Whitney, W.T. *The Baptist Churches of North-West England.* London 1913

Whittle, P. *The History of the Borough of Preston in the County Palatine of Lancaster.* Preston 1837

Wickham, E.R. *Church and People in an Industrial City.* London 1957

Wickwar, W.H. *The Struggle for the Freedom of the Press, 1819–1832.* London 1928

Wilson, Bryan, ed. *Patterns of Sectarianism: Organization and Ideology in Social and Religious Movements.* London 1967

Index

Abram, W.A. 5, 129
Accrington 117, 118
Ainsworth, A.J. 147n3
Aldridge, James 165n128
Anderson, Michael 158n10
Anderton, Henry 49, 55
anti-Catholicism 25, 26, 32, 33, 57, 75, 89-90, 97, 102, 106, 122
Anti-Corn Law League 34-5, 74-5
anti-Mormon tracts 54, 162n82
Ashworth, Henry 6, 13, 15, 26, 34, 70, 71, 151nn18, 19, 166n144

Baker, Franklin 13, 33, 157n94
Bank Street Chapel, Bolton 12-15, 157n95
Baptists 47, 50, 79-80, 117
Barlee, Ellen 134
Bath 142, 181n12
Best, Geoffrey 16, 140
Birmingham 121, 140, 141, 172n87, 181n6
Blackburn 7, 68, 89, 107-39, 144, 174-80; Anglican and Nonconformist elites 107, 109, 112-15, 116, 117, 120, 122-5, 126-8, 133, 136; anti-Irish attitudes 135; Church question 119-20; class tension 107, 110-11, 114-15, 120, 122, 134-5; economic development 107-9; education 115, 120-2; election of 1868 138; electorate 124-5, 139; factory owners 108-9, 111, 112-14, 117, 123, 124, 127, 136, 138, 180nn102, 112; friendly societies 119; gentry 136, 176n33; Improvement Acts of 1841 and 1847 125; incorporation 125-6; municipal politics 122-3, 125-35; number and growth of denominations 111-12, 116; old mercantile families 107-9; parliamentary politics 135-9; parochial centralization 112, 175 n24; Poor Law Union 124, 134, 135; pre-Reform government 122-4, 125; Puritan regime 128-32; social background of Baptists 117, Churchmen 112-15, 120, 177n58, Congregationalists 115-16, Methodists 117, Mormons 118, Presbyterians 116-17, Roman Catholics 118, Swedenborgians 118; social background of Conservatives and Liberals 122, 125, 126-39; social conditions 114, 123; tradesmen/shopkeepers 107, 109-10, 117-18, 122, 124, 125, 128, 132-3, 138, 139; Watch

204 Index

Committee 129, 131, 134; working class 109, 110-11, 114-15, 117, 118-19, 133-5, 139
Blackburn Academy 115, 176n36
Blackburn Gazette 136
Blackburn Relief Committee 134
Blackburn Standard 136
Blackburn Times 134
Bolton 7, 10-36, 47, 69, 89, 98, 105, 111, 122, 149-57; Anglican and Nonconformist elites 11-12, 14, 16-17, 19-23, 27-8, 29, 30-2, 35; anti-Irish attitudes 17, 26, 32, 156n83; Civil War 10; class tension 23-4, 29, 35; Courts Leet 27, 28, 155n69; economic development 22, 23; education 19, 25-6; factory owners 19-23, 150n14; 'gas and water' socialism 30; improvement trustees 28, 155n68; incorporation 27-8; municipal politics 27-33; number and growth of denominations 10-12, 15-17, 18, 19-22, 25; parliamentary politics 32-6; Poor Law Union 32-3; population increase 149n1; River Weaver bill 30; social background of Churchmen 11-12, Congregationalists 15, Methodists 15-16, Mormons 17-18, Quakers 13-14, Roman Catholics 17, Secularists 18-19, Swedenborgians 18, 152n37, Unitarians 12-15; social background of Liberals and Conservatives 30-3, 35; social mobility 23-4, 151n19; social problems 29, 30; town hall 30; tradesmen/shopkeepers 12-13, 28, 35, 150n13; working class 16-18, 23-5, 29, 150n16, 152n44
Bolton Chronicle 34, 156n93
Bolton Evening News 34
Bolton Hesperus Literary and Christian Association 25

Bolton Massacre 10
Bowen, Desmond 5
Bowring, John 135-7
Boyle, James 128, 179n82
Boyson, Rhodes 151n18
Bradford 141
Briggs, Asa 141
Bristol 142
building trade 83-4
Bythell, Duncan 73

Calvinism 56, 80
Canon Street Chapel, Preston 48, 50, 51
Catholic emancipation 25, 33, 111, 122
Census of Places of Worship not of the Church of England, 1829 20, 41, 76, 112
Census of Religious Worship, 1851 6, 21, 41-2, 76, 113, 159n28, 183
centralism 32, 59, 81
Chadwick, Owen 5
Chamberlain, Walter 11, 112, 150n6
chapel migration 50-1
Chapel Street Chapel, Blackburn 116
Chartism 24, 29, 68, 74-5, 78, 87, 99, 110-11, 115, 169n26
Chorley 120
Church and King clubs 33
Church building commissioners 75
Church Institutes 25, 56, 86, 171n57
Church of England 4, 6; in Blackburn 109, 112-15, 119-21; in Bolton 10-12, 22-3, 28; in Preston 39-46, 57-8; in Stockport 75-8, 90; in other areas 140-4
Church of Ireland question 32, 135, 136
church rates 25, 56, 75, 85, 120, 137, 170n56, 177n55
churches: general social position and role 5-7; attendance 6, 19; doctrinal

conflict 4, 25, 51; working classes 5–7, 43, 50, 78, 113–15; general growth in Blackburn, Bolton, Preston, and Stockport 145 (appendix)
'Circle,' The 13, 150n15
Clark, G. Kitson 5, 25, 74
Clarke, P.F. 4, 36
class: definition of 149n17
class conflict 6–9, 52–3, 64–5, 68–71, 73–5, 89–90, 110–11, 139; causes of 7–9, 38; measurement of 8; *see also* entries for Blackburn, Bolton, Preston, and Stockport
Clay, John 38
Cobbett, William 64, 135, 178n70
Cobden, Richard 19, 105, 134
Communism 14, 70
Congregationalism 15, 48, 50, 79, 115–16
Conservative operative associations 32, 33, 92, 138, 180n109
Conservative party: and the Church 5, 9, 25, 27, 29–30, 32–5, 57–8, 60–1, 62–3, 66, 67, 78, 94–6, 97, 99–106, 122–39, 140–4; ideals 30, 32–3, 92, 94, 97–9, 143; leadership and organization 27, 39–40, 92, 99, 132, 138, 140; newspapers 66, 105, 173n110; and Orangeism 32, 34, 67, 135, 141; *see also* Conservative operative associations and entries for Blackburn, Bolton, Preston, and Stockport
co-operation 18–19, 70, 85
Coppock, Henry 80–1, 88, 92, 93, 94, 99, 103, 105, 172n83
Coppock, James 81, 104, 170n43
cotton industry: labour supply 23, 38, 73, 108, 158n11; millowners 11, 19, 23, 31–2, 38–40, 64, 90, 91, 101–2, 107–9, 113–14, 117, 127, 132, 136, 137, 159n25, 180n102; specialization in 7,

23, 38, 72–3, 158n10; wages 64, 70–1, 110–11, 167n148; *see also* handloom weavers *and* entries for Blackburn, Bolton, Preston, and Stockport
Cotton Famine 16, 19, 36, 67, 79, 103, 111, 117, 120–1, 133–4, 175n22
Courts Leet 27, 28, 91, 123, 155n69, 163n103
Coventry 142
Crossick, Geoffrey 8
'crossing-over' 56

Darbishire, C.J. 27, 28, 32, 33, 155nn72, 82
Davison, William Hope 15, 34
Dewhurst, George 109–10, 117, 119, 120, 122, 126, 128, 133, 135–6, 138, 139, 174n12
Disestablishment 67, 153n56, 177n60
Dissent *see* Nonconformity

Eccles, William 109
Ecclesiastical Titles Act 66, 89
Education Act of 1870 3, 26, 56–7, 86, 121
educational disputes 26, 56–7, 86–7, 103, 120–2
elections: corruption at 33, 65, 99, 136–7, 138, 156n86, 164n118, 180n112; municipal 29, 30–2, 58, 60, 61, 99, 126–7, 135; parliamentary 17, 34–5, 64–6, 103–5, 135–8; poor law unions 32–3, 59, 91, 124; school boards 26, 86; voting behaviour 34–5, 105–6, 138, 164n117, 165n124; *see also* franchise
elites, theory of 9, 22–3, 149n19, 150n4, 155n75
embourgeoisement 8, 68
Engels, Frederick 6, 57
Evangelical revivals 7, 16, 25

Exeter 142

factory paternalism 8, 19–23, 108–9
Feilden family 123, 124, 137
Finney, Charles G. 16
Foster, John 7, 16, 23, 57, 148n14
franchise: parliamentary 5, 64–5, 68, 155n79, 164nn115, 116, 121, 173n103; municipal 30, 154n61, 155n79, 164n15, 173n103
Fraser, Derek 125, 155n75, 156n85
Fraser, James 3, 4, 140, 147n1
free trade 33, 66, 67, 105, 137, 165n128, 180n112

gas and water socialism *see* municipal socialism
gentry *see* landed interest
Gilbert, A.D. 4, 6, 183
Gill, Conrad 141, 143
Glossop 6
gospel of civic improvement 31
grammar schools 56, 88–9

handloom weavers 38, 72–3, 74, 108, 109–10, 135, 167n4, 174nn1, 16
Hanham, H.J. 97, 98, 143, 159n25
Hanover Congregational Chapel, Stockport 79
Hanover Street Congregational Chapel, Bolton 25
Hanson, Joseph 64, 166n137
Harrison, Brian 162nn85, 88
Harrison, Joseph 79, 88
Hargreaves' spinning jenny 108
hat manufacturing 73, 168n18
Head, Sir George 49
Heald, James 78, 99, 172n83
Helmstadter, R.J. 140, 184
Hennock, E.P. 141, 142

Hewitson, Anthony (pseudo. 'Atticus') 43–6, 50–1
Heywood, Robert 28, 30, 155n76
Holyoake, George Jacob 36, 84, 133
Hook, W.F. 142
Hoole, William 115, 129, 179n80
Hornby, William Henry 113, 126, 127, 132, 137, 179n78
Horrocks, John 38, 39, 41, 47, 64, 157n6, 159nn17, 20
Howard, Lord Edward 67, 166n133
Hume, Abraham 50, 161n59
Hunt, Henry ('Orator') 64–5

improvement commissioners 28, 38, 61, 90, 122–3, 124–6
Independency *see* Congregationalism
industrial suburbs 23, 109
Inglis, K.S. 5
Irish: political activities 32, 34, 67, 102, 141; relations with English 17, 26, 32, 57, 61, 84, 89–90, 102, 135; Roman Catholic church 17, 52, 83, 89, 118; social conditions 17, 52, 83–4, 89, 170nn48, 49; *see also* anti-Catholicism, Liberal party, *and* entries for Blackburn, Bolton, Preston, and Stockport

Joyce, Patrick 19–20, 109, 116, 132, 153n46

labour aristocracy 8, 13, 149n17
labour relations 13–14, 72, 74, 91, 110–11, 120
landed interest 30, 37, 39–40, 52, 57–8, 64, 91, 136, 159n25
Langley, John Baxter 105, 173n107
Laqueur, T.W. 6, 87
Leeds 22, 120, 141, 142, 172n87
Leicester 39, 142, 144

Liberal party: ideals 30, 34, 58, 61, 66, 93, 97–8, 131–2, 135; leadership and organization 27, 28, 53, 59, 66, 91–2, 98, 133, 134, 135–6, 138–9; newspapers 66, 105; and Nonconformity 5, 9, 25, 27, 28–29, 30–5, 56, 59–60, 61, 62–3, 66, 91–4, 96–8, 102–5, 128–32, 133, 135, 137–9, 140–4; and Roman Catholicism 5, 33–4, 66–7, 102, 105, 141; *see also* Blackburn, Bolton, Preston, and Stockport

Liberator 22–3
literary and philosophical societies 178n64
Liverpool 140, 141
Livesey, Joseph 47, 55, 56, 58, 61, 66, 160n49, 162nn89, 94, 163nn97, 107, 112, 165n131
localism 32, 59, 66, 80–1, 91, 97–8, 101, 103, 156n85
Lomax, James 105
London 59, 140
Lowe, J.C. 6, 132, 138
lower middle class *see* entries for tradesmen/shopkeepers in Blackburn, Bolton, Preston, and Stockport
Luddism 24, 74, 110, 153n52, 168n14

MacLaren, A.A. 19
McLeod, Hugh 141
Manchester 7, 74, 90, 140, 167n1, 170n49, 181n5
Mann, Horace 21
Marshall, J.D. 165n128, 180n102
Marsland, Henry 72, 92, 104
Marx, Karl 6
Mayer, Joseph 86–7
mechanics' institutes 17, 56, 86, 120, 121, 152n31
Melly, George 65, 66, 67

merchants 23, 37, 107, 108, 126, 140
Methodism 4, 5, 7, 16–17, 24, 49, 51, 78–9, 86–7, 117, 137–8, 142
middle-class ethos 54
Mormonism 17, 53–4, 84, 118
municipal reform 58, 90–2, 163n103
municipal socialism 30, 96, 98
Murphy, William 32, 135, 156n83

National Society 11, 42, 114, 115, 123, 184
New Church 18, 54, 84, 144
Newman, John Henry 97
Newton, Robert 142
Nonconformist conscience 61, 96, 128–31
Nonconformity 4, 9; governing and financing of chapels 13, 16–17, 47–8, 50–1, 80–3, 109, 116; in Blackburn 107, 109, 114, 115–17, 127–8, 144; in Bolton 12–17, 22–3, 27–8; in Preston 39–40, 46–51, 53, 58; in Stockport 78–83, 90; in other places 140–4
North Cheshire Reformer 105
Nottingham 158n16

Oastler, Richard 110
Oddfellows 85
Oldham 7, 16, 23
Oldknow, Samuel 72, 79
Orangeism 32, 34, 57, 90, 102, 105, 119, 122, 156nn83, 88, 177n54
Owenism 18, 84, 119

Papal Aggression 34, 57, 89
Park Road Chapel, Blackburn 116
parochial centralization 11, 112, 175n24
Parr, Owen 43, 56, 57, 67, 159n29
Patterson, A. Temple 39, 142, 144
Perkin, Harold 6, 36, 148n12

208 Index

philanthropy 16-17, 29, 42, 46, 52, 74, 77, 79, 134
Pilkington, James 109, 116, 124, 126, 132-3, 136, 137
police commissioners *see* improvement commissioners
political corruption *see* elections
poor law unions 32, 59, 93, 124, 172n80
Power, Alfred 124, 178n72
Presbyterianism 116-17, 141
Prescot, Charles 78, 79, 168nn23, 24, 170n48
Prest, John 142
Preston 7, 8, 9, 16, 18, 37-71, 107, 122, 134, 144, 157-67; Anglican elite 39, 40, 41, 46, 53, 56, 57-8, 60-1, 67; Anti-Easter Dues Association 162n94; anti-Irish attitudes 57, 61; Civil War 41; class tension 52, 61, 64, 67-71, 158n10; early history 37; economic development 37-8, 40, 157n2; education 42-3, 52, 56-7; electorate 61, 65, 164nn115-17, 121; factory owners 38-40, 47, 61, 66, 68-71; Independent (Radical) party 64; landed interest 37, 39-40, 57, 64, 159nn25, 26; municipal politics 39, 57-9; old corporation 38, 39-40, 57-8, 158nn12, 15; parliamentary politics 64-8; poor law union 59; population growth 157n4; race track issue 61; social background of Baptists 47, 50, Churchmen 40, 41-3, 46, Congregationalists 48, 50, Methodists 49, 51, Mormons 53-4, Quakers 48-9, Roman Catholics 51-3, Secularists 55-6, Swedenborgians 54, Teetotallers 54-5, 162nn85-9, 91, 92, Unitarians 46, 47; social background of Conservatives and Liberals 39, 40, 57-66; social conditions 38, 70, 157n5; town improvements 61; tradesmen/shopkeepers 38-9, 48, 52, 53, 55, 58, 59, 60, 64, 66; working class 43, 46, 47, 48, 49, 50-3, 54-5, 57, 61, 64-5, 68-71, 162n85
Preston Chronicle 43, 88
Preston Guardian 66, 165n129, 173n107
Preston Guild 163n103
Preston Observer 68, 166n138, 177n52
Preston Pilot 66, 165n129
Preston strike of 1853-4 43, 61, 69-71, 166nn143-6
Pugsley, N.K. 75, 78, 79
Puritanism 10, 128-31; *see also* Nonconformist conscience

Quakerism 13, 15, 48-9, 80, 92, 151n18, 160n54

Ratepayers' associations 99, 101, 172nn82, 93
Rating of Tenements Act of 1850 30, 154n61, 164n115
Read, Donald 143
Reform Act of 1832 3, 25, 64; of 1867 36, 134, 155n79
Rimmer, W.G. 22
riots 4, 24, 32, 67, 74-5, 89-90, 110, 111, 133-4, 135, 138
Rochdale 16, 18, 119, 177n55
Roman Catholicism 4; in Blackburn 118, 121, 122; in Bolton 17, 25, 26; in Preston 51-3, 57, 66-7; in Stockport 83-4, 89-90, 170n46; in other places 141, 142
Royle, Edward 152n41
Rushton, John 121, 180n97

'sect-type' 3, 18, 59
Secularism 18-19, 55-6, 84-5, 119, 133, 144

self-improvement 54, 162n85
Sellers, Ian 140
'Seven Men' of Preston 55, 162n87
silk manufacturing 72-3
Skinner, Francis 116-17
Smith, J.B. 105, 173n106
social mobility 8, 23
Socialism *see* Owenism
Society for the Protection of the Poor 29, 155n73
Stanley family (earls of Derby) 39, 40, 64-5, 159n22, 164n119
Stearns, Peter 71
Steele, E.D. 102
Stephens, J.R. 84, 104
Stockport 7, 47, 69, 72-106, 107, 111, 122, 166n146, 167-73; Anglican and Nonconformist elites 75-8, 80-3, 88, 90, 98, 103-6; anti-Irish attitudes 84, 89-90, 102; burial board 103; class tension 72, 73-5, 90; county magistrates 91; economic development 72-3, 75, 83-4, 168n18; education 75, 86-8; electorate 173n103; factory owners 72, 76-83, 88, 90, 91, 96, 99, 101-2, 172n80; friendly societies 85; gentry 91; house ownership 172n83; Improvement Act of 1837 93; Improvement Act of 1847 97; Local Government Act (adopted 1863) 103; Manorial Tolls bill 98; market hall 101; municipal politics 88, 90-103; municipal expenditure issue 93-7, 100-1; number and growth of denominations 75-7; parliamentary politics 103-6; Poor Law Union 93; pre-Reform government 90-2; Protestant Association of Stockport 102, 105; Public Libraries Act 103; secret societies 74; social background of Baptists 79-80, Churchmen 75-8, 168n23, Congregationalists 79, 80, Methodists 78-9, Quakers 80, Roman Catholics 83-4, 170nn46, 48, Secularists 84-5, Unitarians 80-3; social background of Conservatives and Liberals 94-6, 99-102, 105-6; social conditions 73-4, 75, 83-4, 170n49; town magistracy 96; tradesmen/shopkeepers 80, 92, 94-6, 98, 99-101; Waterworks Act 103; working class 75, 78, 79-80, 82-5, 87-90, 93, 99, 101, 106
Stockport Advertiser 105, 173n110
Stockport Grammar School 88, 103
Stockport High School 88
Stockport Mercury 102-3, 105
Stockport Ministerial Association 80, 169n37
Stockport Sunday school 86-8
Stockport Unitarian Chapel 80-3, 104
Stonyhurst College 122
strikes 43, 68-71, 74, 111, 120
Swedenborgianism *see* New Church

Taylor, W. Cooke 6, 10, 17, 69
Teetotallers 18, 29, 54-5, 56, 58-9, 64, 67, 68, 122, 144, 162nn85-9, 91, 92
Ten Hours bill 68, 83, 110
Test and Corporations Acts 25, 33, 67
Thernstrom, Stephan 140
Tholfsen, Trygve 8, 181n6
Thomasson, Thomas 15, 29, 30-2, 35-6, 152n43, 155n82
Thomis, Malcolm 153n52, 168n14
Thompson, E.P. 153n52
Thwaites, Daniel 112
Tiviot Dale Chapel, Stockport 78
trade unionism 15, 24, 68-71, 74, 111, 168n12
Troeltsch, Ernest 147n2
Trollope, Frances 167n3

Unitarianism 12–13, 46–7, 80–3, 92, 94, 104, 117, 140, 150nn15, 16
university religious tests (Oxford, Cambridge) 122
Ure, Andrew 6, 87

Verity, E.A. 26, 138, 180n110
Vincent, J.R. 65, 138, 143
Voluntaryism 56

Walkden, James 136

Walker, R.B. 16, 77
Ward, W.R. 6–7, 16, 25, 49
Weber, Max 59
Whitaker, Thomas 114–15, 123, 176n33
Whitehead, E. 11
Whittaker, J.W. 110, 111, 112, 115, 122
Wigan 41
Wiltshire 56, 142
working classes *see* entries for Blackburn, Bolton, Preston, and Stockport